'Raises *Sopranos* discussion to a ⌐ the "close up" of an individual ⌐ an overview or context proves the show's seriousness and depth. The writers' critical perspectives are so varied that even the most devoted fans should find something new and provocative. The arguments are all original, insightful, well supported. In the parlance of the academic Family, this is "a palpable hit".'

Maurice Yacowar, author of **The Sopranos on the Couch**

Reading Contemporary Television

Series Editors: Kim Akass and Janet McCabe

The *Reading Contemporary Television* series aims to offer a varied, intellectually groundbreaking and often polemical response to what is happening in television today. This series is distinct in that it sets out to immediately comment upon the TV zeitgeist while providing an intellectual and creative platform for thinking differently and ingeniously writing about contemporary television culture. The books in the series seek to establish a critical space where new voices are heard and fresh perspectives offered. Innovation is encouraged and intellectual curiosity demanded.

Reading THE Sopranos

Hit TV from HBO

EDITED BY **David Lavery**

I.B. TAURIS

LONDON · NEW YORK

Published in 2006 by I.B.Tauris & Co Ltd
6 Salem Road, London W2 4BU
175 Fifth Avenue, New York NY 10010
www.ibtauris.com

In the United States of America and in Canada distributed by
Palgrave Macmillan, a division of St Martin's Press
175 Fifth Avenue, New York NY 10010

ISBN 1 84511 121 4
EAN 978 1 84511 121 2

A full CIP record for this book is available from the British Library
A full CIP record for this book is available from the Library of Congress

Library of Congress catalog card: available

Typeset in Goudy Old Style by Steve Tribe, Andover
Printed and bound in the United States

CONTENTS

ACKNOWLEDGEMENTS

The rapid development of this book made me envious of the amount of time David Chase and company have to create a new season of *The Sopranos*. It could not have been completed without the contributions of many.

For their discerning and insightful essays, my thanks to all the book's authors: David Johansson, Janet McCabe and Kim Akass, Gwyn Symonds, Chris Kocela, Brian Gibson, Valerie Palmer-Mehta, Bruce Plourde, Dean DeFino, Jessica Baldini, Cameron Golden, Chris Neal, Doug Howard, Michael Epstein, Jimmie Reeves, and Mark Rogers. Particular thanks to the "two-timers"—McCabe, Akass, Epstein, Reeves, Rogers, Howard—who have contributed to both of my *Sopranos* books.

Thanks to Janet for the "brilliant" subtitle.

Thanks to Jimmie Cain for many wonderful "water cooler" discussions of *The Sopranos*.

Special thanks to Michael Prete for his excellent photographs.

Philippa Brewster at I.B.Tauris, a joy to work with, and Janet McCabe and Kim Akass, the *Reading Contemporary Television* series editors, always considerate and understanding, even during the heat of our accelerated publishing schedule, are the finest of taskmasters. Thanks, too, to Steve Tribe for his hard work on the manuscript.

Unlike Tony, I have only one family, a wonderful trio of brilliant and independent women. This book is dedicated to them.

David Lavery

CONTRIBUTORS

Kim Akass is Senior Lecturer in Film Studies at London Metropolitan University. She has written with Janet McCabe on female narratives and narration in American TV drama and is currently working on motherhood in contemporary American television. She has co-edited and contributed to *Reading* Sex and the City (I.B.Tauris, 2003) and *Reading* Six Feet Under: *TV to Die For* (I.B.Tauris, 2005) and is one of the founding editors of *Critical Studies in Television*.

Jessica Baldanzi is a Visiting Lecturer in the English Department at Indiana University, Bloomington. Her research and writing focus on eugenics, reproduction, and stereotype in Twentieth Century American literature. Her most recent publication, "Stillborns, Orphans, and Self-Proclaimed Virgins," appeared in *Genders* in Fall 2005.

Dean DeFino is Assistant Professor of English and director of Film Studies at Iona College. He earned his PhD at SUNY Binghamton.
Michael M. Epstein is Associate Professor at the Southwestern University School of Law, where he teaches courses on media and entertainment law. With Reeves and Rogers, he has authored articles on *The X-Files*, *The Sopranos*, and *Seinfeld*.

Brian Gibson is a PhD candidate at the Department of English and Film Studies at the University of Alberta in Edmonton. He has published papers on African masculinities, the male gaze in *Patriot Games*, and Jim Hawkins' adolescence in *Treasure Island*. He is writing his dissertation on Saki (H. H. Munro). His first novel, *Bleeding Daylight*, was published in 2004.

Cameron Golden is completing her Ph.D. in English at the University of North Carolina at Greensboro. Her dissertation looks closely at autobiographical writer figures within the novels of Paul Auster, Charles Baxter, Philip Roth, and Mark Leyner. She has published articles in *Mosaic*, *Critique* (forthcoming), and *The Midwest Quarterly* (forthcoming).

Douglas L. Howard is Writing Center Coordinator and Honors Program Professor at SUNY Suffolk. His work has appeared in *Literature and Theology*, *The Chronicle of Higher Education*, *PopPolitics*, and in *This Thing of Ours: Investigating The Sopranos*. He is currently co-editing and contributing to a forthcoming volume on racial and social representations of the Gothic Other.

David Johansson's work appears in *Issues and Identities in Literature*, *Masterplots I and II*, and *Cyclopedia of World Authors*. In 2005 he lectured on drama at Lund University, Sweden and on poetry at the University of Edinburgh, Scotland. He currently teaches literature and film at Brevard Community College on the Atlantic coast of Florida.

Christopher Kocela earned his PhD at McGill University. He teaches courses in 20th Century American literature, contemporary theory, and popular culture at Georgia State University in Atlanta. He has published in *Pynchon Notes*, *Genders*, and *The Steinbeck Newsletter*.

David Lavery is professor of English at Middle Tennessee State University and the author of over ninety published essays and reviews and author/editor/co-editor of eleven books, including *Full of Secrets: Critical Approaches to* Twin Peaks and *Reading* Deadwood. He co-edits the e-journal *Slayage: The Online International Journal of Buffy Studies* and is one of the founding editors of the new journal *Critical Studies in Television: Scholarly Studies of Small Screen Fictions.*

Janet McCabe is a Research Fellow in television drama at Manchester Metropolitan University and Managing Editor of *Critical Studies in Television.* She has written on American TV drama on British screens, as well as with Kim Akass on female narratives and narration in American TV drama. She is author of *Feminist Film Theory: Writing the Woman into Cinema* (Wallflower), and has co-edited (with Akass) and contributed to *Reading Sex and the City* (I.B.Tauris, 2003) and *Reading Six Feet Under: TV to Die For* (I.B.Tauris, 2005).

Chris Neal is the Director of Bands at McMurry University. Additionally, he teaches courses in the Music Education sequence, including Orchestration and Arranging, Instrumental Practicum, and Brass Methods.

Valerie Palmer-Mehta (Ph.D., Wayne State University) teaches communication theory, persuasion and multicultural communication at Oakland University in Michigan. Her research focuses on the intersection of hegemony, ideology, and the representation of gender, race, and sexuality in the media.

Bruce Plourde is a doctoral candidate in English at Temple University.

Jimmie L. Reeves is Associate Professor of Mass Communication at Texas Tech University. In addition to articles on subjects ranging from Mr. T to *The X-Files, Twin Peaks, The Sopranos,* and *Seinfeld,* he is the co-author of *Cracked Coverage: Television News, the Anti-Cocaine Crusade, and the Reagan Legacy* (1994).

Franco Ricci teaches in the department of Languages and Literature at the University of Ottawa. He is the editor of *Calvino Revisited* and author of *Difficult Games: A Reading of I racconti by Italo Calvino* and

Painting with Words, Writing with Pictures: Word and Image Relations in the Work of Italo Calvino.

Mark C. Rogers is an Associate Professor of Communication at Walsh University. His previous publications include collaborative pieces on *Twin Peaks, The X-Files, The Sopranos,* and *Seinfeld.*

Gwyn Symonds is a special education teacher and doctoral candidate in the Department of English, University of Sydney. Her essays have appeared in *Refractory: A Journal of Entertainment Media* and *Slayage: The Online International Journal of Buffy Studies.*

INTRODUCTORY

Pulaski Skyway, New Jersey. Photograph by Michael Prete.

Introduction

CAN THIS BE
THE END OF TONY SOPRANO?

David Lavery

I. LOATHING TV

> I've got to watch TV to figure out the world?
> *Paulie Walnuts*

Early in "Mr. Ruggiero's Neighborhood" (3.01), the first episode of
Season Three of *The Sopranos*, Tony and his crew sit down for lunch. As
salad and pasta are dispensed, the obsessive-compulsive, macho-prissy,
extravagantly coiffed psycho Paulie Walnuts washes his hands, again.
When asked why, he holds forth, literally ad nauseam, on the dangers
of tying shoelaces, the disturbing hygiene of "your average men's
shit house," and the spread of disease. Both appalled and amazed,
Christopher Moltisanti, curious where his frequent nemesis has
acquired such esoteric knowledge, asks "You saw this on TV?" "I've got
to watch TV to figure out the world?" Paulie responds, rhetorically.

In Season Four's "Watching Too Much Television" (4.06), mob-
wife-in-training Adriana, watching a rerun of *Murder One*, gets the
notion that if she and Christopher marry (long her hope) she cannot
be forced by the FBI to testify against him. When she later learns that
expectation is false, the title of the episode finally become clear.

Season Five's "In Camelot" (5.07) finds Christopher alternately
supporting/bankrupting J. T. (Tim Daley), a friend from rehab. At a
twelve-step meeting, J. T. introduces himself as "a TV writer, which by

default makes me a douche bag." (J. T. mentions missing a deadline for *Nash Bridges* as the result of his addiction.) Desperate for money after a horrible night at the poker table, he will later try to pawn an Emmy statue only to be told it is practically worthless. "If it was an Oscar," the pawnbroker suggests, "maybe I could give you something, an Academy Award, but TV?"

Airing on HBO, already pre-branded as "not TV," in a series created by David Chase, a man who scorns the medium in which he has spent his career ("I loathe and despise almost every second of [television]" [Rucker interview]; see Lavery and Thompson), these medium-specific, self-referential slams should come as no surprise. *The Sopranos*, however, is no *Nash Bridges*, and, as the essays in this book, the latest contribution to the already extensive scholarly/critical discourse about a landmark series—the highest-ranked drama in the history of American television ("50 Greatest Shows")—demonstrate, there is much to learn about the world, both the mediated small-screen cosmos and the real world too, from at least the best of TV.

II. NOT TV

> Not only will ordinary folks watch a show [like *The Sopranos*] that demands
> constant attention, resists easy closure, relies on subtext and is rich with
> metaphor—they will pay near usurious subscription fees for it.
>
> *James Poniewozik*

In a March 2004 interview on National Public Radio's *Fresh Air*, Chase, a thirty-year, once nearly invisible veteran, in his pre-HBO life, of network television—before, that is, he destroyed his anonymity by creating HBO's signature dramatic series—reiterates his unhappiness with the current state of American television.[1] Sick and tired of the complaints of Chase's former employers the networks—all of whom had passed on his story about a New Jersey gangster and his two families—that HBO cable shows have an unfair, censorship-free advantage (see Levinson), Chase lists instead some of the freedoms network television fails to exercise:

[A]ll of us have the freedom to do story lines that unfold slowly. We all have the freedom to create characters that are complex and contradictory. The FCC doesn't govern that. We all have the freedom to tell stupid, bad jokes that may actually turn out to be funny. And we all have the freedom to let the audience figure out what's going on rather than telling them what's going on.

Any regular viewer of *The Sopranos* will immediately recognize that Chase is actually spelling out the mission statement of his own masterpiece.

"You get bored," Chase confessed several years ago to James Longworth, "and I don't know if you can tell it from looking at *The Sopranos*, but I had just had it up to here with all the niceties of network television. I couldn't take it anymore. And I don't mean language and I don't mean violence. I just mean storytelling, inventiveness, something that really could entertain and surprise people. I just couldn't take it anymore" (34). Network television fails, Chase goes on to say, because it has forgotten its first obligation as a storyteller in order to pursue a not-so-hidden agenda:

I think the first priority is to push a lifestyle. I think there's something they're trying to sell all the time ... I think what they're trying to sell is that everything's OK all the time, that this is just a great nation and a wonderful society, and everything's OK and it's OK to buy stuff. Let's just go buy some stuff ... There's some indefinable image of America that they're constantly trying to push as opposed to actually being entertaining.

In love with cinema, determined to make a "little movie" every week, Chase and company only grudgingly surrendered to the conventions of episodic storytelling but, from the very beginning, *The Sopranos* has been a character-driven, darkly funny, supremely ironic, frequently subversive, wholly democratic series with no "palpable design upon us," insisting we make up our own minds about all its often deeply conflicted, never wholly admirable characters and the culture that created and sustains them.

Chase fails to disclose, however, one undeniable, inequitable advantage working on HBO does offer him. A *Sopranos* season is only thirteen episodes, and HBO has acquiesced in Chase's ever-increasing demands for longer-than-customary hiatuses between seasons. *The Sopranos* returned for its fourth season in September 2002, after sixteen months of replenishing the creative juices. Season Five aired after fifteen months off the air. The hiatus preceding Season Six will be only three months short of two years.[2]

We will soon learn what Chase, writers Robin Green, Mitchell Burgess, and Terence Winter; directors Allen Coulter and Tim Van Patten,[3] to name only Chase's longest-running collaborators, have made out of their longest gestation period. We will learn, too, whether Season Six will be the end of Tony Soprano. It will almost certainly not be the end of *Sopranos* Studies.

III. TELEVISION STUDIES/*SOPRANOS* STUDIES

In "Life with (God)Father," an essay in Regina Barreca's collection of essays on Italian-American culture in *The Sopranos*, renowned feminist literary scholar Sandra Gilbert (co-author, with Susan Gubar, of the watershed study *The Madwoman in the Attic: The Woman Writer and the Nineteenth Century Literary Imagination* and numerous other books) stoops to conquer *The Sopranos*. Not a happy watcher, she finds *The Sopranos* to be the latest precipitation in "a rain of cultural messages excluding me from imaginative authority." Forced to watch it, she find herself "relegated to a somewhat comic, perhaps even grotesque underclass" (13). Along the way, bemused by the serious attention paid to television in general and *The Sopranos* in particular, she takes unbecoming, admittedly ignorant, and sometimes *ad hominen* swings at critics and scholars. Offended by television critic Joyce Millman's suggestion (in *Salon.com*) that even non-Italians can identify with *The Sopranos*, she responds by characterizing her ideas as "burbling." Bemused by my own attempt in the online journal *PopPolitics* ("Coming Heavy") to identify *The Sopranos*' characteristically postmodern intertextuality, she takes fussy pot shots at a quotation of Eco and then, embarrassingly, changes a quotation from my essay through a bracketed insertion that alters my meaning.[4] Later, she admits, evidently proud of the fact, that "I write this ... without having seen *a single frame* of the third season of *The Sopranos* ..." (25; my italics), even though Barreca's collection, appearing in 2002, covered the first three seasons of the series. Would she brag about not having read, say, all of Emily Dickinson's published poetry prior to writing about her work? (Because I have no desire to be petty, I will not bother to point out the problem in Gilbert's phrasing: that television doesn't come in frames.)

The condescending, dismissive tone of Gilbert's essay should be familiar to anyone who follows the reception of television studies in the popular press. The vast majority of US reviews of important studies of significant television series, from *Buffy the Vampire Slayer* to *Six Feet Under*, are written by the nonplussed and incredulous. Committed to self-fulfilling prophecy, newspapers and magazines, it seems, wouldn't think of assigning a review to a friend of television. Even though the field continues to proliferate—*Buffy the Vampire Slayer* and its sequel *Angel*, for example, have already generated over a dozen scholarly books, four international conferences, and well over a hundred published essays—Television Studies in general can't get no respect.

The emerging field of *Sopranos* Studies,[5] only three years old as I write, has seen the publication of over fifty individual essays in such scholarly journals as *The Journal of Popular Film and Television, The Journal of Popular Culture,* and *Film Quarterly* and three edited collections, my own, *This Thing of Ours: Investigating The Sopranos* (2002); Barreca's *A Sitdown with the Sopranos: Watching Italian American Culture on TV's Most Talked-About Series* (2002); and Richard Greene and Peter Vernezze's *The Sopranos and Philosophy: I Kill, Therefore I Am* (2004); as well as monographs like Glen O. Gabbard's *The Psychology of The Sopranos: Love, Death, and Betrayal in America's Favorite Gangster Family* (2002), Maurice Yacowar's *The Sopranos on the Couch: Analyzing Television's Greatest Series* (2002, 2003), and David Simon's *Tony Soprano's America* (2002).[6]

Study of a television series is not comparable to, say, investigation of the human genome. Chromosomes and genes are not methodically allocated to appropriate experts for definitive assessment. No one is coordinating *Sopranos* Studies. No one is calling the shots; there is no boss to this mob. Still, trends are discernible.

Tony. More essays have been written on Tony Soprano himself than on any other single topic, almost all seeking to come to grips, in one way or another, with the central question of the morality of the series' anti-hero. Noel Carroll's "Sympathy for the Devil," for example, grapples with the apparent contradiction of the audience's identification with Tony's clearly criminal behavior. James Harold's "A Moral Never-Never Land: Identifying with Tony Soprano" and Mike Lippman's "Know Thyself, Asshole: Tony Soprano as an Aristotelian Tragic Hero" cover similar territory, the former implementing Tolstoy's aesthetics (from *What is Art?*), the latter examining Tony as a tragic hero according to Aristotle's *Poetics*. Sheila Lintott's "Tony Soprano's Moral Sympathy (or Lack Thereof): *The Sopranos* and Subjectivist Ethics" and Scott D. Wilson's "Staying within the Family: Tony Soprano's Ethical Obligations" offer additional assessments of Tony's moral code. Ronald M. Green seeks to understand the nature of Tony Soprano's business ethics in "'I Dunno About Morals, but I Do Got Rules': Tony Soprano as Ethical Manager." Richard Greene offers a tightly argued assessment of Tony Soprano's own fallibility in "Is Tony Soprano Self-Blind?"—he is, Greene concludes definitively. Jennifer Baker applies classical notions of the nature of human happiness in seeking to understand the motives of Tony Soprano in "The Unhappiness of Tony Soprano: An Ancient Analysis."

Feminist. Feminists have of course had a great deal to say about *The Sopranos*. Lisa Cassidy's "Is Carmela Soprano a Feminist? Carmela's Care Ethics" unequivocally finds *The Sopranos'* most important female character an "anti-feminist," but one potentially capable of reform. Kim Akass and Janet McCabe's "Beyond the Bada Bing! Negotiating Female Narrative Authority in *The Sopranos*" and Cindy Donatelli and Sharon Alward's "'I Dread You': Married to the mob in *The Godfather*, *GoodFellas*, and *The Sopranos*" both offer arguments (narratological/genre-based) for the surprising and unprecedented strength of women in the series. Regina Barreca seeks to account for her counter-intuitive/feminism-subverting attraction to the females of *The Sopranos* in "Why I like the Women in *The Sopranos* Even though I'm Not Supposed to."

HBO and Television. Both Paul Levinson's "Naked Bodies, Three Showings a Week, and No Commercials: *The Sopranos* as a Nuts-and-

Bolts Triumph of Non-Network TV" and "*The Sopranos* as HBO Brand Equity: The Art of Commerce in the Age of Digital Reproduction" by Mark C. Rogers, Michael M. Epstein, and Jimmie R. Reeves explore the series as a product of a premium cable channel. In "Bada-Being and Nothingness: Murderous Melodrama or Morality Play?" Al Gini brings a variety of media critics—Neil Postman, Susan Sontag, Marshall McLuhan—and thinkers like Jean-Paul Sartre and Ernest Becker into play in trying to ascertain the appeal of *The Sopranos*. David Lavery and Robert J. Thompson's "David Chase, *The Sopranos*, and Television Creativity" takes a careful look at the "television auteur" who created *The Sopranos*.

The Gangster Genre. Comparing and contrasting the series to earlier manifestations of the gangster film or to true crime gangsters has been the focus of over a dozen published essays: Albert Auster, "*The Sopranos*: The Gangster Redux"; Ellen Willis, "Our Mobsters, Ourselves"; David Pattie, "Mobbed Up: *The Sopranos* and the Intertextual Gangster"; Glen Creeber, "'TV Ruined the Movies': Television, Tarantino, and The Intimate World of *The Sopranos*"; two essays by Martha P. Nochimson ("'Waddaya Lookin' At?': Re-Reading the Gangster Genre through *The Sopranos*" and "Tony's Options: *The Sopranos* and the Televisuality of the Gangster Genre"); Lee Siegel, "The Attraction of Repulsion"; David Remnick, "Is This the End of Rico? With *The Sopranos* the Mob Genre is on the Brink"; Fred Gardaphé, "Fresh Garbage: The Gangster as Suburban Trickster"; and Ingrid Walker Fields, "Family Values and Feudal Codes: The Social Politics of America's Twenty-First Century Gangster" (which offers an extensive comparison of Jim Jarmusch's film *Ghost Dog* [1999] and *The Sopranos*); Chris Messenger, "*The Godfather* Sung by *The Sopranos*" (a chapter in The Godfather *and American Culture*). George Anastasia, one of the premier organized crime journalists in the USA, assesses the real-world accuracy of *The Sopranos* in a wide-ranging essay entitled "If Shakespeare were Alive Today, He'd be Writing for *The Sopranos*."

Italianness. One book—Barreca's *Sitdown with The Sopranos*—and several essays—Jonathan J. Cavellero's "Gangsters, Fessos, Tricksters, and Sopranos: The Historical Roots of Italian American Stereotype Anxiety"; Roseanne Giannini Quinn's "Mothers, Molls, and Misogynists: Resisting Italian American Womanhood in *The Sopranos*"; B. Beck's "The Myth That Would Not Die: *The Sopranos*, Mafia Movies, and Italians in America"—examine the series' Italianness, most simultaneously considering the role of the gangster genre in perpetuating cultural stereotypes. E. Anthony Rotundo's "Wonderbread and Stugots: Italian American Manhood and *The Sopranos*" examines men and manhood in the show.

Language. In "This Thing of Ours: Language Use in *The Sopranos*," Michael E. Gettings applies the "speech act" theory of philosopher J. L. Austin to an examination of the underworld slang and waste management jargon of *The Sopranos*. "'Soprano-speak': Language and Silence in *The Sopranos*" by Douglas L. Howard examines communication and miscommunication in the narrative.

Psychotherapy. One book, Gabbard's *The Psychology of The Sopranos*, and at least two essays—Peter Mattessi's "The Strong, Silent Type: Psychoanalysis in *The Sopranos*," and Michael Flamini's "'Pa cent' anni, 'Dr. Melfi': Psychotherapy in the Italian American Community"—assess the central role of psychotherapy in *The Sopranos*.

Religion. Carla Gardina Pestana examines the important role of the church and the nature of belief in the series in "Catholicism, Identity, and Ethics in *The Sopranos*." Peter H. Hare's "'What Kind of God Does This...?'" offers an overview of some of the series' theological questions and problems. And Peter Vernezze provides a Dantesque map of Sopranoland in "Tony Soprano in Hell: Chase's Mob in Dante's *Inferno*."

Sui Generis. Many essays on *The Sopranos* are one of a kind. Jeremy Creedon's "The Greening of Tony Soprano" is an ecopyschological reading of Tony's malaise. Steven Hayward and Andrew Biro's "The Eighteenth Brumaire of Tony Soprano" is a neo-Marxist reading of the series. "Unmade Men: *The Sopranos* After Whiteness" by Christopher Kocela explores the complex role of race in *The Sopranos*. Lance Strate's "No(rth Jersey) Sense of Place: The Cultural Geography (and Media Ecology) of *The Sopranos*" seeks to delineate all the many environments of the series. In "The Cultural Work of *The Sopranos*," Jay Parini outlines the many ways in which the show interrogates modern American culture by "draw[ing] ing attention to the fault lines in family and community life" (80). Inspired by Tony's reading of Sun Tzu's *The Art of War* (recommended by Dr. Melfi) in Season Three, Steven C. Combs' "Tony Soprano and the Art of War: New Jersey Meets the East" compares the struggle of organized crime in New Jersey to the Spring-Autumn (circa 770–476 BC) and Warring States (circa 475–221 BC) periods of Chinese history. David Hahn's "The Prince and I: Some Musings on Machiavelli" draws some parallels between Machiavelli's *The Prince* and goings-on in Sopranoland. H. Peter Steeves offers a Hobbesian/Cartesian-influenced reading of the individual and the community in "Dying in Our Own Arms: Liberalism, Communitarianism, and the Construction of Identity on *The Sopranos*." Avi Santo's "'Why Don't you take a look in the mirror, you insensitive prick': Weight, Body Image and Masculinity in *The Sopranos*" enacts its own title by considering obesity in the series. Joanne Lacey's ethnographic study, "One for the Boys? *The Sopranos* and Its Male, British Audience," assesses the way ten men in Brighton, England watched and understood the show. Dawn Elizabeth B. Johnston's "Way North of New Jersey: A Canadian Experience of *The Soprano*" offers an account of the reception of *The Sopranos* in Canada. Kevin Fellezs's "Wiseguy Opera: Music for *Sopranos*" listens to the role of Italian music in the show. Joseph S. Walker's "'Cunnilingus and Psychoanalysis Have Brought Us To This': Livia and the Logic of False Hoods" carefully examines the structure and themes of the series' first season. J. Gattuso Hendin's "Tony and Meadow: The Sopranos as Father-Daughter Drama" considers the mob boss as parent. Kevin L. Stoehr reads the series as both an existential drama and a manifestation of *film noir* in "'It's All a Big Nothing': The Nihilistic Vision of *The Sopranos*." And, as the title suggests, Sara Lewis Dunne's "'The Brutality of Meat' and 'the Abruptness of Seafood': Food, Violence, and Family in *The Sopranos*" digests the central role of food in the show.

The present volume, with the first five seasons of *The Sopranos* on the table, builds upon earlier work on the series and opens up new territory for exploration. The present essay is followed by two other introductory essays, "Surviving the 'Hit': Will *The Sopranos* Still Sing for HBO?" in which Epstein, Reeves, and Rogers continue their examination of *The Sopranos* and HBO (begun in *This Thing of Ours*), this time considering what the end of the series means for both *The Sopranos* and HBO brands; and David Johansson's "Homeward Bound: Those *Sopranos* Titles Come Heavy," which presents a close reading of the series' famous opening credit sequence.

The book's second section, "Sopranos Women," includes readings of key females in the series. Janet McCabe and Kim Akass extend their earlier feminist interpretation of the show in *This Thing*, this time seeking an answer to the question "What has Carmela Ever Done for Feminism?" Valerie Palmer-Mehta's "Disciplining the Masculine: The Disruptive Power of Janice Soprano" considers Tony's unruly older sister. In "Eve of Destruction: Dr. Melfi as Reader of *The Sopranos*," Bruce Plourde offers a reader-response take on the series' resident psychiatrist.

"Episodes," the third section, gathers essays that take hard looks at individual hours of *The Sopranos*: "Employee of the Month" and "Another Toothpick" in Jessica Baldanzi's "Bloodlust for the Common Man: *The Sopranos* Confronts Its Vengeful Audience"; "The Test Dream" in Cameron Golden's "'You're Annette Bening?': Dreams and Hollywood as Subtext in *The Sopranos*"; and "Christopher" in Christopher Kocela's "From Columbus to Gary Cooper: Mourning the Lost White Father in *The Sopranos*," a continuation of the author's earlier essay on whiteness in the show.

"Music, Theatricality, Aesthetics," *Reading* The Sopranos' fourth section, includes three more essays. Chris Neal—in "Gangstas, Divas, and Breaking Tony's Balls: Musical Reference in *The Sopranos*"—contemplates the significant role of music. Gwyn Symonds reflects on the staging of its larger-than-life personae in "Show Business or Dirty Business?: The Theatrics of Mafia Narrative and Empathy for the Last Mob Boss Standing in *The Sopranos*." And in "Art Imitating Life Imitating Art: Aesthetics and Ammunition in *The Sopranos*," Franco Ricci exhaustively foregrounds the paintings, statues, photographs so often overlooked in *Sopranos*' mise-en-scéne.

Reading The Sopranos' final section—"Criminal Justice, Power, Homophobia, Race"—is comprised of Douglas Howard's close look at the Bureau and the mob in the series: "Tasting Brylcreem: Law,

Disorder, and the FBI in *The Sopranos*"; Dean DeFino's consideration of Tony Soprano's Machiavellian side: "The Prince of North Jersey"; and Brian Gibson's examination of bigotry and homophobia: "'Black Guys My Ass': The Queerness of Racism in *The Sopranos*."

Three appendices (a complete list of *Sopranos* episodes, writers, and directors; a catalog of Intertextual Moments and Allusions in *The Sopranos*, updating a similar catalog in *This Things of Ours*, this time covering Seasons Four and Five; and a list of characters); a composite bibliography; and an index complete the book.[8]

IV. THE END

> Two endings for a high profile guy like me: dead or in the can.
>
> *"For All Debts Public or Private"* (4.01)

How then does a "high-profile" show like *The Sopranos* end? As I have shown elsewhere ("Apocalyptic Apocalypses"), the "narrative eschatology" of any long-running television series is complex, offering "a variety of 'little deaths,' mini-apocalypses": those sub-climaxes network and basic capable narratives require for commercial breaks (absent, of course on HBO); the wait-until-next-week climax of each episode (Melfi's vengeance-denying "No" to Tony's "Is there something you want to say?" ["Employee of the Month," 3.04); the culmination of a particular narrative arc (Adriana's stint as an FBI info whacked by Silvio ["Long Term Parking," 5.12]); the ending of each season (that shot of the ocean, the new home of Big Pussy, at the end of Season Two ["Funhouse," 2.13), and, most apocalyptic of all, the finale of a series.

Such finales—of M*A*S*H, of *Seinfeld*, of *Sex and the City*—have, of course, become "cultural spectacles" (Morreale), and no doubt *The Sopranos* will inspire yet another. The book you hold, however, was written in ignorance of the end of *The Sopranos*. As it was being completed, word came down from on high that a deal had been reached between HBO and David Chase to produce eight additional "bonus" episodes of *The Sopranos* to air about nine months (January 2007) after the previously thought-to-be-final, twelve-episode Season Six, already set to begin in March 2006.

None of this book's contributors has seen a single episode; none knows the answer to the question (inspired by the lament of Caesar Enrico Bandello in *Little Caesar* [1931]), posed in the title to this introduction. We don't know on which horn of the dilemma Tony predicts to Melfi he (and the narrative) will be impaled. We are not even certain that Governor Chase may not, once again, grant a last minute reprieve, extending the life of the condemned.[8]

I.

SURVIVING "THE HIT"

WILL *THE SOPRANOS*
STILL SING FOR HBO?

Michael M. Epstein, Jimmie L. Reeves,
and Mark C. Rogers

"A Hit is a Hit"—the tenth episode of the inaugural season of *The Sopranos*—examines some of the same connotations of the word "hit" that we elaborate in this essay. The episode begins with Tony's minions executing a classic gangland "hit" that produces a suitcase full of cash. But the more relevant spin on the word "hit" occurs near the end of the main storyline. After frowning though wannabe rock-band Visiting Day's demo tape (bankrolled by Christopher Moltisanti's share of the blood money from the Mafia "hit"), Hesh Rabkin states the obvious—Visiting Day sucks. When the distraught Christopher asks Hesh to elaborate, Hesh showcases the accumulated wisdom of decades of success finding and exploiting talent in the music business. "A hit is a hit," explains Hesh. "And that's no hit."

Our use of the word "hit," of course, is also an obvious double-entendre relating to both the gangster content of the narrative and to the enormous success of the program itself. Still, as we reflected on the title, it also became apparent that there is a third way to interpret "hit," one that refers to the impact that the end of *The Sopranos*' run on HBO—and its distribution into other windows—will have on the brand equity that, as we examined in a previous essay in *This Thing of Ours*, HBO has worked so hard to build (Rogers, Epstein, and Reeves). Will the loss of *The Sopranos* as a first-run program be a "hit" to the premium cable network? Or has HBO exploited a new system of production and distribution that will allow a show like *The Sopranos*, which has performed magnificently for HBO, to keep on singing, at least in terms of brand building? It is this question, fundamental to the success of artistic creation in the TV III age (Rogers, Epstein, and Reeves 46–7), that this chapter will seek to address.

Few would dispute that *The Sopranos* has done more than any other program to build the HBO brand with American audiences. In terms of traditional measures of success—ratings and new subscriptions—*The Sopranos* has been a bonanza for HBO. Ratings for original airings of the show have been unprecedented for HBO. In September 2002, for example, the fourth season premiere garnered 13.4 million viewers, making it not only the most-watched program in HBO history, but the third-most-watched show on cable since 1994 (Carter, "He Lit Up HBO"). With numbers like that, HBO rapidly expanded its subscriber base, growing from 24 million households in 1999 to 28 million subscribers in 2005 (Atkinson). In the two seasons since 2003, *The Sopranos* has continued to attract unprecedented ratings, outpacing even the final episodes of HBO's other mega-hit, *Sex and the City*, which attracted 10.6 million viewers and was placed third in its timeslot ("Fast Track").

While ratings have remained high, subscriptions have leveled off in the last two years (Carter, "TV Notes"). Why this has happened is a matter of debate. One could speculate that the flattening of subscription increases could be a function of the continued fragmentation of the content distribution emblematic of television in the TV III age. In these same last two years, increased bandwidth capacity and compression efficiency has allowed some digital systems to greatly increase the number of dedicated premium channels available to subscribers (Whitney). HBO itself now commonly bundles six HBO-branded channels to its subscribers, in addition to participating in on-demand services that allow subscribers with digital service to time-shift many HBO programs (Dempsey, "Lonely"). One might think that the proliferation of so many new HBO channels would help the HBO brand by boosting its presence on the cable dial. But it may be that the opposite is true. By competing with itself, in addition to the other channels, HBO may be diluting its audience, which may, in turn, be diluting its brand with new subscribers. The type of appointment television-cum-water cooler experience that characterized a network show like *Seinfeld* or even *The Sopranos* in its early seasons may be harder to sustain in a multichannel environment. This is significant since, unlike the networks, HBO has historically used its highest-rated hits not to sell advertising to a mass audience, but to draw elite audiences willing to pay a fee for a premium service (Brownfield, "At HBO"; Martin). For HBO, a show like *The Sopranos* is all about the water cooler—it is the buzz about the show, and a desire to see it, that had been leading new viewers, at least until recently, to subscribe in large numbers.

Ironically, the enormous success of *The Sopranos* may weaken the HBO brand, at least in the short term. Because *The Sopranos*, and to a lesser extent, *Sex and the City*, have enjoyed a level of unprecedented ratings-generated buzz that HBO has been unable to duplicate with newer programs, the thought persists, discussed frequently in the trades, that HBO's best days may be behind it (Brownfield, "At HBO"). It's hard not to take note that HBO has been unable to attract high ratings with its latest generation of episodic programs, despite their acclaim.

The network has developed a number of original programs since 2001, including, *Six Feet Under*, *The Wire*, *Deadwood*, *Carnivale*, *The Comeback*, and *Entourage*. *Six Feet Under*, which initially had strong ratings and good critical response, has ended its five-season run with a narrative bang, the death of main character Nate Fisher (Peter Krause), but a ratings whimper. The show struggled in the ratings after a short-lived move from Sunday night (long the spot of HBO's premiere original series including *The Sopranos* and *Sex and the City*) to Monday. HBO had intended to try to open a new night for original programming, but this failed. Reversing the move after four episodes did not stem the loss of viewers (Martin, 2005).

Gritty crime drama *The Wire* has received widespread acclaim but has failed to find a mass audience; HBO was on the verge of not bringing the show back for a fourth season. *Deadwood* seemed to follow HBO's *Sopranos* model of allowing a talented writer/producer (David Milch) the creative freedom to put a new spin on an old genre (the western). *Deadwood* has been critically well received and, during its first season, when it aired following *The Sopranos*, it delivered solid ratings. Without the lead-in, however, the second season lost a third of its audience (de Moraes, 2005). *Carnivale* seemed aimed at an *X-Files/Twin Peaks* cult audience. It never managed to break out of this niche and was cancelled after two seasons.

The Comeback and *Entourage* are comedies and represent an attempt to replace the departed *Sex and The City*, but neither has approached the success of their predecessor. Both are self-reflexive programs about the entertainment industry and so garner attention from the media press. *Entourage* has succeeded in generating water-cooler buzz but in its second season it has yet to deliver viewers. *The Comeback*, featuring *Friends* star Lisa Kudrow, has been a bomb, both critically and in the ratings.

None of this is particularly surprising; the failure rate for new television programs is extremely high for all networks; the résumés of successful actors and producers are littered with the corpses of failed pilots and cancelled series. But these particular struggles have dented the bulletproof image that HBO's original programming previously enjoyed. Furthermore, the situation is complicated by the fact that other cable networks are devoting more resources to original programming. FX, in particular, has stolen some of HBO's thunder with edgy programs like *Nip/Tuck*, *The Shield*, and *Rescue Me*.

In many respects, the great emphasis that HBO now places on ratings represents a change in the business model for HBO, a change that underscores the way content providers have had to adapt to a transformed media marketplace in the current TV III era. Before *The Sopranos*, it was sufficient for HBO to have a highly acclaimed but low-rated show—critical buzz for a comedy like *The Larry Sanders Show* or the prison drama *Oz* satisfied the subscriber base and helped increase subscriptions modestly. But that model no longer works in today's fragmented and diluted television dial.

An additional factor in the gradual erosion of the subscriber-based pay cable model is a technical and economic issue that HBO has little control over. While cable multi-system operators have made a significant amount of their revenue from the percentage of premium channel subscription fees that they receive, they are increasingly diversifying into new businesses like broadband internet access and telephony. As a result, a smaller percentage of their revenue comes from premium cable fees and the cable system operators are less inclined to promote pay channels. In twenty years, the percentage of revenue that operators receive from HBO has dropped from thirty-five to five per cent (Atkinson). Marketing resources that could be selling HBO are now selling cable modems and telephone service.

With *The Sopranos*, HBO has realized that the future lies in the development of shows that have larger ratings numbers if it wants to have impact, and make money, in the marketplace (Carter, "He Lit Up HBO"). For HBO today, successful brand building is not about building subscriber numbers anymore; it's about developing highly-rated content and attaching the HBO brand to that content (Brownfield, "Call It Must-Buy TV").

In many ways this strategy is an innovative twist on the concept of "product placement." But the product that is "placed" is not Reese's Pieces (as in *ET*) but the shows themselves. In other words, in the age of TV III, premium cable is becoming a lot like FM radio where getting on the playlist is the first step in reaping the rewards of multiple revenue streams (CD sales, merchandising, concert ticket sales, etc.). Though premium cable is not subject to the kind of payola scandals that continue to haunt the radio business, it is clear that synergies of these new revenue streams for the big media empires determine in large part what appears on the premium cable "playlist." Indeed, by adopting this branding/product-placement/synergy strategy with *The Sopranos*, and with *Sex and the City*, HBO is becoming more like an owner-syndicator and less like a network.

For HBO, *The Sopranos* may be a test case for a new post-Fordist model of brand production and distribution in a TV III age characterized by too many channels, on demand distribution, and DVD sales. While it may be premature to assert that HBO is ready to abandon its dedicated program channels, it may be that the balance between building the network and building its brand as a production identity may have shifted toward the latter. One needs only to follow the money to see that this shift is already underway. In 2004, HBO is reported to have earned profits in excess of $1 billion (Rice). While subscription fees still represented the biggest profit contribution, the recent flattening of subscriptions during *The Sopranos* era reflects a general trend toward limited growth potential in that sector (Rice). In order to maintain or increase its profitability, HBO has turned to syndication, international sales, DVDs, and merchandising as new sources for income (Littleton). In doing this, HBO as a producer may find itself increasingly in competition with itself, with HBO as a network, in much the same way that broadcast networks sometimes are forced to compete with their own production arms. The more a network like HBO places its content into alternative distribution windows such as syndication, hotels, airplanes, and DVD, the less reason subscribers have for tuning into HBO's premium cable service. To a great extent, the impact of these alternative windows can already be seen on the theatrical features that were once the mainstay of Home Box Office. By the time many of these films air on HBO, people have already seen them in another window, or know that they will become available in an alternative window in the near future. The result is that these films no longer have the currency with subscribers they once had.

In other words, in the new converged media world, the time-honored concept of "content exclusivity" (like the notion of "audience flow" in broadcast television) is rapidly becoming obsolete as a programming strategy. As the 2004 numbers suggest, HBO's greatest profit potential lies precisely in these alternative forms of content distribution (Rice). As the owner of *The Sopranos*, HBO's 2005 deal to syndicate the series over five years to A&E is said to have earned HBO at least $2.5 million per episode ("A&E Pays Big Bucks;" Steinberg). With eighty-five episodes expected to be in the can by the close of the show's sixth season, including eight "bonus" episodes to air in 2007, the total take for HBO is estimated to be in excess of $212.5 million (Steinberg; Carter, "HBO Pushes End"). Even factoring the high cost HBO bears in producing the show—$2 million per episode in the first season, and, after contract renegotiations with talent,

$4 million per episode (Higgins and Romano)—$212.5 million is a huge sum for just one alternative distribution window. Indeed, HBO has been raking in profits from a variety of different windows. As of September 2004, DVD sales topped $300 million in profits to HBO (Levin), and are expected to exceed $360 million once the first six seasons become available. Licensing of *The Sopranos* for distribution in foreign markets, according to the trades, is expected to earn HBO an additional $75 million during the show's original run (Higgins and Romano). HBO has even contemplated making the show available for airplane distribution—the original reason for requiring the actors to loop their dialog with sanitized language—although it is unclear what revenue has yet to have been realized from that window (Steinberg).

The evident profit potential of *The Sopranos* program becomes all the greater when one considers that these are only the initial revenues from these alternative windows. In syndication, HBO should expect to continue to make big profits after A&E's five-year deal expires, and for many years to come. Hit series such as *Seinfeld* and *Friends* have shown themselves to be enormously profitable over several licensing cycles, and iconic series such as *I Love Lucy* and *Star Trek* can be cash cows for their owners even decades after production. Whether *The Sopranos*, as a serial drama, will achieve iconic status in syndication remains to be seen; network hits like *The X-Files* and *Dallas*, after all, never performed to expectations in syndication. At least in its initial cycle, *The Sopranos* will have an advantage over these earlier network shows. Since HBO's pay service reaches only a third of the TV audience, the show will be new to roughly two out of three viewers when it airs on A&E ("A&E Pays Big Bucks"). This is an advantage in the long run for HBO since these new viewers likely will mean higher ratings for *The Sopranos* on A&E, and higher fees for HBO when it licenses *The Sopranos* in its second syndication cycle. Moreover, even if *The Sopranos* fails to live up to expectations over the long haul in syndication, HBO still stands to gain, as even under-performing series make profits in syndication, since it costs HBO virtually nothing to participate in the revenue stream.

The prospects for broadening the exposure of *The Sopranos* at A&E should also bode well for DVD sales of the show. The reasons for this are two-fold. On the one hand, the success of a show in syndication functions to promote the DVD to new audiences. The release of the first two seasons of *Seinfeld* on DVD benefited greatly from its success in syndication (*Hollywood Reporter*, 3 May 2005). *Seinfeld*'s producers knew not only that they had a built-in audience for the DVD, but also that they could market the DVD by targeting that audience. In some respects, that is precisely what Twentieth Century Fox Television did with its prematurely canceled series *Family Guy* when it syndicated the show's fifty episodes to Cartoon Network. In that deal, Cartoon Network, in lieu of paying Fox its licensing fee, agreed to heavily promote Fox's *Family Guy* DVD during its highly rated Adult Swim programming block. The deal resulted in the *Family Guy* DVD becoming the bestselling television DVD, as new audiences found the show and created buzz about it (Adalian and Schneider). It's a testimony to the power of DVD sales that Fox also decided to resurrect the show with new episodes on its Fox Broadcasting Network in May 2005. In this light, it was not much of surprise when HBO and David Chase announced in August 2005 that they would extend *The Sopranos* into a de facto seventh season (Carter, "HBO Pushes End"); the production of those eight "bonus" episodes may end up being more of a business decision than a creative one. In the aftermath of the *Family Guy* juggernaut and *The Sopranos* unprecedented per-episode profit in its initial syndication deal, the show's owners ultimately may have found it too lucrative to pass up the opportunity to put more episodes in the can before ending the series.

In addition to the benefits of an expanding audience, *The Sopranos* enjoys a content advantage that may help fuel DVD sales once the program airs on A&E. *The Sopranos*, unlike *Seinfeld* and even *Family Guy*, is a show that was created for a premium cable service. Since A&E is a basic cable channel, and since it must rely on sponsorship, HBO is preparing a sanitized version with alternative dialog and less explicit images that would not alienate mass audiences and advertisers (Martin). If history is a judge, this could be a benefit or a curse in syndication. HBO branded comedies with strong sexual content such as Universal's *Dream On* and Sony's *The Larry Sanders Show* didn't translate well when they were stripped by their respective owners and tamed for mass audiences (Dempsey, "Cablers"). *Sex and the City*, an HBO-owned production which was stripped and edited for syndication on TBS in 2005, has fared very well in the ratings and is advertiser-supported cable's number one sitcom among adults 18 to 34 and 18 to 49, despite mixed reviews (Hill). Interestingly, the more negative reviews have come from fans who have seen the show unedited either on HBO or on DVD; audiences new to the show seem to like it since they either don't know what they are missing, or are happy to be watching a more wholesome version.

In any event, cleaning up *The Sopranos* may prove to be less controversial to viewers, since the explicit sexual content is less important to the show than its graphic violence. While A&E might have to tone down the violence in order to attract advertisers, the channel has already indicated that they may decide to air a more explicit version of the series late at night (Steinberg). Comedy Central, after all, is already deploying such a late-night strategy with its "Secret Stash" programming block. Indeed, it is this same logic of the taboo that may lead new *Sopranos* viewers on A&E to buy original, uncut episodes on DVD from HBO. While it may still be too soon to assess the impact of *Sex and the City*'s syndication on its DVD sales, channels such as Comedy Central have already profited immensely from the sales of uncut, unedited versions of their original series such as *South Park* and *Chappelle's Show* (Dutka).

As lucrative as HBO's syndication and DVD sales have been, they may represent only a small part of the revenue potential that building *The Sopranos* brand can bring. In addition to the profits made from selling distribution rights to the show itself, HBO has the potential for even greater profits through exploitations of *The Sopranos* brand in merchandising, franchising, and derivative works. As far as merchandising goes, the producers early on have carefully cultivated the image of the show and of the characters (*Hollywood Reporter*, 13 September 2002). By the end of the second season, visitors could go to the HBO website with the expectation of buying Sopranos' T-shirts, calendars, baseball jerseys, and gourmet foods. Authorized books, including a bestselling *Soprano's Family Cookbook* written in the voices of the show's characters, have also lined HBO's coffers (Brownfield,

"Nation"). While it appears that the owners are not yet exploiting the brand for high-end goods—they declined a deal for a Tony Soprano sports utility vehicle—there has been talk for some time of a Tony Soprano line of clothing. By 2002, one could even buy a CD-Rom containing the blueprints of the actual suburban house where the show is filmed (Brownfield, "Nation"). In 2004, HBO licensed the rights to *The Sopranos* to Cardini Industries for both a *Sopranos* Trivia game and a *Sopranos* poker set. HBO's director of licensing, Richard Oren, acknowledged that this was part of HBO's branding initiative. In addition to providing undisclosed royalties to HBO, "these products provide fans with fun ways to relive their experiences with the shows," Oren told the trades (Reynolds).

With respect to franchising and derivative works, the potential of *The Sopranos* to become another *Star Trek* has largely been untapped. Certainly, as with *Star Trek* and *The X-Files*, there has been talk about bringing *The Sopranos* to the big screen. Brad Grey, one of the executive producers of the series, has publicly acknowledged that making a feature based on the series would be an "interesting" way to "allow the series to grow" (Brownfield, "Nation") and series creator David Chase has not actively opposed the idea (Carter, "*Sopranos*"; Learmonth). Like *Star Trek* and *The X-Files*, the corporate entity that owns the property also owns a movie studio, so, from a synergy standpoint, it seems that Time Warner could easily make a feature deal. The more interesting question from a branding perspective is whether Time Warner would make the feature under its HBO Films banner, which would certainly help promote the HBO brand, or whether it would use one of its other studio imprints.

What does remain to be seen is whether Time Warner can turn *The Sopranos* phenomenon into the type of enduring, even if somewhat exhausted, franchise that Paramount was able to do with *Star Trek*. Can Time Warner make *The Sopranos* brand strong enough to sustain a series of movies, spin-off series, music soundtracks, and paperback novels? Can the brand survive inevitable cast changes and new settings and still draw audiences? Is America ready for a James Gandolfini album of Italian songs entitled "The Two Sides of Tony Soprano"? And years from now, will fans clamor for Gandolfini and castmates to come out of retirement for one last bada-boom, bada-bing? The answers to questions such as these, unknowable in 2005, are the Holy Grail for HBO's new model of brand building. In the era of TV III, it is just a matter of time before channels such as HBO become a relic of the past, replaced with new technologies of distribution like on-demand program streaming or on-line video file sharing. By building an identity that is separate from the physicality of a conduit, HBO may survive as a brand long after it has lost its relevance as a premium channel. If it succeeds in this new model of brand building, the users who stream on-demand or pay for file downloads may still be willing to pay a premium for content bearing the HBO imprimatur. After all, it will be more than just ordinary TV; it will still be HBO.

Gertrude Stein may be correct in observing that "a rose is a rose." But, as we have demonstrated, Hesh's reductive "a-hit-is-a-hit" insight deserves contestation—especially in the case of popular television. In TV I (the network era), a "hit" (as exemplified by shows like *Gunsmoke* and *I Love Lucy*) was defined in terms of gross ratings numbers; in TV II (the cable era), a "hit" television show was one that attracted quality demographics (as exemplified by NBC's "Must-See" lineup); In TV III (the digital era), "hit" television is not so much about ratings or demographics as it is about brand equity and the synergy of new revenue streams. So, like in baseball, there are "hits" and there are "hits!" Some series on HBO, like *Deadwood* or *Carnivale*, are in-field singles that enhance monthly audience appeal but have not generated exploitable buzz. Other series are doubles or triples. Consider, here, Larry David's *Curb Your Enthusiasm* which is no *Sex and the City* (or *Seinfeld*), but has succeeded in replicating the moderate success of previous HBO comedies like *The Larry Sanders Show*. And then there's a series like *The Sopranos* that achieves the status of a stand-alone brand and has the potential of generating even more profits outside the HBO distribution window. *The Sopranos*, then, is not just a "hit." It is a grand-slam.

Industrial New Jersey. Photograph by Michael Prete.

2.

HOMEWARD BOUND

THOSE *SOPRANOS* TITLES COME HEAVY

David Johansson

Flashback to the 1970s when a snippet of television rose to the level of high art and consider: who can remember the plot of a single episode of the crime-drama *Hawaii Five-0?* Anyone? Yet who can forget the show's brassy theme song, its explosive rhythms and wild crescendos set alongside shots of curling barrels of Pacific surf? The show's title sequence outlived the narratives it introduced and etched itself on cultural memory, and while no *Sopranos* fan is likely to forget the plot of a much-beloved episode, the show's title sequence weaves images and music and acting so deftly as to become a work of art all its own. More than just "opening credits," the title sequence arms every episode with a deadly effective introduction, and the viewer is warned: this television comes heavy.

In opera the overture introduces conflicts, sets up issues and foreshadows themes, establishing patterns and motifs which will run through the work until they collide, crash and climax, ending in resolution. Similarly, the title sequence of *The Sopranos* sets the mood and tone of the show, functions as prologue, and becomes epilogue, the tag by which the viewer remembers the whole series. Specifically, the word "overture" derives from the Latin *apertura*, source of the English word "aperture," suggesting an engagement of the audience as deep or deeper than in the operatic sense. That is, in order to see through an aperture the viewer must actively participate, as if leaning forward to spy through a peephole which, although small, provides a wide-angle view of a world outside the familiar door, a world as alien as it is hostile. Impelled by curiosity, the audience pays attention to the opening credits so as to get a glimpse through this *apertura*, this peephole, to see something forbidden, illegal, criminal.

Indeed, in terms of pure form, that is to say, cinematic technique, the title sequence is a tour de force, a showcase of meticulously edited symbols and images—*le montage magnifique*.[1] And yet as an artistic element discrete from the show, the sequence must overcome an enormous artistic obstacle; that is, given its function as a constant, the title sequence risks boring the audience. It plays every episode and so threatens to leach the energy of an art which relies on suspense for its fuel. That is, in a medium where "cliffhanger" endings are a staple, the reiteration of the sequence might become monotonous were it not for the understated use of the so-called "classical Hollywood style." Simply stated, this style, in which editing and symbolism remain transparent, employs a form, invisible to the untutored eye, in which devices call attention not to their own presentation but to their substance, their narrative importance in the plot. Through this invisibility, this concealment of artifice, the "naive" audience is "educated" and so prepared for the coming episode. Thus by examining this title sequence, this overture and frame, we may come to an appreciation of the art at the very heart of *The Sopranos*.

But first another aesthetic problem must be addressed: that of graceful exposition. In short, if part of the function of the overture is to establish setting and context, the writers must discover a way to release information organically, without awkward insertions which disrupt the natural rhythms of dialogue. The writers must paint *background* without interfering with the action in the *foreground*. On this delicate terrain, what is *not* done is as important as what *is* done. Specifically, dialogue *cannot* be spoken for the audience's benefit. For screenwriters and playwrights, it's known as the "hello, I-know-you-are-my-brother" syndrome, a species of clunky exposition where characters divulge information solely for the benefit of the supposedly unseen audience, amounting to an unfortunate pause in the action as the hapless viewer is brought up to speed. Happily, the title sequence of *The Sopranos* skirts this pitfall and fuses cinematic techniques in a seamless dance of visual and aural rhythms, while also providing plot points and story elements, echoing past tragedies and foreshadowing future conflicts.

In structure, the shots alternate between Tony and what Tony sees, establishing a visual rhythm and a counterpoint between subject and object, thesis and antithesis. Accordingly, the most important values lie in juxtaposition: that is, not in thesis or antithesis, but in *synthesis*, those flashes between subject and object, where the animate meets the inanimate, a metaphor for the struggle of light against dark, life against death.

Structurally, then, the sequence exists as an artistic "compound" born of three elements: the action, consisting of the images themselves divorced from the context of *The Sopranos*; the re-action as these images are processed through Gandolfini's use of method acting—where they signify meanings peculiar to Tony's character and, finally, the music, the catalyst which binds the action to the re-action so as to yield a work of art which releases energy—"energy" the viewer experiences as aesthetic pleasure.

First, and most obviously, the action consists of images which exist outside an HBO series; they are real objects, after all, on a real highway, where they exist as signifiers not only for the fictional history of Tony Soprano but also as recognizable signposts for the audience. From the giant statue of the laborer (who bears a passing resemblance to the legendary giant lumberjack Paul Bunyan) to the well-maintained lawns of suburbia, these are *American* images, from the industrial to the upper class, a running catalog of familiar symbols which initiates the viewer's identification with Tony. What's more, they are viewed from a moving car, again inviting a bond between audience and protagonist because the viewer must travel and endure the same road as the hero; indeed, as Tony emerges from the Lincoln tunnel he enters the most common of American denominators: the lousy business of the long drive home—the shared ordeal of millions fleeing the rat race after another long day.

The sequence opens with the ceiling lights of the Lincoln Tunnel—dim bulbs marking a path out of the underworld, followed by flashes of the roof and wall tiles shot through the windshield of Tony's car as it hurtles toward the bright mouth of the tunnel. Exiting the darkness, the New York skyline appears across the Hudson River through the passenger-side window followed by New Jersey's industrial outskirts, with its enormous fuel tanks, towering smokestacks and dirty waterways, punctuated by shots of highway exit signs. A cemetery passes—the most common of all ground—and the camera continues its tour of the social strata.

For a moment, the entire city is reflected in a hubcap. Further on, more industrial parks, enormous bridges, factory pollution, the tank emblazoned with "Drive Safely"—a caution in wildly ironic contrast to the outlaw at the wheel—then the giant figure of the worker, and the depressingly straightforward "Pizzaland" sign. The sequence ends with shots of working-class, then middle-class city homes, and finally the forested road leading to the driveway of Tony's *nouveau riche*, essentially gaudy home, symbolic of that economic class which is somehow unselfconscious in its naked wish to be noticed and admired.

In filmic terms, this impression is deepened through careful editing. That is, in the course of the sequence, Tony's decades-long background is compressed into moments. Known in film circles as "cutting to continuity," the succession of shots serves to concentrate the narrative and condense time and space. Its principle feature, then, is *economy*. Everything shown stands for everything *not* shown and as a result what is *excluded* is as significant as what is *included*. Accordingly, in *The Sopranos on the Couch*, Maurice Yacowar writes:

> Where is the natural world? All we see is the man-made: factories, icons, bridges. The only animal we see is the fake pig atop Satriale's—a parody of animal life. Without vegetation and natural comfort Tony's industrial empire seems a wasteland. We only see other people in one quick shot, four young men walking abreast. Whether to work or from work or without work, they are a feeble balance against this non-human

characterization of Tony's world ... Driving home from work, Tony takes us from the wasteland to the pocket of luxury that wasteland supports... (170)

Taking Yacowar's point a step further, nature itself is revealed as the incarnation of wealth, once humble countryside suddenly fenced off for the pleasure of the upper class, the owners of things and land. Like all Americans, Tony finds himself thrust into this crowded arena where he must fight for his family's space, their very right to live; thus, *The Sopranos* creates a moral ambiguity, one which invites the viewer to share the character's frustration. In other words, like Tony, modern men and women find themselves crowded into smaller and more expensive spaces, and as the population grows so does pressure and stress. Accordingly, the modern becomes primitive and resorts to violence in the defense of territory, including violence not only physical but also emotional and verbal. Regarding the moral judgment of Tony's violent conduct, then, the images ask us to understand the pain of his struggle upward through the strata of American class, because unless born wealthy, the viewer has also traveled a hard road toward the American Dream and so knows the many bumps and potholes of that drive all too well.

THE RE-ACTION

As a "road movie" in miniature, the title sequence renders the American landscape as an urban, sterile place, deprived of natural wonder yet possessed of all the danger of the jungle, one populated by gangsters and civilians alike, all facing the common problem of survival. It is on this level, then, of identification with the protagonist, that the sequence continues to accrue meaning over time, a deepening of the narrative achieved through the deftly edited reaction shots of James Gandolfini. Indeed, Gandolfini's face conveys as much in silence as when he is speaking—an appealing combination akin to another towering method actor, the late Marlon Brando, whose animal ferocity and volcanic temper were shot through with childlike vulnerability. The quality of that "method" acting here is noteworthy since the acting happens in frame. Accordingly, in close-up the audience enjoys a proximity to the actor impossible in live theatre: the viewer is intensely intimate with him, inside the character's private space, inside the action in a way impossible with an actual stage.

Seen from this distance, Tony's quirks and idiosyncrasies are individual in the extreme, yet he's also representative of the working class, creating a kind of Joe Six Pack on steroids. Over the mass of men and women and their lives of quiet desperation, he has risen from the dark of the tunnel as champion and anti-hero, saluted by the highway lines gliding past at the speed of music, sound and sight, *in concert*. He's a bad guy, certainly—but we're with him, inside the frame with his face, his hairy hands, his brute strength, his air of danger, but within the intimate bounds of the car we get a sense of strength in repose, the alpha male at rest, his guard down, vulnerable. And this deepens the viewer's sympathy for the "hero" because, even though he *is* a bad guy, we're *right there* with him, in tight proximity, where the sense of Tony's physical presence—his aura—feels private, as though we are being trusted. He may be a tough guy but for now he's alone, as naked as the rest of us.

Of course, it's a truism that great actors keep acting even when they're not talking, and Gandolfini's expressive face articulates this principle. His animal magnetism sucks us in, and we follow our unlikely hero on his way home as he skirts deadly hazards both inside himself and in the world. Carpooling with Tony in cinematic space, we watch as the actor descends deeply into the role, chomping his cigar, grabbing the toll ticket with disdain and defiance—a lion among hyenas, a beast in the jungle made so by the fact of other beasts in the jungle. Gandolfini's talent is that we can see him thinking, hear the whisper of his interior monologue, allowing us to imagine his loves and fears and terrors, all the while staring into his unlikely mug. The fake pig above Satriale's, for example, resonates with meaning when we learn the store is the site of the beginning of Tony's panic attacks, the place where he watched his father cut off a debtor's finger ("Fortunate Son," 3.03). These symbols amass meaning over time and take on the same silent menace for us as they do for Tony, and as time progresses our identification deepens further still, and so does our sympathy, our willingness to forgive his transgressions—and this is the heart of the show: given cruel conditioning and a hostile environment: we're all capable of behaving as brutally as Tony.

To reiterate, then, the chief dramatic component of the reaction is Tony's stop at the toll booth, a multi-layered symbol. Indeed, the toll booth is democracy in action—*everybody pays*, even mob bosses. This is America, where, ideally, equality reigns and justice is blind. Accordingly, the ticket machine cannot be intimidated, even by Tony, and so it represents impersonal bureaucracy and faceless government—the system. Tony must enter it like anyone else who wishes to drive down the highway of the American Dream. And in that dream, which is *not* about 2.5 kids and a white picket fence (as so many college freshmen seem to believe), lie the perils and opportunities of class mobility, of living in a country where citizens may take the long road from rags to riches and so achieve in that pursuit what is presumably their happiness.

For Tony is a social climber, and achieving the top of the ladder is meaningless without a sign to advertise it. Implicit within that dream, of course, lies the faith that riches do in fact lead to happiness, a dangerous assumption explored by classics of American literature such as *The Great Gatsby* and *Death of a Salesman*. And while Tony is no Willy Loman, he shares the salesman's stress of maintaining two personas: one for business, one for home. Additionally, he shares an obsession with paternal approval while also struggling to save his own son from suffering a fate like his own, although as in Miller's American tragedy, it's hubris which dooms Tony to repeat his own mistakes, compulsively, no matter his medication and therapy. Like Willy Loman and his son Biff, Tony obsessively tries to root out the bad seed in his son, intent on creating a man without his fatal flaws, only to see the son, like Biff, begin to recapitulate his father's failures. Indeed, the expression on Tony's face gains new meaning as the audience becomes aware of more back story, of Tony's ambivalent feelings toward his own father, of the sense that he's been trapped by fate, whose burden he must shoulder so as to spare his own son a similar end. Of course, on the first viewing none of this derives from the title sequence; it is only after the show has gone on for several seasons that the title sequence increases in richness, as layers of meaning ripple outward over episodes past.

Gandolfini's face as he arrives home is itself a work of art—one composed of acting, cinematography, and creative writing, for even as his character should be reaping his reward and taking his ease after his journey, he arrives at his suburban palace with not so much a look on his face as the absence of a look. Put mildly, he isn't smiling. That Tony must traverse dangerous ground with his family echoes an earlier warning he received: the sign on the enormous industrial fuel tank cheerily exhorting him to "Drive Safely" (a sign which grows in absurdity every time the viewer sees it since this is a world where no one is ever "safe"), a fact Tony understands and which is reflected in the gruff set of his mouth. In his mind, only his fortitude and protection shield his family from the awful knowledge of how the world outside their door really operates.

Faced with death and darkness, all one can do is endure—aspire even—to loyalty, courage, respect, and adherence to the blood bond of family, *this thing of ours*—a bond at its weakest in solitude, that space where doubt creeps in... all this is written across Tony's face as he steers his car toward home and hearth like a modern Odysseus, while below the mantle of his courage lies a soul wracked by doubt, tortured as to the nature of Fate. Must it be fought or accepted? Ascending his driveway, Gandolfini's acting renders the clear expression of decidedly mixed feelings. Filled as much with love as with fear, Tony's homecoming represents an emotional pinnacle, as though he were summiting the peak of his own heart, a climax conveyed through sound as well as space, that crescendo at the top of the hill.

In the shot of Tony's arrival in his driveway, the writers and directors announce themselves and, because these names change, an element of artistic suspense is introduced quite apart from the plot. We learn to spot our favorite "authors" and so become sensitized to their editing styles, choices in music, and preferences in storyline, aware that our pleasure in the show lies not only in identifying with the characters but also in appreciating their creators, whose faces we do not see but whose work we can affirm with a shiver of satisfaction. Then the show's logo appears—*The SopRanos*—the R replaced by a gun, their name branded by violence, the life-blood of their identity—and not so much violence, as *the threat* of violence, the very definition of suspense, of art coming heavy.

THE CATALYST

The visual rhythms are backed throughout the title sequence by the music of A3—also known as Alabama 3—a British acid house band belting out "Woke Up This Morning," the catalyst which accelerates the synthesis of the action with the re-action. As Kevin Fellezs writes in *This Thing of Ours: Investigating the Sopranos*, "Chase is clearly aware of the way soundtracks can increase the interaction between the music and the action onscreen—the music not only cues the audience to any number of interior processes ... the character and the viewer are thus often hearing the music in a similar, if not identical way" (167). Indeed, the song's lyrics provide an apt form for Tony's content: "Born under a bad sign," he vows to overcome the crippling mother who destroyed his father, striving through sheer will to render himself acceptable not only to her but also to himself, a place where he's burnished with a "shotgun shine." The song encourages the viewer to root for Tony as the heroic underdog, the man who will defeat the curse of his birth, the man whose Papa "never told him about right and wrong." Despite his ill-fated nativity, he's got a "blue moon in his eye," a good omen and a sign that he may yet steer clear of disaster and find his way home, an elusive spot at the top of the hill inside himself.

Excerpted from a twenty-five-minute rave mix, "Woke Up This Morning" (aka the theme to *The Sopranos*) has a surprising origin. "It's had a strange and jagged existence," states A3 singer Rob Spragg. The song's beginnings lie in the early 1990s, when Spragg learned of a case in England concerning a wife who, after twenty years of abuse, picked up a gun and killed her husband. Inspired, Spragg composed the song's opening line: "Woke up this morning, and I got myself a gun."

Ironically, while "Woke Up This Morning" began as a tale of female rebellion, it's now tied to outsized manliness, or, as Spragg puts it, "The song went from feminism to gangsterism" (Boehlert 1–3). When *Sopranos* creator David Chase discovered the tune (edited down from its original length) he supposedly announced on the spot that that was going to be the theme song to *The Sopranos*. "Our publisher called and told us about some mob show that wanted to use the song," Spragg says. "We got $40,000, but of course we owed all that to our record company. Then six months later we started getting calls from our friends in New York telling us all about the show" (Boehlert 1–3).

What the band learned was that the show had become an epic, a saga whose hero has been as stalwart in his drive to return home as that other epic hero, the Greek Odysseus. Braving monsters on all sides, Tony has fought many battles and complicated many plots, yet from the pilot to the last episode the same title sequence has rolled, its echo deepening as the years have passed. Why? Because for all his gangster ways, his testosterone-fueled bravado, Tony still has to confront the wife and family, function under their rules, enter a world of ethics on the other side of the galaxy from the laws governing the back room of the Bing. And unlike that earlier Odysseus, Tony's homecoming is fraught with misgiving. His drive up the hill to his house has the tone of a man ascending the gallows, and when the music crescendos, the end comes as suddenly as if a needle had been knocked off a turntable, ripping sound into silence, life into death.

We have, in short, arrived.

And come further still. Over the years, climbing aboard for that same ride home with Tony, it's as if the character has personally trusted us with his address, his family, his secrets, and if only for a while, we are all "made" guys. "Born under a bad sign" though he may be, we begin to root for him because we are now part of his crew. At another level, too, we realize, the creators of the show are inviting us to measure our actions against a code, a system of honor and dishonor which is lethally clear, unlike the foggy gray areas where most of us live, commuting home from our own concerns in the "real" world. Invited into that thing of *theirs*, and its art, we leave the *Sopranos* epic and its overture with our understanding of the human predicament deepened if not illuminated, all The Big Questions asked if not answered, and when the credits roll for the last time, we may see that this art is as "real" as anything else in life.

This is the brilliance of *The Sopranos* title sequence.

SOPRANOS WOMEN

3.

WHAT HAS CARMELA EVER DONE FOR FEMINISM?

CARMELA SOPRANO AND THE POST-FEMINIST DILEMMA

Janet McCabe and Kim Akass

Carmela Soprano. A feminist? *Fuhggedaboutit*. One might, as Lisa Cassidy (97) has already noted, be hard pushed to recruit the social-climbing Mafia housewife from the leafy New Jersey suburbs for the feminist cause. She lives a comfortable upper middle-class existence partly paid for by prostitution; she resolves to establish her independence but remains reliant on Tony Soprano's ill-gotten gains to secure that future; she does charitable deeds only to disapprove of the unwed mothers she is meant to be helping; she is full of pious virtue yet quite prepared to shake down a woman to write a college recommendation for her daughter, Meadow; she supports widowed girlfriends with baked goods and sympathy but only until her husband tells her to terminate the friendship; she continues having sex with her adulterous spouse despite knowing about his sexual indiscretions; and she holds traditional, even conservative moral views while turning a blind eye to what her husband does for a living and enjoying the lifestyle he provides for her and her family. We have no quarrel with Cassidy's basic assessment that Carmela is an embarrassment to the feminist struggle (97–98).

And yet...

There is something utterly compelling about Carmela for two self-confessed feminists like us. But what exactly is it about her that proves so attractive? At first glance she would fit the description of a victim—the woman whose entire life appears mired in compromise. But Carmela is no victim, and neither would she see herself as one. Far removed from the Mafioso wife as a hapless casualty of male (generic) violence, Carmela Soprano possesses a tremendous sense of agency from within the multiple institutions that seek to disenfranchise and even oppress her. Her resistance, or possibly her will-to-empowerment, confirms the work of feminist historians such as Susan Stanford Friedman and Linda Gordon who have identified ways in which women have over time negotiated uncompromising social power that seeks to constrain them. Responding to her friend Rosalie Aprile's assessment of how Hillary Rodham Clinton handled the public humiliation following revelations of Bill Clinton's infidelities—"She took all that negative bullshit he gave her and spun it into gold"—Carmela nods in agreement: "She's a role model for us all" ("Amour Fou," 3.12). Given how Hillary's political career has since developed, the long-suffering Mafia wives who likewise take "all that negative bullshit" know there is more at stake here. As we have argued elsewhere (Akass and McCabe 156), Carmela has indeed long accepted her husband's countless affairs as the cost of her pre-eminent narrative position.

Maybe Carmela is more of a feminist than she thinks. "Doesn't anything ever change?" opines Carmela to Rosalie ("Mergers and Acquisitions," 4.08). "Women are supposed to be partners nowadays. I'm no feminist. I'm not saying fifty/fifty. But Jeez." No surprise that she rejects feminism. But nothing is ever quite that simple when it comes to Carmela Soprano. Expressing her frustration with Tony's intransigence over money matters finds her entangled in contradiction, as in "I am not a feminist, but I believe in some equality for women." It leads us to suggest that the contradictions and paradoxes defining this strong and complicated woman might be symptomatic of a broader dilemma facing women in the post-feminist (media) age. It is our contention, and the subject of this chapter, that what makes Carmela Soprano so pleasurably compelling is how she gives representation to the paradox defining contemporary womanhood, "shaped by struggles between various feminisms as well as by cultural backlash against feminism and activism" (Heywood and Drake 2).

FEMINISM'S DISSENTING DAUGHTERS: MEDIA BACKLASH, CONTESTING VOICES AND POST-FEMINISM

Carmela is not the only woman to be distrustful of feminism. Prevailing wisdom at the end of the 1980s suggested that something had gone seriously awry. Substantial gains had been made; but younger women were turning away from feminism in droves. Refusing the feminist label makes Carmela similar to other women hesitating to adopt the feminist mantle. They see traditional feminism as having little relevance to their lives, their experiences, their familial concerns. Many indeed sense that feminism abandons them once they embrace traditional roles as homemaker, "just a housewife" rather than wage earner—an alleged separation between the public world of the labor market and the private space of domesticity and childrearing (Williams 41). It also bespeaks a lack of radical politicization and a lack of access to what many women like Carmela perceive as an exclusive public sphere where ideological feminism functions—an elitist, Ivy-league world of white, middle-class academic thinking where her daughter Meadow may belong but she certainly never will. Superficially at least Carmela rejects feminism as "an elitist practice" (Siegel, "Reading" 62), caricatured (however wrongly) by Rene Denfeld as "all but inaccessible to the uninitiated" (5).

But where does such an attitude come from? Orthodox wisdom decrees that the media backlash against feminism and feminist activism is responsible (Faludi; Williams; Douglas; Douglas and Michaels). Media reporting translated diverse intellectual thinking, collective political action, and multifaceted dialogue into a monolithic feminism, devalued (often comically) to an image of a strident, man-hating, unattractive militant—possibly lesbian. Writes Susan Faludi, considering how the media "neutralized" (76) feminism: "the press, carried by tides it rarely fathomed, acted as a force that swept the general public, powerfully shaping the way people would think and talk about the feminist legacy and the ailments it supposedly inflicted on women" (77). So successful has the media been in imbibing public opinion in the backlash against feminism that history is forgotten and replaced with created myths. Fabrication is translated into fact, bringing about the retreat from feminism that has subsequently occurred (Faludi 80-1; Heywood and Drake 49). Scores of women have imbibed the antifeminist stereotypes (Findlen xiv-xv), and "bought in to the media demonization of 'sisterhood'" (Heywood and Drake 49), leaving them pitted against each other—divided over the issues in public and conflicted in private.

Carmela Soprano is saturated in and produced through this media-generated paradox. She may belong to a generation of women born into the sexual revolution and the woman's movement, and grew up with "a sense of entitlement so strong that ... denied any form of sexism existed" (42), but she came of age during the cultural backlash and its mix of socio-sexual contradictions embedded in the ideologies of the New Right. Rooted in a tight-knit ethnic community, subject to the laws of alliance codified by Catholicism, marriage, and kinship, and locked into the generic world of the gangster, she is further enclosed in a cultural world where feminist thinking has no place. No wonder she has no sense of belonging with feminism. But Carmela, in so many ways, is an allegory for the paradoxical identities and contradictions confronting contemporary (American) women who "seem to have swallowed [the media-produced backlash] whole" (49). Calls from feminist theorists like Donna Haraway demand that contemporary feminist thinking address this problem and identify "a politics that acknowledges the multiple and contradictory aspects of both individual and collective identities" (quoted in Siegel, "Reading" 53). Contradiction and paradox are not only the preserve of theoretical inquiry but embedded right into the very forms that represent these Generation X women.

Developing third wave feminism is marked, in the words of Deborah L. Siegel "by the politics of ambiguity" (60); its criticism seeks to forge a feminist politics that better understands representational contradictions and is guilty of even transgressive pleasures. Agreeing with Leslie Heywood and Jennifer Drake, we too are "pop-culture babies; we want some pleasure with our critical analysis" (51-2).

Criticism here becomes a form of activism, allowing multiple voices and contesting opinions to co-exist in an unpredictable alliance; and reminding us what the media backlash wanted us to forget: "the power of representation to promote or contest domination" (51). Emerging here is the idea that contradiction and ambiguity manifest in the very representational forms, as in Carmela as textual character. Unlocking the most unpromising representations to pleasure, contradiction is inherent in the travesty of her morality (Nochimson, "Waddaya" 10), her competing desires, her addiction to unattainable men, her lifestyle funded by blood money—and our pleasurable emotional response to a woman who betrays every feminist value we hold dear.

Given that the media creates paradox, Carmela brings that paradox into discourse. Stuck between the self-contained, cause-and-effect generic structure of the gangster film (Warshow 1962) and the more ambiguous and contradictory form associated with melodrama and soap opera (Feuer; Gledhill), forged from competing representational archetypes ranging from domestic goddess, melodramatic victim to Mafia matriarch, Carmela struggles *in* and *through* representation. Such a dilemma is rooted in the third wave feminist project, in which the "subject is always in process" (Siegel, "Reading" 60). Third wave subjectivity, writes Rebecca Walker, seeks "to create identities that accommodate ambiguity and our multiple positionalities; including more than excluding, exploring more than defining, searching more than arriving" (xxxiii). Is this not a perfect description of television characters like Carmela Soprano that we find so truly compelling and terrifyingly like us? Is not the longer television serial format better able to accommodate the ambiguity and a subject in the process of becoming never resolved? Focusing on how Carmela negotiates an empowering subjectivity that embraces paradox and complexity, we will explore the ways in which her choices and actions, seemingly at odds with feminism, push us into new directions for a feminist television criticism in the post-feminist age.

"SHE'S A ROLE MODEL FOR US ALL": CARMELA, IDEAL WOMANHOOD AND THE APPROVED (MEDIA) SCRIPT

Carmela probably feels she has no need of feminism. She has it all.

Content to stay at home raising her children and hosting fun pool parties for family and friends, she has a beautiful home, a designer wardrobe, and expensive Italian strappy sandals to die for. Whiling away her time with shopping sprees, trips to the gym, lunch with girlfriends and attending her local Catholic church, her fridge is always stocked, the beds made, and her nails perfectly manicured. She wants for nothing. Carmela imposes herself as a role model for us all, "enforces the norm and safeguards the truth" (Foucault, *Will* 3) about ideal American womanhood that the media works so hard to promote. Given that America is in the throes of a seismic political and religious shift to the right, shaped by the rise to prominence of the fundamentalist Christian Right with its pro-life, pro-family, anti-gay agenda, Carmela is well rehearsed in its rhetoric. Moving around her ergonomic kitchen, she is saturated in the nostalgic language of the media backlash, seducing us with the promise of simpler, better times when women knew their place and life was less complicated. Tony may say, "[out] there it's the 1990s; in this house, it's 1954" ("Nobody Knows Anything," 1.11), but it is Carmela who compels us to think this way. Superficially at least, as a glossy media representation, she is "simply another impossible contrivance of perfect womanhood" (Walker, *To Be Real* xxxiii).

In the patriarchal world par excellence of the Mafia, where women are unlikely to be running the firm, or even considered important enough to matter beyond providing domestic support, Carmela has long understood the formidable power embedded in roles to which no one pays much attention—and it is worth remembering that the Soprano women do not even figure on the FBI flow chart of Mafia connections. Given that the gangster genre offers us a (filmic) discourse on power, in which the generic codes and conventions compel characters to act and behave in certain ways, Carmela takes great pains to be seen playing by the rules. She operates inside meticulous codes—of marriage sanctified by the Catholic Church, of motherhood extolled by popular media rhetoric, of family valorized by the Mafia and its generic laws. It is a lesson in unseen power whereby the legitimate wife and mother quite literally lay down the law; she is privileged, she *is* privilege. No wonder Tony frustratedly complains that Carmela breaks his balls—yet he can do nothing about it. Her power comes from acting out "that [which] we no longer perceive ... as the effect of power that constrains us" (Foucault, *Will* 60).

Her steely silences and those reproachful looks often speak louder than any words Carmela can utter. One stern look from her can stop Tony dead in his tracks. He often finds it difficult to resist his wife; and even if he does say "no," she will only find another line of attack before he gives in. Season Four opens with Carmela worried about the family finances ("For All Debts Public and Private," 4.01). After seeing Pussy's widow Angie Bonpensiero handing out Kielbasa samples at the local supermarket, Carmela becomes apprehensive about her long-term financial security. She picks her moment. Serenaded by Dean Martin crooning "Time for the Cowboy to Dream," Tony prepares for a quiet evening in front of the television watching *Rio Bravo* (Howard Hawks, 1959) and eating an ice cream sundae. His guard down and mouth full, she moves in. Standing over him, her dour look immediately makes him feel shamefaced. What has he done now? "I'm worried Tony." "About my weight?" "About money," she retorts. As he explains the temporary dip in his fortunes, Carmela cuts him off. What future provision has he made for her and the children? His reassurance fails to placate. She turns off the television and fixes him with resolve. Her silence forces him to further elaborate. The less she says the more he gabbles; and the more questions she asks the less sense he makes. Her suggestions for simple estate planning and trust funds are met with stern refusal. Telling him that if he only watched the news (and as a woman familiar with how the media script works, she knows what she is talking about) he would understand that "everything comes to an end." She retreats. Tony may think that this conversation is at an end, but Carmela knows differently. It will take the entire season, but she will get what she wants. Tearful recriminations, locking herself in the bathroom, afternoons spent curled up on the couch, playing the disrespected wife, the neglected spouse, clandestine trips to the backyard storage bin, and silently pushing papers in front of Tony to sign show Carmela working her angle. Tony may command the sixty-minute narrative but she takes control of the thirteen-episode arc that unsettles any authority he may think he has. By the end of this season she has her diverse portfolio and a second home along the coast. Result.

As "pop-culture babies," we acknowledge that ideal femininity is a scripted cultural performance but yet are utterly beguiled by it at the same time; we get it as a representation that endorses dominant structures of power while deliberately (even to the point of forgetting what we know) taking pleasure in consuming it. Caught in this paradox is Carmela. Our media-savvy Generation X-er knows only too well what the dominant script means and the rewards to be had from living it. She comprehends that mainstream cultural fictions are hostile to anything other than prescribed models of femininity; and she appreciates the hold these images have over the popular imagination as well as generic fictions and a media-literate (television) audience. Her deft ability to play the self-sacrificing angel in the house—"another scripted role to perform in the name of biology and virtue" (Walker, *To be Real* xxxiii)—is Carmela's narrative advantage. Her will-to-empowerment comes not from critiquing such an image of female accomplishment and normalcy, from resisting the representation (of which she embodies), but from being granted legitimacy in and through approved representational forms that are culturally sanctioned and generically privileged.

Heywood and Drake contest that "living up to images of success requires keeping secrets" (41). Who but Carmela knows better about keeping up appearances and her mouth shut? Heavily invested in her construction as a smart (but not overtly clever), attractive, and self-possessed upper-middle-class married woman with children requires her to deny what such a socially privileged image is built on—criminality and the shifting sands of moral relativism. But given that this is television and that the longer serial narrative arc "imposes meticulous rules of self-examination" (Foucault, *Will* 19), disclosure is inevitable. Operating within a longer television serial form, subject to its particular narrative mechanisms, compels Carmela to bring forth that which her representation works so hard to repress. Nowhere is her dilemma more evident than when she seeks counseling ("Second Opinion," 3.07). Referred to a psychiatrist, Dr. Krakower, by Dr. Melfi, Carmela feels liberated enough to confess to knowing about

Tony's involvement in organized crime, about the whores, about the numerous infidelities. Only in this place of tolerance—the other being the confessional—can Carmela say what in other circumstances is clandestine and circumscribed. She says what should never be uttered: namely, the contradictory cost she pays for living the image applauded by dominant culture. Transgressing Mafia law and lifting prohibitions holding the traditional image of femininity in place, there is a pleasure within her dissent. But she does not get the reaction she had hoped. Dr. Krakower suggests that she will never be able to "feel good about herself" while she is an accomplice to her husband's unlawful activities. Carmela retreats into the image: all she does is to "make sure he has clean clothes in his closet and dinner on his table," saying this should grant her immunity. The psychiatrist is having none of it: "Enabler would be a more adequate job description for you than accomplice. My apologies." More shocking still: Dr. Krakower refuses to take Tony's "blood money" in payment for the session. And neither should she. He tells Carmela in no uncertain terms that her only recourse is to "take only the children and go."

Considering Carmela has long been "invested in the work of keeping silent, shoring up images and narrative that [she thinks] help [her] survive" (Heywood and Drake 41), she seems to deliberately mishear what Dr. Krakower is saying to her: "So you think I need to define my boundaries more clearly. Keep a certain distance. Not internalize my..." Lisa Cassidy reads her moral reasoning as indicative of her care ethics, of "[a] feminine voice [speaking] with endless qualifications and compromises" (102). Maybe so. But her dilemma goes to the very heart of living the approved script. Carefully selecting only what she wants to hear reveals the messiness involved in keeping the boundaries that hold her sense of self in place; to inhabit the image of feminine perfection means silence must shroud anything that falls outside this privileged representation. Deciding that "this Jewish doctor 'cannot understand' the Catholic attitude toward marriage" (Nochimson, "Waddaya" 11), she consults her priest instead. His sage advice: "Live on the good part. And forgo those things that lay without it" ("Amour Fou," 3.12). Christian penance is enough; and the confessional proves a safer more discrete space that takes better precautions to safeguard her revelation. And here lies the rub. Carmela is committed to working with contradiction and inconsistency in order to collude "with approved scripts" (Heywood and Drake 14) from which she stands most to benefit. Carmela chooses the advice that will ensure she can remain in her beautiful home; and her ponderous silence reveals the lengths to which she must go to continue living the image she has worked so hard to cultivate—and retain her narrative supremacy.

FOR THE LOVE OF FURIO: SCRIPTING FANTASY AND FEMINIST DILEMMAS

Thinking through further the complexities involved in colluding with approved scripts leads us to consider the role played by fantasy in staging Carmela's dilemmas—and in particular the scripted fantasy of heterosexual romance conditioning her desire. Nowhere is the struggle more evident than in her involvement with Furio Giunta. Season Four finds her captivated by Tony's young, pony-tailed, olive-skinned henchman, who arrived from Naples two seasons before. Turning up each morning to chauffeur her husband to work, and flirting over coffee and home-baked scones, Furio becomes a welcome distraction from the domestic routine. It starts out innocently enough until Carmela decides to take the initiative. Chaperoned by her son, A. J., she calls on Furio under the pretence of helping him with a real-estate problem ("The Weight," 4.04). He ushers his visitors out back where he is assembling a pergola on which to grow grapes. As Furio recounts his memories of when he was at his happiest, Carmela becomes entranced. His talk of working in the fields, toiling as a farm laborer, of the hot sun, of the smell of olives, feeds into her own phallic imaginings. Secretly reveling in the sight of his muscular physique finds her lost in fantasies of erotic pleasure, relishing in the possibilities of mutual intimacy "her" Dionysian hero might offer her, and leaving her quite literally speechless. Regaining her composure, feeling guilt and delight, shame and desire, she starts talking building regulations. But her unease, caught between romantic bliss and cultural remorse, betrays ambivalence: a struggle between the constraints prescribed by class and culture and the pleasures and perils involved in imagining erotic acts that contravene restrictive laws governing appropriate feminine propriety.

Feminist criticism has long grappled with the complexities of romance fictions and their extraordinary appeal for a female readership (Modleski, *Loving* and *Old*; Radway). While feminism has been telling women since the 1970s to break free of the narratives that demand female self-sacrifice and perpetuate socio-sexual subjugation, these stories continue to exert a considerable psychic hold over most of us. Women may be told it is "wrong" to have these fantasies, and feminist criticism may have provided tools to critique the myth of heterosexual romantic love, but the fairy tale of being swept off one's feet remains one women imbibe as a normal pleasure. It is no small coincidence that Carmela chooses to fall for the archetypal bad boy—the dark brooding phallic hero that has long populated cultural myths and the visual arts. As an audience we are privy, in a dramatic irony, to the fact that he is a brutal killer not averse to beating up children ("Commendatori," 2.04) and torturing women ("Big Girls Don't Cry," 2.05). Crikey. But it is worth noting here that we too get caught up in Carmela's longing for Furio; that we come to see him in an entirely different, more romantic light. Suggested here is that even while feminism has taught us to be suspicious of what he embodies as a male archetype, we are nonetheless implicated in an institutionalized sexism and beguiled for better or worse by old pleasures where "[men] crave power and orgasm, while women seek reciprocity and intimacy" (Echols 53). We are not claiming Carmela—or us for that matter—is suffering from false consciousness, or is simply complicit with patriarchal thinking. (Okay, well, maybe just a little bit.) But instead Carmela's complex articulation of her own yearning may give us insight into how women experience desire and fantasies (possibly erotic).

Third-wave feminists (Wolf; Walter) warn that for feminism to ignore the pleasures that heterosexual women gain from dominant cultural fantasies would be perilous. Driven by a generational entitlement to pursue sexual pleasures, their work demands that feminism grant, in the words of Merri Lisa Johnson, "permission to explore our sexuality and the sex limits we transgress" (44). The third wave's particular contribution to feminism has been to navigate a new sexual politics. Opening up new avenues for thinking and writing about sex and sexual pleasures has disrupted norms surrounding the body, troubled rigid gender identities and taken liberties with the language when talking dirty (Walker, *To Be Real*; Damsky; Johnson). Despite championing (however precariously) an empowered vision of female sexuality, women of this generation "hesitate to own up to the romantic binds [they] find [themselves] in, the emotional entanglements that compromise [their] principles" (Johnson 14). What lies not too far beneath the surface of hard-won rights and progress for women is our struggle with theorizing heterosexual desire and being aroused by romantic fictions that walk a fine line between erotic indulgence and rape.

bell hooks lays down the gauntlet here: "[One] major obstacle preventing us from transforming ... culture is that heterosexual women have not unlearned a heterosexist-based 'eroticism' that constructs desire in such a way that many of us can only respond rhetorically to male behavior that has already been coded as masculine within the sexist framework" (111). But is this possible from inside discourses that institutionalize heterosexuality? As Carmela finds out to her cost in Season Five when she wants out, there is no outside the cultural law; she is in fact always "inside" power (of the Mafia, of Catholicism, of media representation, of the television narrative) and subject to its rules, prohibitions and controls. Her romantic dilemma represents resistance; but only because it is represented through fictional forms that find it difficult to conceive of desire as anything other than straight.

It seems to us that despite proving adept at knowing how media fictions work, and despite arguing elsewhere for "Carmela's formal authority over a savvy, media-saturated series that is punctuated with film references, pop songs, and media-hip gangsters" (Akass and McCabe 161), she remains at the same time inescapably bound by the meticulous rules governing these media forms. The delight and awkwardness Carmela experiences in fantasizing about Furio while having to relate to him reveal the conflicts and contradictions inherent in imagining desire from within a rigid representational system. Represented in and through prescribed media narrative and generic conventions, her fantasy is regulated and managed. Egged on by Tony, Carmela accepts Furio's invitation to take part in a traditional Neapolitan dance during his housewarming party ("The Weight," 4.04). The mobsters may be embroiled in talk of conspiracy and oblivious to the drama unfolding in front of them, but the women—and the television audience—observe the erotic frisson between Furio and Carmela as they touch for the very first time. Echoing other cultural narratives of epic feudal power and strong but forbidden love, from *Romeo and Juliet* through to *The Godfather* (Frances Ford Coppola, 1972), the scene finds Carmela no longer reading the romantic fiction or watching the film but performing the desire. Infatuation and a palpable anticipation are scripted into the *mise-en-scène*: the incandescent and incendiary music played by Spaccanapoli speaks of the old country and the unrequited passion of dispossessed rebellious souls; the choreography of the highly coded dance ritualistically keeps the couple separated but moving as one; the editing patterns resonating with the conspiracy of power against the subterfuge of love; and the close-up fetishising intimacy. Who could imagine anything other than this operatic vocabulary of heterosexual desire for making visible the dense emotional landscape of a formidable woman like Carmela?

Over the course of Season Four these elements are reactivated again and again as she continually revises and modifies the real events into an illusory courtship; and time after time it is a particular media form that activates her pleasurable imaginings (a television show about Italian cookery, a reprisal of the Spaccanapoli music or an oil painting of old Naples). These representational forms shaped by an unseen patriarchal "omnipotent armature" (Foucault, *Discipline* 301) that celebrates a compulsory heterosexuality make women work hard for their pleasures. Carmela may not be offering us anything new—besides the culture she performs would deem any transgression perverse—but she offers us a lesson in self-regulating behavior, shoring up boundaries, and taking pleasure in potentially violating what she represents. Carmela continues to visit Furio under the pretence of helping him decorate his newly converted garage. Poring over a glossy interior design magazine finds Carmela talking romance. Chatter about cozy pillows and plush furnishing becomes code for romantic possibilities and secret trysts. Carmela knows she has gone too far: "But, it's for your mother." The couple exchange glances. A pregnant pause. The romantic cocoon Carmela has been building suddenly becomes desperately inappropriate—but thrillingly erotic. Furio looks deep into her eyes and in his halting Italian accent tells her "You are a very special lady." Without skipping a beat Carmela responds: "Have you thought about flooring?" The moment is pure Carmela. Raging emotional hinterland becomes corralled into civilized restraint and feminine propriety.

Carmela may be devastated on hearing the news that Furio has fled to Naples, but has not the emotional entanglement compromised her position enough? She may flee from a lunch with Rosalie distressed and in tears but there was no way this was ever going to end well. Later in the "Eloise" episode (4.12) she takes tea with Meadow at the Plaza. Cosseted in an aura of gentility and female refinement—with its linen tablecloths, willow patterned china and harpist—the interior of the hotel's Palm Court provides a tranquil setting after the turbulence of her infatuation. A long-standing tradition for Soprano mother and daughter, it is a moment of narrative reclamation. Performing her fantasy of feminine perfection, she returns to a role that she knows only too well—and the source of her considerable narrative authority. Long has Carmela imbibed Meadow into her vision of femininity with those white gloves—signifier of genteel manners, old-style sophistication and formal elegance. It is the performance of a femininity that Carmela does so well: the etiquette of the afternoon tea. But Meadow is having none of it. "Soprano tradition notwithstanding," she refuses to don the gloves. Is not such an ideal anachronistic nowadays? Her rejection comes as no surprise to her mother. Despite this, Carmela puts on her gloves and finds some comfort in the continuation of a tradition that excludes men and celebrates the matriarchal line.

But the annual visit soon dissolves into seething resentments over the French pastries and chocolate éclairs. It starts with Carmela rebuking her daughter for adopting a "superior attitude" ever since she started at Columbia and quickly degenerates into bickering over arrangements for a skiing trip to Canada. But what lies beneath the squabbling is a generational conflict that goes much deeper than Meadow's sleeping arrangements. Cultural myths of romance have long divided women, pitching the virginal princess against the old crone. Reworking the idea here finds mother and daughter at opposite ends of the romantic spectrum. Whereas Meadow may be starting out on her fairy-tale romance complete with skiing trips, roaring fires, the promise of an engagement ring from Tiffany's, Carmela abruptly finds herself forcibly at the end left with nothing but a broken heart and color swatches. Meadow's barbed comment, "Excuse me, Mrs. Danvers. What do you have against love?" is an interesting choice of words. Evoking an asexual, formidable and intimidating housekeeper (from Alfred Hitchcock's *Rebecca* [1940]) speaks in part of a divide in feminism. Dispute (often translated as division) shapes contemporary feminism, with younger women habitually distancing themselves from what came before. For them—as for Meadow—feminism is often perceived as a stern authority figure and an uptight prude. It also speaks of an intellectual divide between the women. Meadow now has an educated (elitist) feminist language to explain, narrate, her daily experience. Achieving a fluency not available to her mother lends clout to Meadow's cruelly questioning her mother's choices: "Would you rather I go to Montclair State? Then maybe I could drop out like you did." Hurtful words.

But it presents us with a central paradox shaping Carmela. As Tony tells her later that day: "[Meadow's] becoming a wonderful woman, Carm. Smart. Beautiful. Independent woman that you created. Isn't that what you dreamed about?" Yes, but... Meadow has opportunities Carmela never will. While Meadow has choices, Carmela is living with the decisions she has made; and whereas Meadow "can do whatever she wants," Carmela's options are closing down. And here is the uncomfortable dilemma—a television character unable to blow the whistle on approved scripted cultural performances that praise particular models of female achievement and normalcy because there is no language within her representation to articulate it.

But our culture is not yet done with the fairy tales: the anticipation of what romance promises, the lure of a happy ending, and the hope that the love of a good man will bring completion. Good grief—has nothing changed? But why should it? Carmela returns home at the end of a long seasonal arc that finds her trying to divorce Tony. Hearing that her attorney has bailed on her she sees Tony's car parked in the drive ("Unidentified Black Males," 5.09). Silently moving around her home she hears the phone ring. It is Meadow. Finn DeTrolio has proposed. She is engaged. "Wonderful news. I'm surprised." Forever the pragmatist, Carmela asks if Finn will finish dental school. There is a party to plan. Parents to meet. "I'm going to cry," she says. But are these tears of joy? In an inversion of the final moments of *Stella Dallas* (King Vidor, 1938) when Stella (Barbara Stanwyck) looks in at her daughter's society wedding, Carmela looks out the window watching Tony floating on his inflatable in the pool. She silently sobs. The sparseness of the final moments with Carmela shuddering with aching discontent and engulfing frustration is one of pure melodrama. How can she jeopardize Meadow's faith in the dominant narrative that promises American women a dashing prince, economic security and beautiful children? How can she tell her that the dream may end with an unfaithful husband and cancelled credit cards? And how can she reveal the truth that Prince Charming could become nothing more than a fat middle-aged balding man cluttering up the kitchen and requiring constant servicing.

CONCLUSION: CARMELA GETS HER GROOVE BACK

We revel in the ways that Carmela talks to Tony as others cannot (unless you fancy being slapped with a side of beef. Gloria. Gloria. Where did it go so wrong?); we clap with glee at those steely stares which stop Tony dead in his tracks; we delight in the emotional complexity of her tiny gestures; we relish in those no-nonsense rebukes she serves up with coffee; we adore the ways in which she uses marital treachery to outsmart her perennially cheating husband. But we are also stirred (often to tears) to see her frustrated rage, the heavy burden she must bear for knowing about the whores, her righteous anger when Tony belittles her concerns. Who could forget her taking to her bed after A. J.'s academic advisor, Robert Wegler, dumped her because she used "her pussy" to coerce him into helping improve A. J.'s grades (Well, she did, didn't she?) ("In Camelot," 5.07); or the quivering mix of fury and crushing disappointment she displayed on hearing that her attorney must remove himself from her case as no forensic accountant will probe her husband's murky finances ("Unidentified Black Males," 5.09).

A confession: in parts this essay was impossible to write. Days were lost in heated discussion over Carmela's attraction to Furio. (Why?) We became mired in the very heterosexual fantasies that we are working so hard to theorize and understand anew. We became lost for words. Finding no words. Catherine Lumby (sort of) anticipates such a problem for contemporary feminist scholarship. Writing "[if] feminism is to remain engaged with and relevant to the everyday lives of women, then feminism desperately needs the tools to understand everyday culture" (174), she urges us to find new, more appropriate ways of thinking and writing about popular culture; and this might in part explain our difficulties, our limits with language, our limitations. But women like Carmela—no feminist, slipping through the cracks of feminism, not quite making the theoretical cut, representing a dominance many of us find hard to reconcile ourselves with—have much to tell us about our continued investment in approved heterosexual scripts, deals that must be struck, often working with tools that many of us find deplorable, and the contradictions we live with. Carmela's complex dilemmas are ours. She may not be a feminist, but what she represents reveals the limits of what can and cannot be said. In her resistance she holds out the promise of change. But it is a grueling process—and one that Carmela knows only too well. The end of "Second Opinion" (3.07) finds, after her uncomfortable session with Dr. Krakower, Carmela curled up on the couch struggling with the messy realities of her tainted life—again. Tony arrives home. Shocked to find her in this depressed state, he knows there is no messin' with Carmela today. Holding him in her gaze only once she shakes him down for the $50,000 that she has already promised to the dean of Columbia. The deal is sealed with Tony letting her off domestic duties and offering to buy her dinner instead. She is often down but she is never out. As the lyrics playing out this episode tell us: "She wants new shoulders to cry on / A new back seat to lie on / And she always gets her way." Maybe. Hope so. Cheers Carmela.

4.

DISCIPLINING THE MASCULINE

THE DISRUPTIVE POWER OF JANICE SOPRANO

Valerie Palmer-Mehta

> Barbara: I love seeing men like that over a fire.
> Janice: They're better over a spit.
> *"Guy Walks into a Psychiatrist's Office" (2.01)*

WHAT DO WE DO WITH JANICE?

To suggest that Janice Soprano, the older sister of mob boss Tony Soprano, is not the most likable character on *The Sopranos* may seem an understatement to some. Yet few would deny that her arrival failed to portend the complex and defiant character that would eventually unfold. Janice returns to New Jersey in "Guy Walks into a Psychiatrist's Office" (2.01) after learning her mother, Livia, has had a stroke, appearing innocently on Tony's doorstep as a new-age hippie seeking enlightenment (and some cash).[1] Donatelli and Alward describe Janice's debut this way: "Janice ... first enters the series ... as a seemingly harmless, overweight spaced-out hippie chick who doesn't realize that she is far too old for her clothes and lifestyle" (66). Willis recounts Janice's premiere in a similar manner: "Janice, who years ago decamped to Seattle, became a Buddhist, and changed her name to Parvati, shows up at [Tony's] door flaunting her postcounterculture reinvented self" (3). Although Janice's debut appears less than noteworthy, as time weaves on an interesting sequence of events begins to reveal a persona that is neither simple nor benign.

Indeed, Janice shoots Richie Aprile, her fiancé, at point-blank range in retribution for an act of domestic violence ("The Knight in White Satin Armor," 2.12). A subsequent boyfriend, Ralph Cifaretto, is almost killed after Janice pushes him down a flight of stairs ("Christopher," 4.03). Her eventual marriage to Bobby Baccilieri, Jr., whom Janice dominates and manipulates, appears to be another avenue to power for Janice, as she "guides" (perhaps "goads" is a better word) him to advance through the ranks of the Mafia. Her violent temper gets her banned from the corner store and garners the Soprano family some unwanted publicity on the local news when she gets into a brawl with a soccer mom ("Cold Cuts," 5.10). Janice even steals the prosthetic leg of Svetlana Kirrilenko, Livia's former domestic aid, as leverage to recoup some music records that Janice believes were pilfered from her mother's basement ("Fortunate Son," 3.03).

As Carroll observes "if [Janice] does not cause as much damage as Tony that is only because her theater of operations is much smaller. One senses that in Tony's position, she would be far more dangerous" (131). And Vernezze muses "the list of Janice Soprano's transgressions make it difficult to know exactly what to do with her" (192), a statement that may indicate why there is so little critical work specifically on Janice, despite the deluge of writing on *The Sopranos*. Indeed, *what do we do with Janice?*

To understand Janice, one must first understand her parallel to Livia Soprano, the malevolent matriarch of the Soprano family, played by Nancy Marchand in Seasons One and Two. *Sopranos* writer and long-time David Chase collaborator Robin Green reports that Janice was created "in part to bridge the relationship between Tony and [his] mom" as Marchand's failing health and eventual death necessitated Livia's own decline on the program. Of course, bridging that infamous relationship was no easy task because, as Tony says to his mother, "Everybody thought dad was the ruthless one. But I gotta hand it to you, if you had been born after those feminists, you would have been the *real* gangster" ("Down Neck," 1.07). In many ways, Janice is clearly the spawn of Livia: calculating, unpredictable, and dangerous, and Tony finds it difficult to escape either of them, bound as he is to his dutiful roles as son and brother. In the spirit of Livia, Janice's frequent appropriation of the behaviors and tactics of her male Mafia counterparts suggests that she might be the better mobster, but she is seemingly contained. As an Italian American Catholic woman within the Mafia tradition, she is encouraged to take on the traditional, "respectable" roles of wife and mother.

Taking on traditional roles, however, is no easy task for Janice. While she does attempt to perform some stereotypical feminine behaviors, it is clear that she does so either begrudgingly or in self-interest. Consequently, her performance emerges as a conspicuous appropriation of traditional femininity, a feminine masquerade. Doane asserts that a feminine masquerade "constitutes an acknowledgement that it is femininity itself which is constructed as a mask" (426). "The masquerade, in flaunting femininity, holds it at a distance," manufacturing a "lack in the form of a certain distance between oneself and one's image," creating a slippage (427). Janice's vacillation between appropriating performances of femininity and appropriating the behaviors and appetites of her male counterparts disrupts gender normativity. As Judith Butler has argued, "To the extent that gender is an assignment, it is an assignment which is never quite carried out to expectation, whose addressee never quite inhabits the ideal s/he is compelled to approximate" (231). Janice recognizes that she is compelled to perform traditional femininity, but her performances are frequently not "carried out to expectation" and even ignored in favor of the appropriation of her male counterparts' performances of masculinity. As a result, Janice's vacillating, ambivalent performances challenge the notion that masculinity naturally inheres to male bodies and that womanliness is natural, normal, or even achievable. In what follows, I investigate the ways in which Janice alternatively appropriates a feminine masquerade and the behaviors of her male counterparts within the context of her relationships in the major storylines involving the character. Janice's relationships are an ideal location to examine her performance as she attempts to construct a "respectable" heteronormative feminine identity through her roles as fiancée, mistress, wife, and mother.

RICHIE

The most notorious of Janice's liaisons is with Richie Aprile, a made man, brother of the late boss Jackie Aprile, who is released from prison in Season Two. Shortly after Janice and Richie reignite their relationship (they had dated in high school), they become engaged. Tony does not approve, but he and Carmela feel obliged to hold an engagement party for them. During her toast at the party, Janice declares her love for Richie, which will be brutally undercut by the end of the episode. "I've been looking for my soul mate all my life ... I just wanted to say, you knock my socks off!" ("Knight in White Satin Armor," 2.12). This display torments Carmela, who has been emotionally wrestling with Tony's numerous mistresses, and her distress emerges in a comment made to Janice at the bridal shop. Carmela advises Janice that she should enjoy herself now because, "in a year tops, you're gonna have to accept a *goomah* [mistress]." Janice scoffs at this idea. "Oh yeah, well, I'd like to see a *goomah* that's gonna let him hold a gun to her head when they fuck." Carmela is shocked to hear that Janice allows this, saying, "I thought you were a feminist." Janice doesn't perceive this detail as compromising her power, comparing it, using her usual psychobabble, to wearing garter belts and nonchalantly stating, "Usually he takes the clip out. ... It's a ritual. It's fetishistic. That's all." Indeed, one might perceive this interaction as acceptable currency for Janice.

Janice may be willing to tolerate a gun being pointed to her head during sex, but she is not willing to make any compromises when it comes to the new luxurious home she and Richie are building. When Richie advises her that she should slow down on the spending because a decision that did not go his way will be affecting him financially, she becomes furious. "But we're still going ahead with everything at the house right? ... [Tony] just can't handle that our house is gonna be nicer than his fuckin' house!" ("Knight in White Satin Armor," 2.12). In a move reminiscent of Livia, Janice decides to reveal that the real reason Tony's son did not attend the dirt bike championship with Richie is because Tony does not want Richie around his kids. Janice recognizes this will push Richie over the edge since "this shit with your brother's been building since I been out." As Janice surely must have foreseen, Richie begins to plot Tony's demise. When Uncle Junior advises Tony that Richie plans to kill him and take over, Tony says, "You know that asshole's marrying my sister," to which Uncle Junior replies, "You gotta wonder where *she* is in all of this, my little niece!"

Janice will place her brother in harm's way to ensure a lavish lifestyle, but she isn't willing under any circumstances to accept abuse from Richie. While preparing to eat dinner, Janice and Richie get into a fight over the acceptability of his son's possible sexual preference. In the process, Janice demonstrates the extreme vacillation in her character between traditional feminine behaviors, such as cooking dinner and looking after her mother, acts which she begrudgingly performs, and masculine behaviors, such as tranquilizing her mother with Nembutals so she can fulfill her sexual appetite. Upset at Richie's mood, Janice tells him off: "You came home with a fuckin' attitude. I been in this house fuckin' cooking your dinner and taking care of that fuckin' black hole upstairs all day!" Richie, angry at Janice's insistence that he need not be ashamed if his son is gay—"Just because he's a ballroom dancer you think your son is gay? And even if he was, what difference would it make? You feel threatened?"—calls her a "fucking sow" and then punches her. As Richie nonchalantly prepares himself a plate of food, Janice is uncharacteristically speechless. For her, there is nothing left to say. She retrieves a gun—the same gun he had earlier held to her head during sex—and looms over him. Richie says, "Get the fuck out of here, I'm not in the mood for any of these fuckin' dramat-", and Janice shoots him twice in the heart at point-blank range, killing him. Then she calls her brother to dispose of the body.

The next morning, Tony comes back to the house to take Janice to the bus station so she can disappear. Livia questions why Tony has appeared so early. "Richie didn't come home last night. She's worried about him." Livia responds, "Oh sure, he probably jilted her. That's the story of her life." Tony jumps to Janice's defense, "What kind of a fuckin' chance did she have with you as her mother?" While Janice is one of the only persons on the program to defend Livia, such as when she subtly scolds Tony for not inviting Livia to her engagement party and when she encourages everyone to say something in remembrance of Livia at her funeral ("Proshai, Livushka," 3.02), she also recognizes the pathology that exists in the family and its effects on her. At the bus station, Janice asks Tony, "What's wrong with our family?" and then becomes grossly sentimental at Tony's sarcastic account of the disposal of Richie's body: "We buried him. On a little hill, overlooking a river. There's pine cones all around." (In fact, Christopher and Furio have sliced up Richie at Satriale's.)

In the social world inhabited by Janice, women are expected to acquiesce to mistresses and endure domestic abuse or intimidation, whether they transgress boundaries or not, as demonstrated by Adriana La Cerva, who is beaten up by her fiancé Christopher Moltisanti simply because he thought she might have had an encounter with Tony ("Irregular Around the Margins," 5.05).[2] Janice is sometimes willing to appropriate a feminine masquerade to fit into her environment and achieve a particular end, but she chooses not to engage in the masquerade in this instance. As Barreca states, Janice "has learned that the pretty ways taught to privileged little girls will not work for her. Learning partly from experience and partly from instinct, Janice comes to the conclusion that it is in her interest to challenge, rather than observe or submit to, the world around her" ("Why" 44). She gains control of her life and cultivates power in the same way the men around her do: through intimidation, manipulation, and murder. In this instance, she appropriates the behavior and tactics of her male counterparts not by simply refusing to be disrespected and injured, but by murdering the perpetrator of her distress and then calling Tony to help her clean up the murder scene and dispose of the body. Barreca recalls that this scene provoked responses that varied according to gender. "The next day's conversation around the water cooler heard many men saying that Janice was nuts and had drastically overreacted and equally as many women saying they hadn't watched such a satisfying response to domestic abuse since *Thelma and Louise*" (44). Indeed, by forcing male viewers into the "object" position, Janice's actions demand a rethinking of traditional power relationships and oppression.

RALPHIE

Janice also engages in violence to rid herself of her next boyfriend, Ralph Cifaretto. First, however, she seduces him away from her friend, Rosie Aprile. In "No Show" (4.02), Janice follows Ralph to the bathroom during a dinner at Tony's house, pushes her way in, and finds him snorting cocaine, which they begin snorting together. Even though she knows that Ralph is dating Rosie, who is sitting downstairs at the dinner table (and who is still grieving over her murdered son), Janice seduces him. The relationship continues, becoming more intense in "Christopher" (4.03), which features Janice and Ralph in bed, Janice in control of the sexual situation, using a vibrator on Ralph. Their interaction proceeds in the following dialogue, indicating that even her sexuality has a violent, transgressive edge:

> Janice: How much money did you make today slut?
> Ralph: $300.
> Janice: That's all, bitch? I'm going to put you back on the street ho, make you work that ass ... Work that ass you little cunt ... Momma's little tramp. Momma's little who? I'm gonna pimp you out bitch!

In contrast with her previous relationship with Richie, who held a gun to her head during sex, Janice is dominating this sexual situation, reversing the previous power relationship and prompting the audience to consider that men are not the only aggressors in sexual situations.

While Tony and his men are frequently shown enjoying the company of other, sometimes random, women, this kind of behavior is discouraged for wives and women in the family in general. The other Mafia women typically do not engage in affairs, and when they do, they speak of it in guilty terms. In Season Three, for instance, Rosie Aprile discourages Tony's wife, Carmela, from engaging in an affair with Furio Giunta, recalling that the guilt from her own one-time affair was just too much to bear and suggesting that Carmela will be similarly overcome, even though her husband has engaged in numerous affairs. In contrast, Janice appropriates the sexual appetite and behavior of her male counterparts, thinking first of her own pleasure and empowerment. Additionally, she has little concern for what others think about her. When Tony indicates to Janice that he knows about her affair and discourages her from seeing Ralph, Janice tells him, "Why don't you mind your goddamn business?" ("No Show," 4.02).[3]

In the next scene, Janice is waiting for Ralph to come home; she is anticipating breaking up with him after an appointment with her therapist who suggests that Janice is repeating dysfunctional dating patterns. Ralph, however, reports enthusiastically that he has just broken off his relationship with Rosie so he can devote himself completely to Janice and begins to kiss her. Janice knows that tonight is her night to bring food over to Bobby Baccilieri, whose wife has just died in a tragic car accident—a gesture performed by all the women in his network of family and friends. She says, "Oh shit! Oh shit! Tonight's my night I gotta bring food over to Bobby Baccala's ... What should I do?" She pauses only a moment before she laughs and they go upstairs to bed. In contrast to Hartley, who suggests that "Women are still raised in our society to be nurturers. They are taught to tend first to the needs of others and only then to themselves" (69), Janice is concerned first and foremost with her own needs, mirroring Tony's tendency to think of himself first.

Later, Janice is shown bringing Kentucky Fried Chicken over to Bobby's house instead of the traditional home-cooked Italian meal. Referring to her choice to have sex with Ralph rather than bring food to Bobby's house, she says: "Sorry I didn't make it last night. My bible group had a pot luck for the homeless and I was on clean up crew, so..." Because she understands that it was egregious as an Italian woman to have ignored this duty for the sake of her own pleasure, Janice blatantly lies to Bobby in a feminine masquerade. In her negotiation of her own desires and ambitions and those relegated to her by her culture, Janice highlights the confining nature of traditional femininity.

Bobby is not concerned with food at this juncture because he is distraught about the loss of his wife and fraught with guilt because he was angry with her when she died. Janice encourages him to talk to her. Crying, Bobby tells her, "She was up the road ahead of me lying in twisted metal. But I didn't know and I could've been with her. I should've been there to help her. But I was mad at her. Oh my sweet Karen, my sweet girl!" ("Christopher," 4.03). The contrast in femininities is significant here. Janice has just told a lie about attending a church event in order to get out of missing her "womanly" duty of bringing food to Bobby. In contrast, Bobby's deceased wife, Karen, who was characterized as a caring, selfless woman who took care of the extended family, was killed coming home from an actual church event. Janice is juxtaposed with Karen, who is positioned as the (Italian-American) feminine archetype, highlighting her distance from the feminine norm.

Like the other mob women, Janice is touched by Bobby's display of love for his late wife, so much so that she decides to "dispose" of Ralph so that she can pursue Bobby. When Ralph comes home, Janice is shown towering over him at the top of the stairs. With a suitcase in his hands, Ralph happily states, "Janutsky! Janice! This is it hon, this is the last stuff I had at Ro's." Looking annoyed, Janice scolds, "Your shoes ... Didn't I ask you to take off your shoes when you come into this house?" Surprised by her sharp response, Ralph apologizes. He smiles as he proceeds up the stairs with his arms open to embrace her, but Janice becomes increasingly agitated as she says, "Forgot. So that's just it. You fucking forgot!" Reflecting her male colleagues approach to disposing of undesirable relationships, Janice aggressively pushes Ralph down the staircase. The audience sees him lying immobile at the bottom of the stairs, seemingly dead until he mutters in agony. Janice continues yelling at Ralph, "Get out! Get out!" In pain, Ralph, however, cannot move, crying out "My back! My back! I'll kill you, you crazy bitch! I'll kill you, you bitch! You crazy cunt!" Again, Janice yells, "Get out!!" before she runs away into her bedroom and locks herself in. Any other woman or man who did this (or something much less severe) to Ralph surely would have been killed at his hands, which underscores Janice's ability to wield power far beyond that available for most women in *The Sopranos*.

BOBBY

In "Calling All Cars" (4.10) Janice, in full feminine masquerade, has been attempting to establish a romantic relationship with Bobby Baccilieri. She has been bringing over food, even claiming she made a dinner dish actually made by Carmela, and trying to act as a mother figure to his children. Bobby is positioned differently from most of the men on the program. While a member of the Mafia, a made man, his role has been confined to taking care of Uncle Junior, and he is typically "soft-spoken and shy ... trusting and kind" (Santo 82). Additionally, he is the only one of the men who never had a *goomah*. In this particular scene, Bobby and Janice are eating as Janice drops her masquerade in favor of appropriating the confrontation, intimidation, and manipulation characteristic of her male counterparts. Bobby asks if she liked the movie, and Janice completely changes the subject, asking him if he went to the cemetery today to see his wife. Even though she brought up the subject, she says, "This is exactly what I mean. We have a nice evening and we end up talking about your dead wife." Surprised, Bobby says, "You invited me." Janice then tries to bring Bobby's children into her stratagem, referencing an incident that occurred at Tony's house. "The other night at Tony's your kids were trying to contact Karen on the Ouija board. What do you expect, you're talking to her headstone!" Bobby replies, "She's my wife." To which Janice says, "Well she's dead and I'm here." Uncharacteristically, Bobby tells her to "Shut the fuck up," and she tells him the same.

While Janice provides a tough love stance in this interaction, her next move demonstrates she is not about to let go of what she perceives as a good thing. Employing an ambiguous username and instant messaging, Janice prompts Bobby's children to get out the Ouija board, leading the children to think their mother is trying to contact them. In so doing, Janice creates chaos in Bobby's house, spurring him to get over his wife in order to make room for her without regard for the emotional consequences for Bobby or the kids.

The plan begins to work as Bobby confides in her that they've been playing with the Ouija board. Janice defers to Bobby, again putting on the feminine masquerade. "I came over with some pound cake. I thought this is not good. But after the other night, I didn't want to overstep my bounds." In an interesting contrast of cruelty and kindness, Janice says, "The dead have nothing to say to us. It is our own narcissism that makes us think they even care. It does get better with time. ... Did you get anything to eat at least? Can I fix you something?" Bobby indicates that it is too much trouble. Janice replies, "No it's not. I'm starving too. There's probably something in here." She looks into the freezer and retrieves what she knows to be Karen's last legacy, which Bobby has been saving. She offers it to him. "Karen's ziti," Bobby acknowledges. "It's the last one she made." As a tear flows down his cheek, she offers it up to him again, and he nods yes. In a symbolic, almost cannibalistic moment, they ingest the tangible remains of Karen's memory.

After she marries Bobby, Janice has some difficulty settling into her role as wife and stepmother. The children clearly are distressed by her presence, as evidenced by Bobby Jr.'s bedwetting after her arrival and Sophia's embarrassment at a soccer match at which Janice initiates a brawl with a soccer mom whose daughter was playing too rough. This incident appears on the nightly news as Janice is shown savagely beating the other mother while shouting "How you like it now, bitch?" but also running from the police ("Cold Cuts," 5.10). When confronted by Tony about the unwanted publicity, Janice states, "That bitch is lucky I didn't kill her!" To which Tony responds, "Well, we know that." Interestingly, Tony advises Bobby to "get control of your wife" because he feels that the family needs no further exposure in the media. This command is humorous for the viewer because we recognize that not even Tony, the boss, is effective in placing limits on Janice or on his own anger. Although Bobby does insist she take anger management classes—after all, she's been banned from the corner store because of the ruckus she caused over burnt coffee beans—one suspects that its effects may be short-lived. This suspicion is confirmed when, after Tony purposefully provokes her, anxious to prove her new anger management skills are for naught, she charges after Tony with a fork. The scene is reminiscent of Tony's childhood when his mother menacingly responds to his request for an electric organ by saying, "I could stick this fork in your eye!" ("Down Neck," 1.07). The distress Janice causes Bobby's children and the abandonment of her own son, Harpo, suggest that her motherly presence may be as toxic as Livia's.

Few would argue that it is in her relationship with Bobby and his children that Janice appears at her most unscrupulous. Some might applaud Janice's killing of the unsavory Richie, who belittled and humiliated her, and the beating of the similarly sordid Ralphie. Her manipulation of Bobby, who is positioned as a good guy, and his children, makes her malevolent. Because women are expected to be the nurturing caretakers of children, especially in the context of this patriarchal text, she is particularly demonized for her role in their emotional distress.

THE DISRUPTIVE POTENTIAL OF JANICE SOPRANO
Janice is a complicated character. On one level, her vacillation between the appropriation of feminine masquerade and masculine behaviors, creates an ambivalence that places gendered normativity into question. Her performance suggests that Janice does not enjoy adopting stereotypical roles or behaviors for women. In certain circumstances, however, she recognizes that performing traditional femininity is the most direct route to acquire what she desires. Additionally, she is aware that she will be ostracized from her family if she does not offer such performances. Consequently, her femininity emerges as exaggerated, conspicuous, unnatural and, ultimately, subversive. Scheie states, "a subversive performativity is ... a sort of obedience in bad faith, one which conforms to the rules under protest in order to reveal their exclusionary and brutal nature" (156). In the figure of Janice Soprano we recognize that stereotypical femininity is neither natural, nor normal, but is stifling and provides only indirect routes to power.

Additionally, Janice's behavior reflects the brutality of male behavior as she appropriates it in her disciplining of the men in her life—indeed in her disciplining of the masculine. When Janice desires more direct routes to power, she appropriates the very appetites, behaviors, and tactics of her male counterparts, as exemplified in her killing of Richie, her beating of Ralphie and her exploitation of Bobby. She uses the tactics such men have used on countless women and each other, but in her performance of these behaviors as a *woman*, she forces audiences to view the behavior from a different angle of vision—from the margins. Audiences are not used to seeing women engage in such behavior, and it becomes all the more startling as a result, particularly for men who are accustomed to being the subject of violence only at the hands of other men. Perhaps this is why, as Barreca notes, men were disturbed by Janice's killing of Richie and women found it liberating. As people watch Janice's behavior, it cannot be divorced from the other violent acts on the program and, consequently, the viewer is prompted to be more conscious of the brutality enacted by the men. Additionally, the notion that violence and sexual aggression are naturally the acts of male bodies is put into relief.

On another level, Janice offers a long overdue representation of corpulent women as desirable, sexy and in control: she is never without a relationship if she wants one. She decides when relationships will begin and when they will end (at least so far) and never has to purchase the affection or attention of her companions. As such, Janice offers an important alternative to the stereotypical representation of large women in contemporary US media culture.

Janice's distance from traditional femininity, made emphatic when she manipulates Bobby's children into thinking their deceased mother is trying to contact them, thus forcing Bobby to give up his grieving in order to make room for her in their lives, is too disconcerting to make her a feminist role model. Indeed, it makes her look too pathological, framing her as an aberration, completely self-interested and willing to use any means to achieve her ends, regardless of whom she may hurt. This very framing suggests that the reason Janice is unruly is not because she is as strong and capable as her male counterparts but because she lacks the ethical and mental foundation of her female companions.

Janice Soprano disrupts conventional notions of feminine embodiment and behavior and prompts the audience to reflect on the brutality of her male counterparts, but not even the most malevolent men on the program stoop to her levels of manipulation. Consequently, Janice emerges as disruptive, unruly, but not transformative, thus containing her feminist potential.

5

EVE OF DESTRUCTION

DR MELFI AS READER OF *THE SOPRANOS*

Bruce Plourde

Genetic predispositions are only that, predispositions. It's not a destiny written in stone. People have choices! ... You think that everything that happens is preordained? You don't think that human beings possess free will?

Dr Melfi, "Down Neck" (1.07)

When Satan still in gaze, as first he stood,
Scarce thus at length fail'd speech recover'd sad.

John Milton, *Paradise Lost* (Book IV, ll. 356–357)

Bent on destroying God's good work, Satan pauses in his mission of vengeance, struck dumb by the beauty and innocence which confront him. This dark presence, the very embodiment of Christian evil, feels genuine doubt about his enterprise, revealing the deep conflict within. Hatred has moved him to strike against God, but the beauty he discovers seems too perfect to destroy. Observing Eve in her garden, the very image of domesticity, he is almost swayed from his purpose. Yet once he regains his power of speech; he soliloquizes that he cannot turn back. He has fashioned his resolve from "Honour and Empire with revenge enlarg'd," though he regrets having "To do what else though damn'd I should abhor" (Book IV, l. 392). Driven by a combination of rage and dismay, he seems all too human, marveling at the innocent beauty before him and regretting the ruination of it. In this reflective moment, the prince of darkness reveals a vulnerable side.

As we read the poem, we read into the very soul of Satan, empathizing with his situation, and finding ourselves, like Eve, similarly seduced (Fish). Only from a distance can we remember the consequent evil that he unleashes upon humanity, but up close and personal this evil matters less. Understanding him, we forgive him, emulating Eve in her moment of original sin. She also succumbs to his linguistic talents, the likes of which Adam did not possess. From the beginning, the word has had great power. The same word which could seduce Eve would also, coming through the voice of an angel, make Mary full with child. Both women, one driving the old testament and one driving the new, willingly accepted the call of the word. The masculine speaks, the feminine translates.

Tony Soprano, like a latter-day Satan, is a charismatic leader driven by honor and empire; like Satan, he has a capacity for malevolence. And yet we, the audience, are charmed by this dark figure because he, too, has a nurturing side he reveals to us through his own narrative. As we come to know the complexities of his life, we too are seduced, often failing to condemn his most criminal behavior. At odds between our moral standards and our personal sympathies, we often give Tony a pass so we can continue to observe a life by turns ordinary and disturbing. What normalizes our ambivalent reading of Tony is the intermediary figure of the psychoanalyst, Dr. Jennifer Melfi. Having left the garden for the Garden State, this Eve figure welcomes the seducer into the rarified space of her office, the center from which all narrative threads radiate, and encourages Tony to produce his story. At times fascinated and repulsed, she *wants* to be seduced by language. As a professional, she listens and observes, becoming familiar with his soul in a process of transference and counter-transference, distance and empathy, learning to read and diagnose him. At first only an interesting case, the mobster becomes a favorite patient, and nearly a love interest, situating her in a morally ambiguous position. Remaining within the bounds of her professionalism, however, she maintains a better reading posture than the audience is capable of. As a perceptive reader for a charming narrative, Dr. Melfi acts as a kind of Greek chorus, fulfilling the role of both audience and commentator.

The interplay of psychiatrist and analysand produces a compelling drama. The psychiatric method, after all, requires the production of a personal narrative, and creator David Chase once contemplated having the entire story unfold as flashback in Melfi's office (Lavery and Thompson 21). Such a premise becomes problematic, however, in the actual production of a coherent narrative, and so did not survive the pilot. It is also problematic because we know from gangster movies that telling tales to strangers violates the cultural imprimatur of *omerta*. At one critical juncture, when Tony and his uncle have gone to war over rumors, Tony tells Carmela that "cunnilingus and psychiatry got us to this" ("I Dream of Jeannie Cusamano," 1.13) and, culturally speaking, he is correct. Both activities are unsanctioned forms of tongue-wagging, one suggesting that a man is a weak finooch [homosexual], the other suggesting that a man is venting family secrets. In either case, confidentiality is essential. Junior's love interest, Bobbi Sanfillipo, cannot keep her secret, while Tony has better luck, turning not only to a professional, but to a fellow paisan [countryman] like himself, someone familiar with Italian-Americana. As Alane Salierno Smith puts it, "It is a love and a rage" (62) to be a modern-day Italian-American, with one nostalgic foot in the old country and one resistant foot in the new. Melfi can appreciate Tony's conflicts and function accordingly as a kind of priest, a figure who does have cultural authority. As Michael Flamini points out, "Therapy and confession do, though, have two important things in common" (116), confidentiality and professional distance. In the confessional, as in the psychiatrist's office, a person is expected to unburden the soul through divulging secrets. One offers forgiveness, the other awareness, but both offer relief from guilt and stress, the root causes of Tony's problems. In order to become more functional, he *must* unburden his soul, or "sing," which is, as Maurice Yacowar points out, "the series' basic pun" (16). If Melfi is the chorus whose dramatic function is to "sing" to us, Tony is the character who sings to her. His family name, Soprano, describes a singer at the highest range, a role difficult for a powerful man to assume, and a dangerous one for a criminal who is not supposed to sing. Even though Carmine, the boss of New York, tells Tony that "there's no stigmata these days" ("Fortunate Son," 3.03), and one of his capos [captains], Paulie, will admit to undergoing therapy for "some coping skills" ("I Dream of Jeannie Cusamano," 1.13), his bi-weekly visits to Melfi suggest feebleness and incompetence. A don of a group of thugs who wags his tongue to a psychiatrist places himself in a precarious position.

Thus, the dramatic stage is set for the production of narratives which constitutes the show. In the interplay between therapy sessions and real life—between gangster and upper-middle-class suburbanite—the show offers a decidedly new twist on the gangster genre, in which *The Sopranos* participates joyfully. It demonstrates a postmodern awareness of this participation by referencing elements from a variety of sources, from *The Godfather* trilogy to *I, Claudius*, and any number of other Italian or gangster contexts. *The Sopranos*, however, offers a richer portrait of the Italian-American gangster by exposing the limitations of men and, more importantly, by demonstrating the agency of women. An essay by Kim Akass and Janet McCabe discusses this agency by explicating the various strategies with which women negotiate the power available to them, focusing upon the two most powerful women, "Carmela Soprano, his long-suffering wife and most trusted confidante, and Dr. Jennifer Melfi, his analyst and the other woman to whom he unburdens himself" (148). In one sense, these women are the most capable because they are most sibylline at reading the masculine presence. This dyad of feminine power also is bound ironically through an awareness of past gangster movie roles. Their common link is Suzanne Shepherd, the actress who plays the mother role in both the film *GoodFellas* and *The Sopranos*. Mother to Karen Hill (Lorraine Bracco) in the film, Shepherd steps into the role of Mary de Angelis ("Mary of the Angels"), mother to Carmela Soprano. In both roles, she plays a harpie who has not mastered the subtle power of language. Carmela and Melfi (Bracco), however, are masterful readers. Carmela (Edie Falco) assumes the role that Bracco had, and Bracco becomes a different, but no less able, reader as Tony's counselor.

Although both women are effective readers, Carmela is limited through her emotional ties to Tony. She "knew the deal" ("Whitecaps," 4.13) and has made a conscious choice to willfully ignore her husband's crime and immorality while enjoying the material benefits of them. Melfi does not have this emotional or financial connection, and so is freer to confront him on character issues. She has clearly been designated as Tony's reader, evidenced from the manner in which Bracco often speaks her lines in a slightly stilted, precisely enunciated manner which sounds like a woman reading. Also, she has been given an apt symbol in her reading glasses, a personal article that she does not wear outside her office. The glasses come on when Tony appears for his session, the better able to read him. Twice, these glasses disappear, and she becomes vulnerable to his seductions. Once, in Season Three ("Employee of the Month," 3.04), she is raped, and the assailant is released through an error in processing his case. Once, in Season Five ("The Two Tonys," 5.01), she begins having erotic dreams about Tony. In consequent sessions with Tony, she fails to don her glasses, and nearly gives in to her inner desires, the one for revenge, the other for lust. Later, having put her glasses back on, she reasserts her professional distance and can focus on her therapeutic reading, but there is a lingering tension between the intellectual and the passionate.

It is this humanity which ultimately makes her not simply a good reader and counselor, but a good audience. She is a professional, but she also grasps the dualities in his life that we all deal with. Without her own duality, Melfi could not draw out Tony's narrative, and it is this duality which from the start has promised complications. While she draws a firm line in professional conduct, she also allows Tony to subtly transgress that line. In the first episode, when Tony mentions "the matter of an outstanding loan" ("The Sopranos," 1.01), Melfi stops him and explains that her confidentiality does not extend to criminal violence. Tony adjusts his language, explaining that he and the gambler Mahaffey "had coffee." The ensuing scene flashes to coffee cups splattering to the ground as Mahaffey runs from Tony, who breaks the man's leg by running him over. When the camera cuts back to Melfi, she is smirking. "So you had coffee," suggesting that she has interpreted his euphemism and has gotten a good idea of what actually transpired.

Tony can use his linguistic power to generate lies transparent enough for his psychiatrist to see through. We, the audience, have a less limited point of view and can see the actual events replayed, but Melfi must make her own interpretation of the events from what Tony tells her. Though dependent upon Tony's narration, she comprehends her subject in ways that often elude us. In any kind of reading, whether it is a book or a movie, the narrator provides to the reader "information that we must accept without question if we are to grasp the story that is to follow" (Booth 3). The reader must then adopt the narrator's point of view to some extent in order to follow the story. Tony is most often the narrator of his own life, and often an unreliable narrator, a man who regularly deceives himself as often as the people around him. Whereas our more omniscient position actually limits our ability to judge Tony's behavior, Melfi's more limited but more insightful reading of Tony stems from her better ability to see through his deceptive language and to read his malevolence, serving as a corrective to our more accommodating perspective. Also, her morality is more firmly fixed. In her system of social values, she recognizes Tony as a manipulator, sociopath, and a crook from New Jersey. For the viewing audience, he is both a figure of entertainment and a wish fulfillment, a man with the clout to get a speeding ticket expunged and the traffic officer removed from duty. Whereas the viewing audience is often swayed by what seem like reasonable justifications for criminal behavior, Melfi reminds us of Tony's regular violations of the social contract.

As she reads her patient, she cues us as to how we should judge Tony. During the first four seasons, the camera shows us flashes of Melfi, particularly her body language and facial expressions. These are meant to educate our own responses to Tony's seductions. For example, early in their analytic relationship, Melfi asks Tony if he ever has "any qualms about how you actually ... make a living" ("The Sopranos," 1.01). She is trying to lead him toward an exploration of the harm he causes to others through his involvement in gambling, prostitution, and extortion. Instead, Tony describes himself as the "sad clown," the man who laughs on the outside and cries on the inside. His emotions are turbulent, not because of his own anti-social activities, but because his colleagues are more willing to "sing" to the authorities than silently accept their prison sentences. "Nowadays, no values. Guys today have no room for the penal experience" as the code dictates. What disturbs him is not his own violence and pathological behavior, but the disloyalty of his associates. Although she does not say anything in rebuttal, Melfi's facial expression clearly indicates her disappointment at his inability to confront his own malicious conduct. It's not that he willfully refuses to see; it's that he feels justified in how he puts food on the table. The family man who nurtures ducks in his pool, deals with the normal problems of raising teenagers, and negotiates a separate peace with his wife seems like a regular, reasonable guy. This average life blends with his criminal life to lend validity to those rationalizations of his criminality. Melfi's corrective reading reminds us that Tony is not simply a regular guy but also a narcissistic bad guy capable of violence and murder.

What makes Melfi the best reader of Tony, however, is her proximity to the audience's own fascination with this bad guy. Like Carmela, she feels she must often put her own judgments aside if she is to help Tony work through his therapy. Accommodating his moral blindness for a greater good, she sometimes finds herself silently condoning his explanations. Even this capable reader of the human soul can become seduced by a sociopath, as she confesses to her own therapist, Dr. Kupferberg. "It's like watching a train wreck. I'm repulsed by what he might tell me but somehow I can't stop myself from wanting to hear it" ("House Arrest," 2.11). Melfi experiences the same morbid fascination we do, curious about a lifestyle that both disturbs and entices. As Season Two begins, she has sworn off him, having experienced up close the very real danger immanent in organized crime, but her morbid curiosity draws her back into her relationship with this charismatic, articulate man. Another practicing psychotherapist, Dr. Glen O. Gabbard, claims that the central question of the series is, "Is Tony redeemable?" (45), and early in the relationship Melfi might have had the same thought. But for her, as well as for most fans, the questions become more visceral over time: Who will get whacked this week? And when will Tony get his? Melfi is more politic in her curiosity, managing a delicate balance between the personal and the professional, but her attitude is closer to ours than to Gabbard's.

Thus Dr. Melfi, the woman who willingly welcomes Satan into her safe space, propels the narrative until the end of the fifth season, when she all but disappears from the scene. When Tony has a lengthy dream about his cousin Tony B. ("The Test Dream," 5.11), he is able to interpret its significance himself, as are we, the observers who have internalized Melfi's past readings. Suddenly unneeded, Melfi makes only fleeting appearances in the last three episodes. In one of these appearances, she berates Tony for his reluctance to share more of his private details with her. As demanding as a jealous lover, she now wants him to transgress the professional boundary she had established long ago so that she can elicit from him a richer narrative. The end of the season seems to suggest that, while Melfi has come under his sway, Tony has outgrown her. With Melfi cast aside, the audience has assumed her position. In a sense, we have been trained to read Tony without the help of an interlocutor. But ultimately, Melfi cannot disappear.

At the end of the season, Tony comes to the conclusion that he must murder Tony B., the cousin he grew up with. Following the course of events and the problems inherent in keeping him alive, we understand the decision. Murdering a beloved relative makes sense to us because it will set right a business wrong. We are saddened, but we know it was for the best: more than ever, Melfi has a job to do. Fortunately, this Satan figure, whose troubles arise from "family" connections, must rely upon the power of language for his curse as well as his power. Tony needs his personal, feminine reader to keep his singing act together. Without that need, he is simply another snake in the grass.

EPISODES

Entrance to the Lincoln Tunnel, New York. Photograph by Michael Prete.

6.

BLOODLUST FOR THE COMMON MAN

THE SOPRANOS CONFRONTS ITS VOLATILE AMERICAN AUDIENCE

Jessica Baldanzi

In *The Sopranos on the Couch*, a close analysis of the first four seasons of the series, Maurice Yacowar argues that "Employee of the Month" (3.04), one of the most emotionally intense episodes of the series, "centers on the fragile state of our civilization" (136). This episode, in which Tony's psychiatrist Dr. Jennifer Melfi is raped, certainly exposes a rare fragility in an otherwise formidable character. Yet the episode as a whole is much more about violence than fragility. An examination of this episode in tandem with "Another Toothpick" (3.05), the exceptionally violent episode which follows, marks "Employee of the Month" as the series' most scathing critique not just of the glamorized violence that characterizes representations of the Mafia, but more pointedly, of the viewers' complicity in that violence, a collusion occasioned by their misguided nostalgia for the vigilante, yet brutally rigid, systems of justice that kick into action in traditional Italian American narratives. In forcing viewers to acknowledge their own desire for revenge against Melfi's rapist—and to confront and examine their reactions to the Italian American stereotypes that help fuel this desire—these two episodes do more to deflate such stereotypes than high-profile attempts by the American Italian Defense Association and other organizations to publicly denounce *The Sopranos*, a response that shuts down productive discussion of how those stereotypes work and what they might mean.[1]

The multi-tiered critique of "Employee of the Month" is packaged into the single small word that abruptly ends the episode. Bewildered by Melfi's sudden crying fit when Tony agrees that he might be ready to move on to a behavioral therapist as she suggested in an earlier session, he asks her, "You wanna say something?" Melfi's steel-jawed "No" clearly shows her mustering control over her own impulses and also signals a refusal to other characters—her ex-husband, her son—who have tried to lay claim to a very personally devastating experience that the justice system has failed to rectify. Yet the main force of her refusal is aimed at the audience. As the episode develops, the viewer watches Melfi's fear and frustration build; as our own anger intensifies along with Melfi's, Tony is dangled in front of the audience as a potential solution at key moments of tension. By the end of the episode, the viewer is rooting for Melfi to tell Tony about the rape, to have "that asshole," as Melfi herself calls her rapist, "squashed like a bug." This angry phrasing, which Melfi vents to her own therapist, Dr. Kupferberg, shows us that we are not alone in such impulses if one of the most morally upstanding characters on the series fantasizes about vigilante justice when the American justice system falls flat.

That single "No," however, represents a chastisement of the audience more than a simple identification with it, and that reprimand works on multiple levels. First, of course, Melfi is saying "No" to the audience for wanting her to enter into Tony's morally corrupt system of justice. In a broader sense, however, she also refuses the audience's desire to embark on the well-known narrative direction that her confession to Tony would set into motion. More than refusing her status as damaged property that necessitates "reimbursement" in the form of revenge, she also refuses the audience's desire to sail off into the bloody sunset of the traditional and hackneyed Italian American revenge narrative. A close examination of these two harrowing episodes thus reveals that "No" really does mean no for Melfi, and her refusal not only allows her to maintain control of her own narrative—a challenge for a female character in any Mafia narrative—but also critiques the viewing audience: first, for its assumptions about Italian Americans and Italian American narratives and, further, for that audience's refusal to acknowledge its own role in fueling these stereotypes. In part, Melfi's refusal to sic Tony and his Mafia connections on her attacker stems from the knowledge that women, traditionally, don't fare too well in the pop-culture Mafia world. As Cindy Donatelli and Sharon Alward note, for women "to appear on the screen of the *Godfather* films is to experience the danger of trespassing in a dangerously male world" (67). As Melfi regains control of her emotions to muster that final "No," she also regains control of women's autonomy, usurped by generations of Italian American films, with their track record of portraying women not only as property, but as property violently used and "protected."[2]

Melfi's refusal has emerged from a complicated emotional history. She admits to her own therapist that taking Richard back shows that on some level she, like the audience waiting for "justice" to be served, is also longing for a "simpler life," a life run and protected by a dominant male figure. Ironically, the episode shows how Richard's overprotectiveness is largely at fault for the rape. When Richard engages in the all-too-common practice of blaming the victim—he asks the recovering Melfi, "How many times did I tell you to call the security guard when you left late?"—Melfi shoots back that not only was she on her cell phone with Richard mere seconds before she was attacked, but their discussion—a recurrence of his insistence that she drop her unnamed Mafia client before she gets hurt—distracted her from her surroundings. Perhaps she would have been able to escape if she'd been more focused—and particularly, more focused on "real" dangers to her safety, rather than vague dangers generated by Richard's stereotyped ranting about her client. This scene also demonizes Richard further by harking back to an earlier point in the episode when he argues with Melfi about the Mafia's perpetuation of stereotypes about Italian Americans. In doing so, however, Richard is clearly labeled a hypocrite: he makes a number of assumptions about Melfi's unnamed patient, thus not only engaging in but also fueling Mafia stereotypes himself. By putting the arguments about Italian

American "defamation" into the mouth of this overprotective and generally unlikable character, the episode both anticipates its critics and attempts to check the viewer's own tendencies to stereotype.

Yet the viewer is already guilty of stereotyping Tony and also of controlling that stereotype by picking and choosing when his violent impulses should and shouldn't be employed. When Melfi dreams of a rottweiler mauling her attacker, Jesus Rossi, she later explains to her therapist that her subconscious must have chosen that breed not only because of its viciousness, but because of its "Italian" history as a Roman guard dog. The choice is, however, even more appropriate than we realize. Melfi remarks that in the dream she's afraid at first that the dog will attack her, yet rottweilers today are rarely unleashed; police dogs, impeccably trained, their violence is always under control, as we want to believe Tony's violence will be.

The impotence of Richard, as well as of Richard and Melfi's scrawny but blustering son Jason, is explicitly contrasted in this episode with Tony's potential power, which is made visible to the viewer even outside the realm of Mafia "warfare" and within the suburban domestic sphere. Tony's unsprung ability to take action and "fix" the problem that has allowed Rossi to go free is highlighted when Melfi calls to cancel her appointment with Tony a few days after the rape. While Carmela takes the message, Tony roots through the refrigerator in the background, and emerges furious, yelling that someone has eaten the last piece of cake. Richard's parallel fury when he discovers that the cops have screwed up is certainly more justified, yet also clearly less able to accomplish anything. "They'd put me in jail—that's how messed up things are," says Richard, and as he articulates his fantasy to kill Melfi's attacker, the camera melodramatically zooms in on his clenched, shaking, and ineffective fists. Since Tony can kill without such punishment, the viewer again wishes for Tony to step in and make things "right." We see Tony's anger at something trivial in this scene. How explosive—and how efficient—we wonder, would this anger be if he knew why Melfi was really canceling their session?

Yet despite the angry sputtering of her husband and her son, Melfi remains the gatekeeper of her experience, and the audience likewise remains under Melfi's narrative control. Melfi alone has the power to set the revenge narrative in motion; she is the only one who can tell Tony what has happened, even though the audience, accustomed to the violent emotional narrative of mob movies, somehow expects Tony to guess the source of Melfi's distress and start the train of events that will set everything straight. Realistically, however, how could he possibly guess? Tony's failure to "sense" the cause of Melfi's deeper distress—the way that Mafiosi in the traditional films seem to sense betrayal—rejects more than the viewer's bloodlust: it casts off a whole constellation of expectations that even the casual fan of Hollywood's Italian American has been taught will be fulfilled. As Fred Gardaphé writes, Tony, as a representation of Italian American cultural identity, has moved beyond the "traditional, patriarchal sense of manhood that came from an old European model" (99). For Melfi to tell him that the "car accident" was really a rape would send him hurtling back to the Old World, thus jettisoning the progress they've made in their sessions—and the progress that Italian American gender roles have made in the show as a whole.

The episode also flouts the viewer's expectations in more subtle ways, however, as when the judicial technicality that sets Rossi free proves to be just that—a technicality, and not a manipulation of justice. Since we know how easily Tony can pull strings, we become suspicious the instant we hear a logistical error has allowed Melfi's rapist to walk free. By this third season—and again, with a long history of Mafia narratives under their belts—viewers of *The Sopranos* are well trained to assume that logistical errors, lost evidence, reassignments within law enforcement, hung juries, and other blips in the justice system are rarely accidental. Has someone pulled some strings for Rossi? The viewer, still holding out hope for revenge, also hopes Rossi is mob-connected, however tangentially, so that Tony might be able to circumvent Melfi's authority over the story and find out what really happened through other channels.

That fact that Rossi isn't connected to the mob—that this blip in the justice system really is just a slip-up, however unfortunate in such a serious case—highlights the fact that despite our training by well-controlled film and television narratives, violent and terrifying events in real life can sometimes happen entirely out of our control.

In "Another Toothpick," the episode that follows "Employee of the Month," the theme subtly shifts from control—as with Melfi's triumph in "Employee" over the Italian American stereotypes that fuel the audience's bloodthirsty desires—to lack of control. The only area of Tony's life that seems truly out of control for him is the realm of his emotions—and the vicarious sense of power created by the control he does have over the major events in his life is one reason why the viewer tends to root for him. This episode deflates that association, however, complicating the critique of the viewer who, still emotionally wrecked from the last episode, might be holding out hope for Melfi to be avenged. As we discover in "Another Toothpick," however, Tony's not pulling strings for a matter as serious as rape—he's just trying to get out of a speeding ticket.

While "Employee of the Month" whips up viewers' bloodlust, "Another Toothpick" talks us down and makes us somewhat ashamed of ourselves, of our role in feeding the violence surrounding representations of the mob. The episode justifies Melfi's refusal—a decision that makes the viewing audience, at that instant, feel disappointed and even cheated—by highlighting the worst injustices and moral breaches in the Mafia's system, particularly the racism that slips under the radar of both the positive and negative stereotypes of the mob.[4] Any viewers wishing, with a false nostalgia, for an earlier day when justice for heinous crimes such as rape was (supposedly) served swiftly and harshly with no question—and with no random logistical errors that would let the rapist walk free—realizes in watching "Another Toothpick" that not only did such a perfect justice system never exist, but even if it did, it wasn't in the universe of the mob, an organization run on outdated machinery that functions less predictably in the "New World."[5]

A number of things run "out of control" in this episode. "Another Toothpick" refers to Janice's repeated coarse references to cancer victims within the family circle. We are reminded later in the episode that she adopted this phrasing from her mother, a woman so distressed by her lack of control toward the end of her life that she puts out a hit on her own son. The episode also shows the FBI listening helplessly while Meadow whisks their strategically bugged lamp ("Mr. Ruggerio's

Neighborhood," 3.01), along with all of their hope for incriminating recorded evidence, to her college dorm room ("Another Toothpick"). For Tony, however, most things somehow *don't* seem to run out of control—even a minor annoyance like a speeding ticket is eventually "righted"—but the evils of Tony's world, the episode suggests, aren't worth the predictability, just as those evils weren't worth Melfi fulfilling her desire for revenge.

Leon Wilmore, the policeman who cites Tony for speeding—despite Tony's attempts to flaunt his connections and bribe the officer—is demoted and stripped of his overtime after Tony phones Assemblyman Zellman to complain about the outrage of his being punished like a "citizen." Tony later runs into Wilmore at the Fountains of Wayne—a northern New Jersey retail landmark that serves in this context to signal a minimum-wage employer—and begins to feel guilty for his retribution. When he calls Zellman again, the assemblyman insists that Wilmore isn't just a goody-two-shoes—that he should have been demoted a long time ago because he may have some "serious mental problems." In this corrupt universe, in other words, a policeman attempting to stay in control of the moral high ground is beyond "uptight"—and should be categorized as seriously unstable. The irony is painfully obvious: if a cop like Wilmore who "plays by the rules" had been assigned to Melfi's case, perhaps the procedures would have been followed more carefully, and Rossi would not have been released on a technicality. The audience is once again chastised: how could you root for a guy like Tony Soprano, someone who pulls strings to perpetuate the flaws in the penal system—all for the sake of getting out of a speeding ticket (which, given his budget, would be the equivalent of, for most of us, shelling out for a pack of gum)? Now that you see Tony's code of vigilante justice in action, the episode tells the viewer, how could you have fantasized about letting him "run" things in the first place?

The viewer's guilt is amplified as the episode reminds us of Tony's racism, recently showcased in his anger at Meadow for bringing home—and snuggling on the couch with—Noah Tannenbaum, a fellow Columbia student of both Jewish and African American heritage. When Meadow reports that her bike has been stolen by "some black guy" (a matter of hearsay, since some unnamed people at the dorm claim to have seen the theft), Tony is thrilled to have such solid "evidence" to back up his distaste for the couple's relationship. The audience is slapped in the face with another harsh irony: that Tony's "evidence" is as arbitrary as the logistical mistake that let Rossi off, for he ignores the "evidence" of the truly exceptional moral standards of Officer Wilmore, who is also black.

But it isn't just Tony's system of "evidence" that proves arbitrary. His stereotyped argument reminds us of Richard's vague fear of Mafia retribution when the more immediate danger of a rapist was right in Melfi's face. The arguments of the show's critics likewise seem arbitrary when held up next to these episodes, for Melfi's rape, arguably the most disturbing scene in all of *The Sopranos*, demonizes a racially ambiguous character who isn't Italian American as far as anyone can tell (to Richard's great relief), despite the fact that Rossi sounds like an Italian name. Yet, as Regina Barreca writes, editorial outrage over the show's violence reached a fever pitch after "Employee of the Month" (Barreca 43). The uproar, Barreca posits, was because Melfi is a "civilian." Since there is no evidence, however, that this instance of violence had anything to do with the mob, was the outrage really because of its "gratuitous" nature—because since the rape wasn't avenged, it seemed devoid of any moral purpose? Were the critics who were complaining about all the violence really upset because in this episode, the violence wasn't *completed*? There wasn't, in this case, *enough* violence?

While it's impossible that the show's producers would have had the time to respond to such criticism so quickly, the extreme violence in "Another Toothpick" nevertheless seems to be saying, "And you thought *that* was disturbing!" If the audience was rooting, however secretly, for the Mafia code of justice in the previous episode, this episode seems to show the viewer what her bloodlust has wrought—to remind us just how gruesome vigilantes can get. The gore seems to breed in this episode: a loose cannon named Mustang Sally sends construction worker Bryan Spatafore into a coma with a golf club when Bryan crosses paths with Sally's girlfriend, who is merely looking for a ride to escape a threatening argument. Bryan, the viewer discovers shortly, is the brother of Vito Spatafore, a member of Gigi Cestone's crew, which is under the Soprano umbrella. This is, again, truly "gratuitous" violence, and a truly arbitrary chain of events; this isn't a hit, just a couple's argument, yet one tangential hood happens to bludgeon a mob associate waiting for his friends to pick up some food to go. If *Sopranos* critics wanted to get angry at a particular episode, perhaps they should have chosen this one instead of the previous one, for this episode backs up the argument that the show presents every Italian American as a mobster—swing a golf club in New Jersey, it seems to suggest, and nine times out of ten you'll hit "not just a citizen," as Sally is told, but "a man with friends." The volume of blood multiplies when Sally's godfather, Bobby Baccalieri, Sr.— "another toothpick" suffering from emphysema—kills Sally in a gory, sloppy, and emotionally brutal retaliation (brutal for the audience, at least, although Bobby, Sr. himself seems unruffled by the concept of whacking his godson). In one final nod to the arbitrary, however, death comes in turn for Bobby Sr., not from the violent thrill of the hit, which was successful despite his debilitating coughing fits, but from the bad luck of his inhaler falling to the floor of his car on the way home from the hit, which causes him to crash into a telephone pole. The scene is, of course, exceedingly brutal, even though Bobby, Sr. dies feeling redeemed.

Yacowar makes much of Melfi's repeated observation to Tony that "strong feelings will make their own release, often in the violence of action or language" (143) (or fainting spells, in Tony's case). The extreme violence of these two episodes can be seen as a sort of release in itself. If the series is really an expression of America's sublimated desires—if more broadly, Italian American narratives have been created and fueled by a nation needing such a release—then perhaps these two episodes can prove therapeutic. "You created us," both of these episodes seem to be saying to its American viewers, whether Italian American or not. Italian Americans, perhaps, could have assimilated more rapidly if white America didn't *need* these stereotypes into which to channel their sublimated desires; Americans perpetuated the image of the Mafia long past its relevance.

The viewer who roots for Tony in "Employee of the Month" perhaps slinks off ashamed after "Another Toothpick"; yet, with a (supposedly) characteristic American memory loss, that same viewer forgets it all and returns for the next episode. But perhaps we shouldn't be too hard on the viewer's insatiable penchant for romantic bloodlust. After all, the show's characters themselves, even from their supposedly "authentic" vantage point, seem to cite a gangster film at least once per episode—and the citations aren't always correct. David Ruth's *Inventing the Public Enemy* notes how "New York police detective Remo Franceschini observed during his surveillance of John Gotti that real gangsters had started imitating the characters in *The Godfather* films. After a generation one could hardly tell the difference between the real and artificial gangster" (Ruth 9, as paraphrased by Gardaphé 96). Even real-life mobsters themselves proved influenced by the romantic stereotypes spun out of their experience by Hollywood; even they seemed to like these narratives better than the truly brutal violence of their own worlds—much as we prefer *The Sopranos* to the truly random and unexpected violence of our own worlds.

Sandra Gilbert argues that "*The Sopranos* is artful in the skill with which it simultaneously fulfills guilty as well as innocent wishes and dramatizes the fears that often collect around such wishes" (Gilbert 23). Yet Melfi refuses the viewers' wish for the blood that Tony could have shed. The move into "Another Toothpick" forces the audience to acknowledge that none of its wishes will be fulfilled, and the viewer is instead thoroughly chastised for siding with such a racist, corrupt thug in the first place. This move recurs throughout the show, emphasizing how *little* "fulfillment" the audience receives—and just how often the audience is instead horrified, yet responding to just enough humanity in the characters to return for more. Just when Tony is most endearing—such as when he plays the proud father taking his daughter on college interviews—he turns around and brutally strangles someone minutes later ("College," 1.05). Such scenes remind us that like Melfi, we watch appalled, but with "a kind of fascination" (Gilbert 25) and worse, that we're implicated in this seduction, too easily whipped into an emotional frenzy that leads us to root for vigilante justice.

Yet American viewers in particular need to follow Melfi's lead and refuse this violence. Ellen Willis argues in "Our Mobsters, Ourselves" that one of the reasons that viewers identify so heavily with Melfi is because of the recognition that the horrors that she works to uncover in Tony's life are horrors at work in our own subconscious. As Willis writes, "The therapist's fear is our own collective terror of peeling away those lies. The problem is that we can't live with the lies, either. So facing down the terror, a little at a time, becomes the only route to sanity, if not salvation" (8). Many critics have argued that these "lies" that Melfi helps us uncover reveal cover-ups, flaws, and deception in current American culture. I would argue, however, that the repression runs even deeper than that, into the history of America as a nation. *The Sopranos* reminds us that it is not the Mob but the "mob" to which viewers really respond in watching these two episodes, as well as the series as a whole. The doings and desires of the American mob have developed a long rap sheet: witch dunkings, the attempted extermination of the American Indian, lynchings, and other foundational acts of repressed American violence. When Melfi tells us "No," the word reverberates in the American unconscious, its echo telling us, "Don't go there—you won't like what you'll find." If anyone's unsafe in these episodes, it's the nation—not only implicated, but volatile, always on the verge of that mob violence. If Americans love Mafia movies, this is why: America created the Mob as a means to channel its mob impulses.

The main issue for Melfi in these two episodes is her resolve to build—however gradually and painfully—her own control over the situation. What we forget as viewers, however, is that Melfi is not just the non-gangster conduit into the show with whom so many of us identify. She is also a doctor, who must ensure that her patient travels mostly forward, rather than backward into an emotionally out-of-control narrative of revenge. In which direction is the viewer, and particularly the American viewer, traveling? Are we being trained to be more sophisticated, more sensitive, less emotionally driven viewers by episodes like these, which withhold the fulfillment of our worst impulses and desires? Are we being trained out of our tendency to jump to conclusions when it comes to race and ethnicity? The show withholds clear answers to us, much as it withholds answers to our own questions about Tony's mental health: does he ever actually improve, or will he continue, periodically, to regress? Much like Tony, we need to answer these questions ourselves.

The Real Bada Bing. Photograph by Michael Prete.

7.

"YOU'RE ANNETTE BENING?"

DREAMS AND HOLLYWOOD AS SUBTEXT
IN *THE SOPRANOS*

Cameron Golden

In the Season Five episode of *The Sopranos* entitled "The Test Dream" (5.11), at the beginning of Tony Soprano's landmark twenty-minute dream, Carmela, Tony's estranged wife, asks him to pull himself away for once from watching TV. Carmela insists that Tony stop watching a scene from the film *Chinatown* (Roman Polanski, 1974), telling him "Your head is filled with this stuff." Tony, however, is unable to turn away from the screen. He confesses, "It's so much more interesting than life." Carmela then responds, with an exasperated tone in her voice, "Are you kidding me, it is your life." What Carmela has just underlined for Tony, and for the viewers of the series, is the degree to which Hollywood and dreams fuse together in "The Test Dream" to form a significant intertextual counter-narrative for both Tony and the audience.

TV, films, and dreams feature prominently in the lives of other members of the Soprano family. In "Rat Pack" (5.02), for example, Carmela hosts a weekly movie night where her female friends watch the American Film Institute's list of 100 top films, and in "Where's Johnny" (5.03), Junior Soprano becomes confused about who he is after flipping channels to *Curb Your Enthusiasm* and seeing his doppelganger in Larry David (and Tony's in Jeff Greene). In "The Test Dream," however, Tony's response to his dream vision offers proof that he has finally learned how to successfully read his own unconscious motivations while simultaneously rewarding and ratifying the audience's participation in this complex intertextual narrative.

Throughout the run of the show, Tony has been seen watching TV and films, each one specifically chosen to give insight into Tony's life and actions to himself as well as to the viewer. An instructive example of how David Chase and the writers use these intertextual references comes in the episode "Two Tonys" (5.01) as Tony and his girlfriend Valentina come across the film *The Prince of Tides* (Barbara Streisand, 1991) while channel surfing one night. Exhorting her not to change channels, Tony tells Valentina, "I like Nolte," but we can see it is not the masculinity of Nick Nolte he is drawn to but rather the emotional connection Nolte's character builds with his sister's therapist, Dr. Lowenstein (Barbra Streisand), which truly attracts Tony. As Lowenstein remarks to the Nolte character, Tom Wingo, "You feel your mother betrayed you," we see Tony smiling broadly, and the message is clear: this filmic representation of therapy is the version of psychoanalysis he desires for himself, where any real work on the conflicts in his life is superseded by the dream of romance with the elusive Dr. Melfi. In *The Prince of Tides*, Tom Wingo, the brother of Lowenstein's patient, is a strong, rugged football coach, a role that will take on an important function in "The Test Dream," with the feature role played in the dream by Coach Molinaro, Tony's high school football coach. Ostensibly helping Lowenstein understand why her patient, Savannah Wingo, has attempted suicide, an echo of the fate of Season Four's Gloria Trillo, Tony's ex-girlfriend, who also appears in "The Test Dream," Tom embarks upon a romantic relationship with Lowenstein, something that Tony has always wanted but been repeatedly denied by Melfi.

This sequence allows the audience to gain insight into how films operate for Tony: he continually makes very literal connections between what he sees on screen and his own life. Watching this film encourages him to begin romantically pursuing Melfi, an amusing twist since it appears obvious to those who have seen the entire film that Tony has missed the essential point of *The Prince of Tides*: that therapy, not dating your therapist, can be an effective way for a troubled adult to come to terms with events from childhood currently affecting behavior. Instead of recommitting to therapy, Tony sends Dr. Melfi flowers and a huge bottle of Tide detergent along with a card that reads, "Thinking of you, your prince of Tide." Though Tony may misread *The Prince of Tides*, the metalanguage of his encounter with this Hollywood product is clear: for him, films possess a direct one-to-one correspondence with life and provide a very literal blueprint of how to read events in real life.

Of course, viewers of *The Prince of Tides* see that Tony has for the moment missed the point of the film. Thankfully, by the time he awakens from the "The Test Dream," he has grown more skilled at breaking the semiotic code of films and dreams. The *Prince of Tides* reference invokes many recurring themes from Tony's life and therapy sessions (childhood trauma, a strained mother-son relationship, repressed memories, and an attraction between a doctor and a patient), but Tony's response to the film only emphasizes how much he needs therapy in the first place. By ignoring the part of the film about Tom's domineering mother, his conflicted feelings about athletics, and repressed memories, Tony misses the similarities between his life and Tom Wingo's and only considers the romance between Wingo and Lowenstein, paying attention solely to the most superficial component of the narrative. Astute viewers know that the links between these two texts are complex and profound and are empowered to make more of these allusions than Tony. If, as David Pattie asserts, the intertextuality of *The Sopranos* is "obsessively foregrounded" (135), then viewers of the series are being instructed in how to read the film references in *The Sopranos*, such as *The Prince of Tides*, better than Tony himself. By understanding the intertextual nature of the show and engaging the audience on the level of subtext, *The Sopranos* creates its own form of internal commentary and allows its audience the opportunity to actively suture meaning from other narratives.

Unlike most other television dramas, *The Sopranos* has not created a landscape where either dreams or TV and film references simply offer a comment on the action of the show. On *Six Feet Under* ("Making Love Work," 3.06), when Ruth and Arthur watch Arthur's favorite film *Silent Running* (Douglas Trumbull, 1972), it seems obvious that the isolation and alienation they witness on screen are analogous to the emotions experienced by the characters. But in *The Sopranos*, a myriad of narrative threads are knit together in a way that allows multivalent references to illuminate each character's mental landscape and sometimes unconscious motivations. Given the show's reliance on therapy as a way of understanding actions, analyzing the film, TV, and dream references of the characters becomes a way for viewers to assume the importance of a therapist by interpreting these clues and, as we have seen, sometimes reading them better than the characters themselves.

The Sopranos has a devoted online fan base and, after each episode, chat rooms are filled with not just critiques but sophisticated analyses of references and allusions; online interpretive communities have formed a web of exegesis that allows contemporary audiences to join in the therapy sessions and actively collaborate to uncover the subtext of the show. Message boards on sites such as Sopranoland.com have become a way for viewers to become educated in reading the signs of the show, to express praise or disdain, or to show off their insights. "The Test Dream," in particular, provides these online communities with ample material: Tony's lengthy and complex dream, with its ambiguity and limitless interpretive possibilities, allows for endless discussion and debate.

By viewing the subtext-ure of Tony's life as a palimpsest constituted by these intertextual references, audience members are given the opportunity to continually re-write the text of the show, using each new allusion to add another layer of individual interpretation and meaning. Tony Soprano, the inveterate TV watcher, is a product not just of the gangster genre but of a myriad of texts. When we don't see him sitting on the couch with a bowl of ice cream watching the History Channel or a movie, references to history, popular culture, and even sociology creep into his everyday dialogue. In the very first episode of the show ("The Sopranos," 1.01), during his initial meeting with Dr. Melfi, Tony discusses his reluctance to open up in therapy and share his feelings because Gary Cooper wasn't in touch with his emotions: "Whatever happened to Gary Cooper, the strong, silent type? ... Now that was an American." (Tony repeats this speech almost word for word in "Christopher" [4.03]). Gary Cooper is again echoed in "The Test Dream" when Tony sees a clip of High Noon (Fred Zinnemann, 1952) playing in Vesuvio's.

Even more ubiquitous in Tony's world than Gary Cooper, however, are The Godfather films, and the foregrounding of these cinematic versions of Tony's profession has been one of the markers of The Sopranos as a postmodern text filled with allusions to other narratives. According to Chris Messenger, the central link between The Godfather and The Sopranos is the acknowledgement that "America has been totally colonized by The Godfather itself" (255). The Godfather can be viewed as an ur-text that not only gives shape and meaning to the characters' lives, but also serves as the central underpinning to all other texts, becoming, in the language of Roland Barthes, an anchor, a text that serves to "fix the floating chain of signifiers" (39). In Season One, when Christopher proclaims to Big Pussy that "Louis Brasi sleeps with the fishes" (instead of Luca Brasi from The Godfather), this misquoting underscores not only an important fact about Christopher (that he isn't all that bright), but also something about how The Sopranos is using The Godfather. This anchor demonstrates the liberties Chase and company are taking in internalizing, recycling, and rewriting the central text of The Godfather.

In interviews, Chase has acknowledged a debt to another television show in the overall design and look of his series, David Lynch's Twin Peaks, but it seems clear that there is another connection between these two shows. Dreams and the significance accorded to them by the dreaming characters are of great importance in both series. In Twin Peaks, Agent Dale Cooper becomes convinced that he has found the answer to the organizing question, "Who killed Laura Palmer?" in the famous "dancing dwarf" dream: "It seemed to beg for a semiotic rather than a hermeneutic reading of Laura's murder" (Dolan 38).

Tony too sees dreams as semiotic codes that must be read and interpreted correctly in order to solve whatever problem he is currently facing. Tony dreams of his friend and associate Big Pussy in "Funhouse" (2.13) and in his dream logic sees him as a talking fish. This sign must be read correctly by Tony because the talking fish who confesses in Pussy's voice of being an FBI informant is telling the truth and his friend needs to be killed. The dream sequence in "Calling All Cars" (4.11), with its quite blatant subtextual emphasis on transformation (Carmela's hair magically changes from long to short; Gloria's place in the car is assumed by Svetlana Kirilenko; and the caterpillar crawling on Ralph Cifaretto's toupee-free head becomes a butterfly) points Tony towards the changes that will be occurring in the near future, namely the dissolution of his marriage. Like "The Test Dream," "Calling All Cars" revives some dead *Sopranos* regulars: Gloria and Ralph. In Tony's dreams, characters often return from the dead to assist him in making decisions and remind him of the repercussions of his past actions. "The Test Dream" features at least ten dead members of *The Sopranos* cast (Carmine Lupertazzi, Gloria Trillo, Johnny Boy Soprano, Big Pussy Bonpensiero, Mikey Palmice, Richie Aprile, Gigi Cestone, Ralph Cifaretto, Pie-O-My, and Vin Makazian among others). Tony himself believes in the connection between death and those who appear in his dreams so fervently that during his phone call to Carmela after the dream, Tony asks her if anything has happened to Artie Bucco since, in the dream, "He was the only alive guy in this car full of dead guys." Dreams for Tony, unlike films, are texts to be unlocked, and in "The Test Dream" his abilities to read and interpret correctly are among the many things being tested. He must break the code and resolve his most pressing conflicts—deciding what to do about his cousin Tony Blundetto and also his marriage to Carmela.

The dream in "The Test Dream" begins once Tony checks into the Plaza Hotel, learns that Phil Leotardo has killed Angelo Garepe, surmises that Tony B. will try to kill Phil in return, and falls asleep after he is visited by a prostitute. The pop quiz administered to the audience through Tony's misinterpretation of *The Prince of Tides* has now been replaced by the final exam of "The Test Dream." Those—including Tony—willing to do the work, breaking the code of references and allusions, can pass the test; and those who are merely frustrated will fail. Internet message boards were filled with posts after "The Test Dream" aired that vilified the show and David Chase for relying on the hoariest of dramatic conceits—the extended dream sequence. However, even those who viewed this dream as a narrative dead end or a waste of valuable screen time near the end of the season that could have been devoted to resolving various plotlines must have been impressed with the depth and breadth of Tony's dream vision. Within it are references to movies, books, television shows, celebrities, popular culture, popular music, and other *Sopranos* episodes. Over twenty characters from *The Sopranoverse* appear, some still living, some dead. During the dream, there are ten changes in location, from the Plaza to Tony's high school. At its root are several conflicts, but two of them are central: Tony's separation from Carmela and his problems with Tony B. Both of these dilemmas are linked, however, to Tony's essential internal conflict—his ongoing tension between doing what he wants and doing what he needs to do to retain his power in both of his families. The dream will allow him to work through this struggle and conclude that he needs to kill Tony B. and reconcile with Carmela, this time reading the clues of the dream along with the intertextual references correctly.

Though there is a seemingly endless amount of material to be analyzed in "The Test Dream," the remainder of this essay will focus primarily on the intertextual references that emerge in the dream and how these allusions connect to Tony's conflicts. The dream's second sequence takes place in Dr. Melfi's office, where we think we see Tony telling Dr. Melfi about what Carmine Lupertazzi has said in the dream's initial sequence, but we soon see it isn't Dr. Melfi at all that Tony is talking to but Gloria Trillo. In their ensuing banter, *The Honeymooners* is quoted ("To the moon, Alice!"), and Tony remarks that his cousin "does a mean [Jackie] Gleason" imitation. Their scene ends with Gloria asking him, "You ready for what you have to do?" Tony could read this question as a sign that he has to eliminate his cousin who has also imitated Tony Soprano, the strong, take-charge boss, and whose vigilante actions with the Leotardos have caused Tony's own professional life to unravel. This brief reference to *The Honeymooners* encapsulates many traits of Tony's, not only violence towards and from women, but also his affection for his cousin and his deep regret at having mistaken the surface imitation of Gleason-esque joviality and humor for the real thing.

As Gloria prepares Tony for the next part of his journey (and there is definitely a picaresque quality to the dream, with Tony traveling by car, by foot, or by horse to different locations), she points towards a television in the office. On the screen, Tony sees a version of himself in the back of a car being driven by his father. In one of many examples of mirroring through television screens in the dream, he watches himself. Surrounded by the dead (Johnny Soprano, Ralph Cifaretto, Big Pussy, Mikey Palmice) and the living (Artie Bucco), Tony is informed by Ralph that he is being driven to "the job," which turns out to be his own home, lending credence to the conclusion that his job is to reconcile with Carmela. (This sequence also echoes the dream sequence from "Calling All Cars" [4.11], which features the exact same background process shot as Tony is being driven by Carmela to an actual job as a menial laborer.)

Once they arrive at the Soprano house, Tony walks into the kitchen where Carmela, dressed in black, tells him to get dressed so they can go to meet Finn's parents. Despite Carmela's urging, he finds himself transfixed by another TV, this time a small portable showing a scene from *Chinatown*. There are many possible interpretations behind this reference, perhaps the most obvious being the idea that the film is all about one man's fruitless attempt to expose the corruption, both private and public, that surrounds him. But the use of *Chinatown* becomes clarified later in the dream when Tony witnesses a scene from *High Noon* on the television at Vesuvio's. In his book *Habits of the Heart*, Robert Bellah mentions—only sentences apart—both Jake Gittes of *Chinatown* and Will Kane of *High Noon* as avatars of mythic American Individualism, asserting that these two men perfectly illustrate the "connection of moral courage and lonely individualism." Both the detective and the cowboy act as one "who again and again saves a society he can never completely fit into" (145), and it is this conflict that resonates so clearly with Tony. He must act to save his family, while simultaneously knowing that he can't really fit into either his professional family or his biological one. (As an HBO ad insisted, "One family or another will kill him.") Still, his loyalty to these institutions is so deeply ingrained he cannot turn his back on his commitments to either of them. The concept of self-reliance which Tony cleaves to so strongly, as evidenced by his repeated references to Gary Cooper, is in complete opposition to the oath of loyalty he has taken both professionally and personally. Carmela is absolutely correct when she tells Tony that this stuff—this scene from *Chinatown*—is indeed his life.

The scene on the small TV then changes abruptly to *A Christmas Carol* (Desmond Hurst, 1951), a reference even Tony would be capable of reading correctly, understanding his dream will be a journey through his past, present, and future to help him change his life's direction. Significantly, this clip shows Scrooge after he has awakened, ready to put what he has learned from his dream into action. But before Tony can wake and act on his dream, he is once again mirrored on the screen. By watching himself on the television screen, Tony's dream echoes Jean Baudrillard's thoughts on the effect of technology on our lives: "It is well known how the simple presence of the television changes the rest of the habitat into a kind of archaic envelope, a vestige of human relations" (129). As Tony is displaced by his mirror image on television, he can clearly see the vestiges of both of his families and, upon waking, will try to rebuild both houses.

Once Tony and Carmela arrive at Vesuvio's for dinner with Meadow, Finn, and Finn's parents, Tony's dream logic takes a turn that has been discussed avidly in chat rooms and on discussion boards. Appearing as Finn's parents, Mr. and Mrs. DeTrolio, are John Heard, the actor who portrayed troubled cop Vin Makazian in Season One (he committed suicide in "Nobody Knows Anything" [1.11]), and Annette Bening who, in contrast to Carmela, is dressed entirely in white. (The credits for this episode interestingly list "Annette Bening as Herself" and "John Heard as Vin Makazian.") Makazian's appearance as Mr. DeTrolio is difficult to unknot, but one possible interpretation lies in the fact that Tony once assigned Makazian to tail Dr. Melfi. Makazian not only reports to Tony that Dr. Melfi does not have much of a sex life, he assaults one of her dates ("Meadowands," 1.04). After this incident, according to Glen O. Gabbard, Dr. Melfi "is more revealing of herself than ever as she tells Tony the details ... Tony is beginning to take care of his doctor" (53). If, as Freud claimed, dreams are "the royal road to an understanding of the unconscious" (Gabbard 180), then Makazian signifies Tony's reluctance to relinquish his role as Meadow's protector to Finn now that they are engaged. Makazian was used as a tool by Tony to protect Dr. Melfi and to bind her more closely to him, just as giving Finn employment at one of his construction sites ultimately ensures that Meadow will remain a part of the Soprano family.

After showing everyone at the table the tooth he lost while back at the house, Tony tells Meadow that having a husband in dental school means that Finn will be able to fix her mouth and then immediately loses another tooth of his own. Embarrassed by the bloody tooth falling from his mouth, Tony quickly removes the tooth only to be told, in a kindly voice, by Mrs. DeTrolio, "We know all about you and I think it's great." Though her meaning remains indeterminate, Mrs. DeTrolio is clearly being established as an idealized version of motherhood (the supportive, understanding mother dressed in white, as opposed to Carmela's black dress). Earlier in this episode, in a conversation with his cousin, Tony mentions that he has been thinking about Charmaine Bucco, claiming that, by virtue of being a good cook *and* a notary public, she "is the kind of woman I need." But in his dream, Tony creates another woman whose public persona attracts him, one who stands in stark contrast to Carmela. As Mrs. DeTrolio states that "People always told us that Finn wouldn't amount to much," Finn is abruptly replaced at the table by A. J., and Carmela responds, "He won't. I think the die is cast." After this harsh indictment, Mrs. DeTrolio, who is intent upon keeping up public appearances at this dinner, defuses an argument with her husband, and asks Meadow an innocuous question about whether or not she can play a musical instrument. In this sequence of the dream, as he conjoins dentistry, sons, and nurturing-yet-critical mothers, Tony reminds viewers of another episode from Season One, "Isabella" (1.12), where, in a lithium-induced haze, Tony hallucinates meeting the beautiful young dental student staying next door at the Cusamano's house. According to Dr. Melfi, this vision of Tony's appears at the exact moment when he is in need of an idealized maternal figure. And just like Isabella,

Annette Bening appears here to offer him another version of the kind of woman he needs.

As Mr. DeTrolio launches into an a cappella version of The Commodores' "Three Times a Lady," Tony taps on the shoulder of Mrs. DeTrolio. "You're Annette Bening?" he asks; she nods affirmatively. In this moment of disruption, Hollywood, dream logic, and Tony's subconscious all collide. Among some of the theories floating around the internet about "Why Annette Bening?" are her role in the film *Bugsy* (Barry Levinson, 1991) about a gangster with a glamorous lifestyle and ties to Hollywood, or perhaps, even more plausibly, her part in *American Beauty* (Sam Mendes, 1999), a film about the decrepitude hiding behind the perfectly manicured lawns of the suburbs. The respectability Tony has tried to buy with his home in the suburbs and a daughter attending an Ivy-league university is constantly in danger of being disrupted as violently as the life of Lester Burnham (Kevin Spacey) in *American Beauty*. Even her real-life role as the woman who tamed one of Hollywood's most notorious bachelors, Warren Beatty, could have been on Tony's mind. Bening made a family man out of Beatty, a wish that Tony has for Finn in order to ensure that Meadow will not be removed from the Soprano family. The seemingly random appearance of the actress Bening and her dual role as herself and Finn's mother can be more fully understood, however, in light of Tony's ambivalence towards the performing mandated by each of his roles. The meeting of the parents and the ensuing confrontation in the street between Tony Blundetto and Phil Leotardo—the next episode in the dream and the second appearance of Bening—are both public performances, and indeed most of Tony's life as a mobster involves the playing of a role whose conventions originated long ago in many other texts.

Once her husband's song is (finally) over, Mrs. DeTrolio rewrites a very familiar quote from *The Godfather*. After Mr. DeTrolio tells everyone he "could use a nice tinkle," Bening, knowingly joining in the play, reprises Sonny Corleone's famous bit of dialogue, insisting "I don't want my husband coming out of there with just his cock in his hand." Tony, too, evokes *The Godfather*, when, in the bathroom of Vesuvio's, he imitates Michael Corleone and looks for the gun that should be hidden behind the toilet tank. Unfortunately for Tony, there is nothing there. Unlike Michael, Tony is unarmed and unprepared to deal with what will happen next. With only a copy of *The Valachi Papers* instead of a gun, Tony is unable to prevent the shooting of Phil Leotardo by Tony Blundetto. Tony's dream reveals him as a postmodern version of Michael Corleone: a boss tormented by doubt and anxiety, whose efforts to rule his family are finally revealed to the public as wholly ineffectual.

Outside of Vesuvio's, apparently drawn to the scene by the sounds of gunshots, a crowd has gathered to witness what will happen next: Tony B.'s violent attack on Phil. Reversing the logic of the Soprano family's usual activities, the murder takes place in broad daylight in front of the assembled crowd. As Tony B. fires multiple shots, Tony S. pushes through a mass of people, arriving too late to prevent Phil's murder. Tony Soprano, not Tony Blundetto, however, is held responsible by the crowd. Immediately after Tony states, "I knew this was gonna happen," a man steps forward to confront him, asking "Why didn't you stop him?" Before Tony can answer, Phil exits the car and stumbles into the street. Phil's bloody execution scene now takes a darkly comic turn as Tony B. pretends to shoot Phil again with his finger. Tony B. then demands that Tony S. tell the crowd what happened twenty years ago, which Tony S., clearly not prepared to admit publicly to the panic attack that kept him from being arrested along with his cousin, refuses to do. Phil, who has been lying in the street, then waves his hand and asks, "What do I gotta count to before I can get up?" Though Tony tells him, "You're really dead," Phil continues to argue why he can't be. His responses are made even more public as they are broadcast into a microphone held by Gloria. Tony is next questioned by another member of the crowd, who asks, pointing towards Tony B., "Wasn't that Tony there the guy you were supposed to cap to prevent this from happening?" Tony's responses—that he doesn't know the answer and he doesn't have a gun—are unconvincing, and he seems to sense that the crowd has begun to turn on him. Annette Bening, now a part of the assembled masses, raises her hand and, after being called on to speak, by her real name and as if in a classroom by Gloria, states, "There's something Bugsy about him."

As David Pattie has suggested, references to Mafia movies serve as "a symbolic framework within which Tony ... and most of the other Mafia characters in *The Sopranos* attempt to find a meaning and justification for their lives" (137). By referring to Tony as "Bugsy," an allusion which echoes Hollywood, performance, and Tony's desire to be seen as a brave and honorable leader (the mob definition of the term "Bugsy"), Bening reminds Tony of what he will lose if he refuses to act: his status as boss of the family and, quite possibly, his life. Pursued by the crowd that holds him responsible for the violence they have just witnessed, Tony finally understands that deferring action and responsibility will only end in disaster. After escaping from the angry mob, he is ready (both in the dream and in real life) to return to Carmela and publicly perform his duties as head of both of his families.

After his dream in "Calling All Cars," Tony relates the substance of his vision to Dr. Melfi who tells him, "Dreams are wishes." Though Tony's wishes in "The Test Dream" to reconcile with Carmela and contain the threat posed by Tony Blundetto are granted, the dream illuminates another wish of Tony's: to understand himself. On the phone to Carmela in the last scene of the episode, Tony asks her if it is light where she is yet. The exposure of Tony's unconscious revelations has shed light on his own life and revealed it to be not just another addition to the gangster genre, but instead a hybrid text itself, comprised of a myriad of allusions and illusions, demanding to be read and interpreted.

8

FROM COLUMBUS TO GARY COOPER

MOURNING THE LOST WHITE FATHER
IN *THE SOPRANOS*

Christopher Kocela

In the pilot episode of *The Sopranos*, Tony begins his first session of psychotherapy with Jennifer Melfi by lamenting he did not come into his business on the "ground floor." Perhaps more than any other line in the series, this comment has led critics to locate the originality of *The Sopranos* in its nostalgic and self-conscious brooding over a lost "golden age" in gangster history. Owing to the obsessiveness with which the show references the films of Coppola and Scorsese—particularly in its first two seasons—*The Sopranos* has been read as a "postmodern Mafia tale" (Pattie 144) in which the history of the Mafia is reduced, even for its members, to a series of cinematic images.[1] Yet for all the critical attention paid to the way in which Tony, Sil, Paulie, Christopher, and others yearn for filmic ideals of Italian-American identity, there has been little recognition of the complexity with which *The Sopranos* portrays the relationship between Italian-American ethnicity and whiteness.

That complexity, I suggest, also emerges through cinematic references in Tony's earliest sessions with Jennifer Melfi. Halfway through the pilot episode, shortly before storming out of Jennifer's office for the first of many times, Tony expresses his frustration about the confessional nature of psychotherapy: "Whatever happened to Gary Cooper? The strong, silent type. That was an American. He wasn't in touch with his feelings. He just did what he had to do" ("The Sopranos," 1.01). Like Tony's longing for the "ground floor" and his regret over his lost ducks, Tony's question about Gary Cooper recurs throughout the series and reveals his mourning for a lost ideal of white masculinity that both structures and confounds his efforts to fashion himself as a contemporary godfather. If, as others have argued, the originality of *The Sopranos* stems from the postmodern self-reflexivity with which it treats the gangster genre, I maintain that the series is equally revolutionary by virtue of its thematic focus on the conflicted relationship between Italian-American and white identity. This theme, a central preoccupation of many recent studies of Italian-American history, emerges in numerous subplots throughout the series but receives particular attention in "Christopher" (4.03), to which I devote the majority of the analysis that follows.

Critical commentary on the portrayal of race and ethnicity in *The Sopranos* has rarely gone beyond the question of whether or not the series stereotypes Italian-Americans. Such commentary ranges from outright condemnation of the show to more circumspect studies of the embeddedness of stereotypes within the history of the gangster genre.[2] Not infrequently, the series itself has weighed in on the question of its own stereotyping by portraying characters who give voice to the notion that gangster stories are bad for the Italian-American community.[3] I want to argue, however, that beyond the self-consciousness of its depiction in the media, *The Sopranos* also reflects a substantial body of recent theoretical and historical work on the relationship between Italian-American ethnicity and whiteness. Matthew Frye Jacobson's influential *Whiteness of a Different Color: European Immigrants and the Alchemy of Race* identifies Italian-Americans as "problematic whites" owing to the fact that they were accepted only gradually, after enduring much racial discrimination, into the class of "Caucasians" that defines twentieth-century American whiteness. The result of this historical "becoming-Caucasian" is that Italian-Americans, like many contemporary "ethnic whites," retain their sense of ethnicity through historical amnesia about the process of inclusion in the white race and the many advantages which that status affords.[4] Supporting this view of Italian-American history, Jennifer Guglielmo introduces her book *Are Italians White? How Race is Made in America* with the observation: "Italians were not always white, and the loss of this memory is one of the tragedies of racism in America" (1).[5] Through its attention to the assimilated status of the Soprano family and crew (dramatized in myriad ways, from Meadow's anxieties about affirmative action to the inability of Tony and crew to conduct themselves with even marginal social success during their visit to Italy).[6] *The Sopranos* provides abundant fuel for interrogating the troubled relationship between Italian-American ethnicity and whiteness. But *The Sopranos* is more than simply a passive object text for such studies. In keeping with its celebrated self-reflexivity, *The Sopranos* occasionally takes up its own direct interrogation of the relationship between Italian-American identity and whiteness.

One of the more interesting and provocative forms of that interrogation is Tony's repeated question, "Whatever happened to Gary Cooper?" Less a query than a mantra, this line always precedes Tony's canned description of Cooper as the "strong, silent type" based on his legendary role in *High Noon* (1952) and other films. When, for example, A. J.'s high school guidance counselor asks Tony why he won't allow his son to go to therapy, Tony replies: "People use it as a crutch. And I always wonder, what happened to Gary Cooper, the strong, silent type?" ("All Happy Families," 5.04). For Tony, formulaic mourning for the "loss" of Gary Cooper is shorthand for all that is wrong with contemporary American culture—particularly its fostering of a victim mentality and its celebration of public (especially broadcast) displays of emotion. Yet despite his frequent appeal to Cooper's legacy of strength and silence, Tony's relationship to that ideal is in fact highly conflicted on several levels.

Most obviously, the fact that Tony is himself a patient of psychotherapy makes Gary Cooper less an inspiration to him than an index of his own weakness and insufficiency. That Cooper's name precipitates Tony's slide into self-pity becomes clear in a heated exchange in Jennifer's office in "The Happy Wanderer" (2.06):

Tony:	Sometimes I resent you making me a victim.
	[...]
Melfi:	I make you feel like a victim?
Tony:	Yeah. Remember the first time I came in here? I said the kind of man I admire is Gary Cooper, the strong, silent type. And how all Americans, all they're doing is crying and confessing and complaining—a bunch of fuckin' pussies. Fuck 'em! And now I'm one of 'em—a *patient!*

Tony's implicit conflation of the terms "victim" and "patient" as signifiers of American group belonging is indicative of his deep distrust of confessional therapy, the antidote to which is Gary Cooper's stoic silence. Naturally enough, Jennifer strenuously contests Tony's opinion that her profession creates victims; but Tony's views are seconded later by Jennifer's former teacher, Dr. Krakower, whose dim view of the contemporary state of psychiatry in America suggests another, deeper level of conflict in Tony's relationship to Gary Cooper.

Dr. Krakower tells Carmela: "Many patients want to be excused for their current predicament because of events that occurred in their childhood. That's what psychiatry has become in America. Visit any shopping mall or ethnic pride parade and witness the results" ("Second Opinion," 3.07). Though Dr. Krakower does not universally equate patients with victims as Tony does, his observation about the relationship between childhood and ethnicity is important because Tony, too, periodically invokes ethnic history as an explanation for his criminal activities. The most forceful example is found in "From Where to Eternity" (2.09), in which Tony defends himself in a session with Jennifer:

> When America opened the floodgates and let all us Italians in, what do you think they were doing it for? ... The Carnegies and the Rockefellers, they needed worker bees and there we were. But some of us didn't want to swarm around their hive and lose who we were. We wanted to stay Italian and preserve the things that meant something to us: honor, and family, and loyalty. ... Now we weren't educated like the Americans, but we had the balls to take what we wanted.[7]

From Dr. Krakower's point of view, Tony's resistance to becoming a victim is compromised by his use of his ethnic past to excuse his present behavior. Furthermore, Tony's view of Italian-American history framed by figures like the Carnegies and Rockefellers reflects on Tony's appeal to Gary Cooper as both a defense against, and verification of, his descent into the common pool of American "victims."

If, as Tony maintains, resistance to "swarming around the hive" of the Rockefellers and Carnegies led to the formation of the Mafia, it is perhaps not surprising that the qualities Tony reveres most in Gary Cooper are his strength and silence—silence which reflects the Mafia's policy of *omerta* through which "honor and family and loyalty" are preserved. Yet the undeniable fact of Cooper's whiteness—a trait that places him in league with the Carnegies and Rockefellers—surely problematizes Tony's reverence for an anti-assimilationist model of Italian-American history. That Tony recognizes this inherent conflict of loyalties is revealed, I suggest, in his own conspicuous silence about Cooper's racial identity. With the exception of one instance which I will discuss later, Tony never acknowledges the whiteness of his symbolic American father. And while this implicit denial enables Tony to maintain belief in his ethnic resistance to assimilation, it also reveals his repeated "Whatever happened to Gary Cooper?" question to be a symptom of his racial anxiety. Like whiteness itself as described in some studies, Gary Cooper takes on a kind of ghostly existence in *The Sopranos*, paradoxically present through remarks about his absence, frequently referred to but seen only once (and that in a dream).[8]

The tension between Italian-American ethnicity and white racial consciousness emerges in various forms throughout the series and marks one of *The Sopranos'* most original contributions to the gangster genre. For the most part, this tension is manifested by Tony and rarely emerges outside the discussions in Jennifer's office or the occasional subplot or flashback.[9] In "Christopher" (4.03), however, the relationship of ethnicity to victimization takes center stage. Through its portrayal of the political furor surrounding the annual Columbus Day parade in Newark, "Christopher" provides ample support for Dr. Krakower's thesis that the ethnic pride parade represents, at root, a celebration of victimhood. Yet far from simply mocking the sentiments of characters like Sil and Tony (although it does do that), the episode also directs attention to the roles played by several symbolic American father-figures (from Christopher Columbus to George Washington to Gary Cooper) in structuring contemporary white racial consciousness. Through their conflicted relationships to these symbolic figures, characters like Tony and Sil emerge as unique in the history of the gangster genre—as Italian-American gangsters torn by devotion to their white American "founding" fathers and their Italian godfathers.

The avenues through which "Christopher" develops the relationship between ethnic identity and the celebration of victimhood are manifold. At perhaps the most obvious level, "Christopher," like earlier episodes in the series, incorporates outside criticism of the show for its role in perpetrating Italian-American stereotypes. Early in the episode Carmela attends a church lunch and lecture on the subject of Italian-American women and pride, given in honor of Columbus Day. The core of the lecturing professor's message is that pride depends on counteracting media stereotypes: "A Princeton study showed that seventy-four per cent of Americans associated Italian-Americans with organized crime. Why would they do this? Because of the way the media depict us." Ironically, Carmela and her friends are outraged when Professor Murphy goes on to announce that the "true" Italian-American is the one who obeys the law. In a parodic reversal of accusations leveled against *The Sopranos*, Rosie Aprile says that Father Phil has "forgotten who his friends are" by inviting such an offensive speaker to his church.[10]

Attention to Italian-American stereotyping, however, forms only a small part of the episode's more extensive commentary on the relativity of "truth" where racial and ethnic identity is concerned. At the heart of this commentary is an explication of the media's role in reifying ethnic stereotypes by sensationalizing racial and ethnic conflict. The opening scene cuts from a vertical shot of the Soprano crew sitting outside Satriale's to find Bobby Baccalieri reading to the group from a newspaper article describing the New Jersey Council of Indian Affairs and its intention to disrupt the upcoming Columbus Day parade. On hearing the official statement of Council Chairman Del Redclay regarding "Columbus's role in the genocide of America's Native peoples," the crew is outraged at this "anti-Italian discrimination" and decides to take action against Redclay and his group. Later, Sil explains his strategy to Tony: "This battle's gonna be won on the PR level. Hearts and minds. They manipulate your image, Columbus, you manipulate theirs."

In the ensuing battle of images, Sil and crew attempt to discredit the protestors' claims to historical and racial victimization by imputing a mixed racial heritage to Iron-Eyes Cody, "poster boy" for Native American pride. Although Cody's racial ancestry has no logical bearing on the validity of the protest, the effectiveness of Sil's strategy is confirmed by Redclay shortly after he is threatened by Ralph Cifaretto with public exposure of the news about Cody. Redclay confides to his teaching assistant that this news, true or not, is a "major PR boner" and a "fucking disaster." Nor is Redclay the only character in the episode to recognize the inevitability of the media's reduction of racial and ethnic identity to an opposition of victim to victimizer. Sil justifies his war of images, as he tells Tony, through his belief that "we're the victims here." When Carmela learns that A. J.'s history teacher, under the influence of Howard Zinn's *A People's History of the United States*, is portraying Columbus as nothing more than a slave trader, she attempts to broaden her son's historical perspective by observing: "George Washington had slaves, the father of our country." But when this fails to do the trick she falls back on simply excusing Columbus as a "victim of his time." Finally, the lecturing professor at Carmela's church responds to Italian-American stereotyping with an equally simplistic binary formula: "If they say John Gotti, you tell them Rudolph Giuliani." If, as Tony maintains, the USA has become a breeding ground for self-proclaimed victims, "Christopher" leaves no doubt that the media is to blame.

Meanwhile, "Christopher" also directs considerable attention to what becomes of the victimizer once everyone has succeeded in becoming a victim. One of the more interesting patterns to emerge in the episode reflects the way in which differing racial and ethnic groups align and realign themselves relative to Columbus as a master signifier of whiteness.

Three scenes depict a discussion in which two or more characters, first portrayed as allies in their view of Columbus and his legacy, suddenly find themselves at odds with one another owing to an unexpected "historical" turn in the conversation. The first of these scenes is the opening discussion by members of Tony's crew outside Satriale's. Toward the end of this discussion, Furio confesses that, despite his desire to support his friends in their anger about the Columbus Day protest, he nonetheless hates Columbus and all of Northern Italy as a result of the North's historical prejudice against the South. Later in the episode, a comparable about-face occurs when Montel Williams, hosting a television forum on the Columbus Day parade, suddenly turns against the spokesman for the Italian-American perspective, Philip K. Donatti. At first, Montel sides with Donatti about the need to look beyond the pain that all cultures have endured in bringing the "startling economic miracle" of America to life. But their alliance falls apart when Donatti implies a historical equivalence between the injustices endured by Italian- and African Americans:

Phil:	Take my grandparents, two simple people from Sicily, who braved the perilous middle passage-
Montel:	Whoa—middle passage? That's a term for the slave trade.
Phil:	Montel, the Italian people in this country also suffered discrimination-
Montel:	Earth to Phil! We're talking three hundred years of slavery here!

Finally, this pattern is repeated again when Tony approaches his Jewish friend and advisor Hesh for help with the protest. As discussion begins, Hesh and Reuben, his Cuban house guest, are in complete agreement about Columbus's historical crimes. But when Reuben makes an offhand comparison of Columbus to Hitler, Hesh is incredulous: "You're talkin' outta your ass, man! Columbus and Hitler? You're trivializing the Holocaust. Frankly Reuben, if you've got that kind of covert anti-Semitism, I'd like you to leave my house." Though Ralph reminds the two men that they have been "friends for years," the discussion ends with Reuben storming away in a rage.

Viewed together, these scenes depict the struggle for ethnic identity in the age of victimhood as a competition over degrees of historical suffering and persecution. But the fact that it is Christopher Columbus and his legacy that serve as the impetus for each of these struggles also builds the case for a structural analysis of contemporary racial and ethnic identification in which identity is defined relative to a central—and white—symbolic figure. Indeed, the role played by Columbus as America's founding father and the white victimizer in these discussions (and throughout the episode) invites consideration of his function in the capacity designated by Kalpana Seshadri-Crooks as a "master signifier of Whiteness." In Seshadri-Crooks' Lacanian analysis of race, the master signifier of Whiteness organizes the placement of subjects along the signifying chain of racial difference, relegating them to symbolic positions such as "black," "white," "Native," etc. This distribution of racial subjectivities is accomplished through the promise of wholeness which Whiteness always holds out to the raced subject—a promise whose falsity stems from the fact that it offers to fill a "lack" in the subject that does not really exist.

According to Seshadri-Crooks, race is not a category fundamental to human subjectivity; nevertheless we believe in race and the promises made by Whiteness because we misread the conspicuous visibility of racial features as proof of race's biological essentiality. In the context of *The Sopranos*, the value of Seshadri-Crooks' theory is that it enables us to see the often-humorous ironizing of racial and ethnic identity in "Christopher" as, at root, a valuable commentary on the structure of racial fantasy in the USA. If, as the episode suggests, Columbus stands as a prominent master signifier of whiteness in American culture—if not the pre-eminent symbolic white Name of the Father— then the "historical turn" repeatedly dramatized in discussions about his legacy reveals the arbitrary nature of whiteness and what comes to found racial difference. Granted, the historical turns taken by Hesh and Montel are motivated by nothing more than an off-base comparison (Columbus to Hitler, Italian-American immigration to the middle passage). But the deeper suggestion here is that the system of race is always based on culture-specific judgments about likeness and difference—judgments usually based on little more than visual appearance. To subject the central organizing principle of racial difference to historical or cultural analysis is to challenge belief in race itself by "troubl[ing] the relation of the subject to the master signifier" (Seshadri-Crooks 35).

Belief in the self-evidence of racial difference is challenged most directly in "Christopher" when Sil and Tony sit down to dinner with Chief Doug Smith, Tribal Chairman of the Mohunk Indians. Having sought an audience in the hope of persuading him to intervene in the Columbus Day protest, Tony and Sil are surprised to find that this prominent Native American looks just like a white man. After exchanging numerous perplexed glances with Tony, Sil finally cannot help himself and says, "No offense, Chief, but you don't look much like an Indian." Chief Smith replies: "Frankly I passed most of my life as white, until I had a racial awakening and discovered my Mohunk blood. My grandmother on my father's side, her mother was a quarter Mohunk." Although Tony suggests that Smith's racial awakening was conveniently timed to coincide with the build-up of his casino, the irony of white racial "passing" reflects as directly on Sil and Tony here as it does on Chief Smith. Indeed, Smith's response—"Better late than never"—to Tony's snide question implies that Tony and Sil have yet to take a full account of their own racial denials in the course of their battle with Redclay. This implication is borne out by the fact that Sil's war of images, which sought to sully Native American pride through the mixed racial heritage of Iron-Eyes Cody, remains utterly silent on the relationship of Italian-American identity to whiteness. If Chief Smith presents a laughable picture of racial awakening, he is nonetheless more honest about his strategic deployment of racial images than either Sil or Tony.

When that moment of racial awakening does finally come for Sil and Tony, it takes the form of an argument between the two men that draws together the central preoccupations of "Christopher" through attention to the legacies of Columbus and Gary Cooper. To be sure, this argument—in the last scene of the episode—has been brewing for some time, owing to the differing degrees of commitment exhibited by Tony and Sil with regard to the Columbus Day protest. From the start it has been Sil who has felt the strongest need to defend the Columbus Day parade owing to the fact that, as he tells Tony, his father was a Knight of Columbus. Tony, on the other hand, has gotten involved only reluctantly, and only at Sil's request that he show "leadership" to the crew in defense of their Italian heritage.

By the end of the episode, Tony's waning enthusiasm turns to hostility when, driving back from their complimentary weekend of gambling at Chief Smith's casino, he and Sil are reminded of the Columbus Day parade by a radio report describing the success of Redclay's protest. When Sil expresses regret at having missed the parade, Tony accuses him of false posturing and having deliberately skipped the parade for a weekend of blackjack. Sil defends himself:

Sil: I don't know what you're so hot about. They discriminate against all Italians as a group when they disallow Columbus Day.

Tony: Oh will you fucking stop! Group! Group! Whatever the fuck happened to Gary Cooper, that's what I'd like to know! ... The strong, silent type. He did what he had to do. ... And did he complain? Did he say, 'Oh, I come from this poor Texas Irish illiterate background or whatever the fuck, so leave me the fuck out of it, because my people got fucked over?'
          [...]

Sil: T, not for nothing, but you're getting a little confused here. That was the movies.

Tony: And what the fuck difference does that make? Columbus was so long ago he might as well have been a fucking movie. Images you said!

Sil: The point is Gary Cooper, the real Gary Cooper, or anybody named Cooper never suffered like the Italians. *Medigon* [non-Italians] like him, they fucked everybody else—the Italians, the Polacks, the blacks.

Tony: If he was a *medigon* around nowadays he'd be a member of some victims group—the fundamentalist Christians, the abused cowboys, the gays, whatever the fuck.

It is worth noting that this is the only time in the first five seasons of *The Sopranos* that Gary Cooper's whiteness is directly addressed.[11] The fact that Tony reacts to Sil's description of Cooper as a *medigon* by positing a new image of Cooper as the "abused cowboy" indicates the extent to which Tony's forced recognition of Cooper's whiteness disturbs him. For Tony to imagine the epitome of the "strong, silent type" as a member of a contemporary victims group signals a radical re-evaluation of his racial understanding. And this, in short order, leads him to a surprising conclusion which he voices in an effort to cure Sil of his own reliance on ethnic history.

As the argument continues, Sil refuses to dissociate himself from his grandparents, who where "spit on because they were from Calabria." Tony responds by highlighting the comforts of Sil's present life:

> Let me ask you something. All the good things you got in your life, did they come to you because you're Calabrese? I'll tell you the answer. The answer is no. ... You got it 'cause you're *you*, 'cause you're smart, 'cause you're whatever the fuck. Where the fuck is our self-esteem? That shit doesn't come from Columbus or *The Godfather* or Chef-fuckin'-Boy-Ardee.

Tony's list of inspirational father-figures completes the litany of symbolic fathers turned up in the course of the episode, from Columbus to George Washington to Gary Cooper. But his conclusion that self-esteem does not derive from these master signifiers contradicts everything we know about Tony, his friends, and his family. It is *precisely* through reference to Columbus and *The Godfather* in particular that Tony, Sil, Paulie, Christopher, and Pussy (among others) derive their sense of themselves as Italian-Americans and *Mafioso*. So what does Tony mean by this? It is tempting to read Tony's complete rejection of symbolic fathers as evidence of the fact that, in Seshadri-Crooks' terms, he has been deeply "troubled" with relation to these master signifiers of whiteness. In this case, Tony's conclusion would be a hopeful one, evidence of his deep skepticism about the cultural images and structures through which racial subject positions are formed.

But this reading, which would place Tony's shift of stance in line with those "historical turns" discussed earlier, is contradicted by the fact that his explanation for all the good things in Sil's life reinstitutes his earlier silence about whiteness. In his effort to cure Sil of his misguided attachment to his ethnic past, Tony carefully avoids suggesting that Sil's present wealth and success might have anything to do with the fact that he is white. Instead, Tony tells him "you're *you*" and explains Sil's success on that fact alone. Seeking to break Sil's dependence on an ethnic model of history that makes him a victim, Tony offers a model of identity completely devoid of race, ethnicity, or history. Such a model would not, in light of Tony's rejection statement regarding Columbus and Chef-boy-Ardee, need to depend on any Italian-American or white symbolic father for its conferral.

Except, of course, that Sil's new identity *is* conferred by a symbolic father figure—one who is, moreover, both Italian-American and white. Even as Tony denies the need for Columbus and the Godfather, he accords himself the ability to grant identity ("you're *you*"), to inspire self-esteem ("you're smart"), and to occupy the position of both Italian godfather and white American father. Herein lies the most impressive historical sleight-of-hand performed by Tony's announcement of the end of symbolic fathers. For by proclaiming the irrelevance of these symbolic fathers, Tony is able, in effect, to "pass" undetected as one of them and to garner their authority for himself. Moreover, this transfer of authority is re-enacted, in part, every time Tony asks the question, "Whatever happened to Gary Cooper?" Tony paradoxically demonstrates the "leadership" requested by Sil at the start of the parade campaign at the moment that he divests his *consigliere* of any claim to ethnic identity. "Christopher" thus concludes with a subtle demonstration that, in an age in which all Italian-Americans are also white Americans, the authority of a godfather in his own family no longer derives simply from his consanguinity with the old Italian patriarchy. Rather, it also depends on a complex relationship with symbolic white fathers through whom the historical process of becoming-Caucasian is both affirmed and denied.

At the risk of generalizing about a complex and multifaceted series on the basis of one (admittedly uncharacteristic) episode, I will end by suggesting that the picture of Tony painted in "Christopher" likewise describes his role as a contemporary godfather throughout *The Sopranos*.

Tony's relations with the Cusamanos and Massive Genius ("A Hit is a Hit," 1.10), his reaction to Meadow's boyfriend, Noah Tannenbaum ("Proshai, Livushka," 3.02), and his handling of the urban housing development scam ("Watching Too Much Television," 4.07) all testify in different ways to Tony's divided allegiance to Italian-American and white symbolic fathers. Interwoven throughout is Tony's mourning for the "lost" Gary Cooper, whose absent presence reminds us of the extent to which Tony Soprano himself has come to stand in contemporary American culture as a prominent and conflicted image of strength, silence, and whiteness.

MUSIC, THEATRICALITY, AESTHETICS

Satriale's Pork Store. Photograph by Michael Prete.

9.

GANGSTAS, DIVAS, AND BREAKING TONY'S BALLS

MUSICAL REFERENCE IN *THE SOPRANOS*

Chris Neal

The familiar theme to *The Sopranos*, "Woke Up This Morning," effectively sets the stage for this story of gangsters in the modern world. Its heavy, hip beat and low-voiced stanzas paint a picture of urban life even before we see Tony driving through Jersey in the opening credits. The soulful, harmonized chorus lends a visceral energy to the opening, leaving us primed to see some poor bastard get whacked in the opening minutes. He probably deserved it. However, the theme song is not our first musical clue about what to expect in the show. After all, before any of us had watched the first episode, or frothed with anticipation at the snazzy HBO trailers, we had a musical reference in Tony's surname.

Why Soprano? Considering the host of distinctly Italian surnames available, how does "Soprano" help us better understand Tony? By choosing Soprano, Chase and company not only identify Tony as Italian but also appropriate the rich history of opera, which has its roots in early seventeenth-century Italy. The allusion creates a subtext that underscores several of the series' principal themes: the emasculation Tony suffers at the hands of the women in his life, his emotional difficulties, and the softer side of his persona that despises violence.

The operatic reference also supports the notion that incidental music frequently serves an ironic function or commentary on the narrative.

As a musical term, "soprano" refers to the vocal range with the highest tessitura of the four most commonly identified ranges: soprano, alto, tenor, and bass. Although singers with soprano voices participate in choral ensembles, the essence of *sopranoness* is solo singing in an operatic setting. It requires significant vocal power to solo in front of an 80–100-piece orchestra, and performing a leading operatic role is the height of professional achievement for many sopranos. The operatic repertoire (especially that from Italian opera composers such as Rossini, Bellini, and Puccini) affords singers opportunities to explore the entire gamut of musical expression, from sweet love songs accompanied only by string instruments, to sweeping virtuosic melodies with full ensemble accompaniment. The most emotional, most tragic, most conflicted—superlative in every sense, the soprano is the center of dramatic attention. Tony is the ultimate soprano/ Soprano—the *diva*.

The earliest operatic compositions date from the early seventeenth century, with Peri and Caccini's settings of the Orpheus and Eurydice myth, premiered in Florence around 1600. Performance practice at the time dictated that soprano roles (female characters) were sung not by women but by men, an inherent gender confusion mirrored in the imbalance between Tony's macho role as a mob boss and his feminine-associated insecurities and attention to his own feelings. The most promising young male singers in the seventeenth and eighteenth centuries were castrated before their voices changed to facilitate long careers singing female roles in opera houses across Europe. Even in the late twentieth century, Tony the Soprano feels a kinship with the early castrati, thanks to the women in his life ("Pax Soprana," 1.06):

Dr. Melfi: What's the one thing every woman ... your mother, your
               wife, your daughter have in common?
Tony: They all break my balls.

Any masculine prowess associated with his Mafia position is virtually meaningless to these women. While his reference is not literal, Tony's failure as patriarch is clearly a blow to his masculinity. In calling upon the history of castrated Italian operatic male sopranos, Chase and company have broken Tony's balls long before Carmela, Meadow, or Livia utter a caustic line or cast a single disapproving glance.

Of course, many of Tony's struggles relate to maintaining alpha-male status in his *other* family as well. Foremost among these is concealing his standing appointment with his psychiatrist, Dr. Melfi. The need to discuss his feelings with a therapist would be viewed by his peers as weak, and would seriously compromise his leadership position within the organization. In fact, as Tony points out to Carmela, it could even compromise his wellbeing ("The Sopranos," 1.01):

Tony: If the wrong person finds out about this, then I get a steel-jacketed antidepressant right to the back of the head!

Only in Melfi's office can Tony be a real person with real weaknesses and insecurities. However, he spends much of his time between therapy sessions concealing his weakness through vigorous *doing*—taking action, giving orders, being the boss.

The alternation between action outside Melfi's office—advancing the plot—and emoting during therapy—reflecting on past or impending events—resembles the typical structure of traditional Italian opera, which employs the alternation of *recitative* and *aria* musical sections. The lyrics of recitative typically have a spoken quality and serve the dramatic function of advancing the plot. Characters interact in a series of rapid-fire declamatory statements, frequently remaining on one or two notes until the end of the musical phrase, accompanied with thinly textured sounds from the orchestra. This is a form of literary housekeeping—advancing the plot as succinctly as possible while cleansing the musical palette in preparation for the next aria. Recitative reflects the Romantic aesthetic by attaching the less interesting musical material to actions, which are substantially less interesting than feelings.

In contrast, the aria is a solo song with dramatic musical lines and virtuosic, soaring melodies. The aria is designed to convey the emotional state of the singer (most frequently, the soprano—a female character in modern times) in response to the twists of the plot just portrayed in the recitative sections. Tony's visits to Melfi are his arias, where he can be emotional (read "feminine") about his life and career:

Dr. Melfi: Do you have any qualms about how you actually make a
               living?
Tony: Yeah ... I find I have to be the sad clown ... laughing on the
               outside but crying on the inside.

("The Sopranos," 1.01)

The dramatic flow in *The Sopranos*, which follows the recitative-aria (action/emotion) pattern evident in opera, allows us to more fully appreciate the complexity of Tony's inner turmoil. By seeing him participate in two distinctly different modes of behavior, we observe the depth of his character by viewing him through multiple dramatic and interpretive lenses. From this perspective, Tony becomes likable despite his socially abhorrent behavior.

While opera relies heavily on the use of continuous music, this modern television production makes somewhat different use of music in support of the dramatic flow. In an interview included on the Season One DVD set, David Chase discusses the use of background music in *The Sopranos*, indicating that all music is source music—there is no musical score for the series. He states that this is simply his personal preference, citing Martin Scorsese, Woody Allen, and Stanley Kubrick as models for this practice. Although including excellent source music is important to Chase, he admits that there is not an overarching vision driving this decision:

It was important to me to have source music, and from the beginning, I
said, "Listen, I really want to make sure we have a decent source music
budget—music licensing budget." And people would say to me "Why?" and
I could never really answer it, to tell you the truth. I just wanted it.

Nonetheless, the specific musical choices do open some interpretive doors for us. Whether supporting the text with small ironies or setting the mood by matching musical style with the scene it accompanies, the source music provides more than auditory interest. It also adds dramatic texture with ironic interplay between music and drama or even creating full-blown subtext. Examples found in the first episode establish a pattern that invites musical readings of subsequent episodes.

Early in the first episode, Tony marvels at the ducks in his pool while the family sits inside having breakfast in the kitchen. As Tony comes inside, we hear Sting on the kitchen radio singing "I'm So Happy I Can't Stop Crying." Although this song actually deals with a man's recovery after being left by his wife, the song's title and general premise do seem to foretell Tony's "sad clown" confession to Melfi later in the same episode. Similarly, we find a subtle reference to Tony's multi-faceted existence in the next scene, as Tony rides in the car with Christopher. On the car radio, we hear Jefferson Airplane's "The Other Side of this Life." The reference is subtle, particularly given that we hear only the instrumental sections of the song. However, were the song to continue, we would hear lyrics that seem to describe Tony's state of mind:

> Would you like to know a secret just between you and me?
> I don't know where I'm going next, I don't know who I'm gonna be.
> But that's the other side of this life I've been leading
> That's the other side of this life.

Even if we do not hear the lyrics, the reference remains valid, particularly with popular music, which audiences are likely to recognize even without hearing the sections with lyrics.

Musical style also serves its own dramatic function throughout the series. Perhaps most overtly, the use of rock and roll music tends to correspond with some kind of illicit behavior. The aforementioned Jefferson Airplane song, while providing subtle commentary on Tony's inner turmoil, recurs while Tony and Christopher are driving to conduct gang-related business. During their drive, they spy Mahaffey, who owes them money for gambling debts. In the ensuing chase, the music changes suddenly to "I Wonder Why," a fifties doo-wop tune performed by Dion & the Belmonts. The lighter style emphasizes the absurdity of the scene while the rock/pop genre of the song helps remind us that Tony and Christopher are misbehaving. In fact, virtually every scene that includes illicit behavior is accompanied by some kind of rock and roll music: Tony's "business" lunch with Christopher at Artie Bucco's restaurant, Christopher's murder of Emil, and waiting at the Bada Bing strip club for a delivery of stolen DVD players. Socially, rock and roll is the only music that could accompany these dramatic moments. No other musical style has such a checkered past and history of rebellion against the establishment.

Similarly, when we hear classical music, it is typically connected with Tony's vulnerabilities. We hear a Beethoven Minuet in both of Tony's visits to the same restaurant: once with his mistress and once, presumably the very next evening, with Carmela. During the first visit, we are reminded of Tony's vulnerability because he sees Melfi at the restaurant and has a short conversation with her. The next evening, at the same restaurant with the same music, Tony confesses to Carmela that he is taking Prozac and seeing a therapist. The only other classical music in this episode occurs during the cookout for A. J.'s birthday. With a soprano singing an aria-like song, we witness one of Tony's panic attacks. Not only does the more genteel nature of classical music support the dramatic revelations of Tony's weaknesses, it also strengthens the established link with Italian Opera with a general reference to the art music genre.

Whether calling upon earlier musical traditions with Tony's surname or utilizing modern musical selections within the dramatic flow, musical reference abounds in *The Sopranos*. The choices made by Chase and company contribute in important ways to our reading of this text, and because the source music seems carefully chosen to interact with the story, the musical flow ultimately becomes a text of its own. Recognizing this important contribution invites music-based readings of subsequent episodes. Whether these readings support or refute the claims made in this essay, the resulting scholarly dialogue will ideally augment the role of musical interpretation within the discipline of television studies.

10.

SHOW BUSINESS OR DIRTY BUSINESS?

THE THEATRICS OF MAFIA NARRATIVE AND EMPATHY FOR THE LAST MOB BOSS STANDING IN *THE SOPRANOS*

Gwyn Symonds

What must big Joey think of these singing bosses and their new partners, the celebrity feds? Sitting in his Brooklyn cell, awaiting a trial that could send him to prison for life or put him to death, he may be wondering if he chose the wrong line of work in an America where a man who keeps secrets can be worth less than a man who spills them. His one rueful consolation may be that much of the public thinks the Mafia is less dirty business than show business, and that a few will be rooting for him to be the last Don standing.

Richard Corliss and Simon Crittle

Popular culture's fascination with organized crime, in which fictional and actual gangsters share an archetypal theatricality on the same media stage, bespeaks a recognition that the drama of the real life events in gangster lives of crime is inherently theatrical fodder, ripe for aesthetic recasting. As Carmela Soprano says of her Mafia boss spouse Tony, "My husband can be very magnetic, bigger than life" ("All Happy Families," 5.04). The dramatic glamour of their stories, with larger than life characters and classic scenarios of greed, revenge, betrayal, power, survival and execution draws the public gaze and the creativity of storytellers. *The Sopranos* has taken those fascinating theatrics inherent in mob murders, strip club cultures, the destruction of crime families, and the struggle for survival in courtrooms and on the streets, to fashion an aesthetic of gangster drama that retains that archetypal theatricality and reflects on it.

To date, academic criticism of the show has concerned itself with the way the series develops its critique of American capitalism, psychiatry and family suburban life in the context of the mob, in the person of Tony Soprano, going mainstream as the gangster becomes the "galvanizing anti-hero on Prozac" (McCarty 246) with a midlife crisis. In addition, critique has responded to the show's intertextuality. Glen Creeber has noted the show's self-awareness of its own "televisionization" in a narrative that deconstructs itself (Creeber 125). David Pattie has insightfully mined the extensive gangster movie referentiality of the show "as a symbolic framework within which Tony, Paulie, Christopher, Silvio and most of the other Mafia characters in *The Sopranos* attempt to find a meaning and justification for their lives" (Pattie 138). However, insufficient recognition has been given to the unique way the show draws on the theatricality real-life events and characters have always offered the gangster genre. While it does update the genre and its social critique for contemporary audiences and use its gangster media referentiality to explore characterization, *The Sopranos* more interestingly offers a multi-layered critique of the ambivalent performativity of the actual, cultural, and textual gangster-verse with which it shares a stage.

The recent comment from *Time* magazine at the head of this chapter is a typical example of the contradictory theatrical mythologizing of the real-life gangster figure as an archetypal hero and an idealist at the heart of corruption. Even in defeat, with "big Joey" sitting in a cell with his life in the balance, he is nostalgically portrayed as a lone figure battling a justice system subverted by celebrity in an America that does not value the code by which he lives. Racketeer though he is, the focus of a celebrity-hungry media, the partnering of "the singing bosses" and the "celebrity feds" highlights the shared moral dubiousness and common theatricality of the very public narrative in which transgressor and legal system participate. He even seems to stand a little taller than the ostensible good guys who are merely "celebrity feds" because he kept to a code and was betrayed by "an America where a man who keeps secrets can be worth less than a man who spills them." This is the "romantic fatalism" of the "promethean, system defying individual hero" (Leitch 306) that the earliest gangster films originated.

As Jack Shadoian intimates in the title of his book on the American gangster film, it is not hard to identify with an archetype characterized by the pathos of dead-end dreams. Since the prosecution of the Mafia is as much show business as dirty business, as much a compelling story as about a threat to public order, the article recognizes that the public as the audience is going to respond equivocally on the story and mythological level and barrack for a larger than life "big Joey" to be the "last Don standing"—particularly in a society that is not, itself, morally clean enough to make the choice of identification unequivocal. No doubt, because he is in a cell, total audience identification is inhibited, but the article acknowledges reader empathy for the lingering presence of an American archetype of failed aspiration in a tainted system. The problem is succinctly portrayed in *The Sopranos* in the workplace camaraderie between the longtime Mafia informant Raymond Curto and his FBI handlers, in the chattily shared complaints Pussy and his FBI contact have about their very similar workplace problems, and in the brutal, eventually fatal, exploitation of Adriana, Christopher's girlfriend, by the FBI. Adriana's handler's claim that "Nowhere but at the FBI is the line clearer between the good guys and the bad guys" ("Rat Pack," 5.02) does not reflect the ambiguity of the situation.

Despite the documented devastation of the real life-and-death consequences of gangster behavior, the mob's fictional history in popular culture, inspired by intra-familial Mafia warfare and crime family legal battles, is one of mythologized codes and archetypal characters that sit on that overlapping boundary posited by performance theory where "Social dramas affect aesthetic dramas, aesthetic dramas affect social dramas" (Schechner 214). *The Sopranos* itself satirizes the theatrical goldmine provided by actual Mafia events when giving a syndicated columnist's book the title *Mafia: America's Longest Running Soap Opera* ("The Legend of Tennessee Moltisanti," 1.08). As Richard Maltby notes in his analysis of golden-age gangster films in the 1930s: "Beginning with the funeral of Big Jim Colosimo in Chicago in May 1920, big gangster funerals became media events, while police raids and gangland wars supplied the melodrama on which the tabloids and sensational magazines thrived" (125). The theatricality conveyed by real-life mobster stories in inspirations for the fictionalized versions was also used by mobsters who role-played versions of themselves in the press and media: "Al Capone achieved national prominence not because he was particularly successful in his chosen field of endeavor, but because he so assiduously courted media attention" (125).

Promotion of *The Sopranos* engages with its own fictional theatricality in relationship to real-life gangsterism. In a DVD feature for the second season of *The Sopranos*, the show is promoted as "The Real Deal" in its image of gangsterism, quoting reporters on crime who have also heard the same claim from the mobsters they have interviewed. The "real deal" is not explicitly defined but seems to be posited as its ability to capture something of the personalities of real gangsters and how they operate, rather than claiming that the fictional is reality television. It is the performativity of the real gangsters' behavior in the context of what they do, that they are entertaining characters as well as killers, that is emphasized. For example, John Miller, one of those quoted, an ABC reporter who has covered the Colombo and Gambino crime families, describes them as paradoxical figures: "They would tell stories and make you laugh until tears were streaming down your face. ... months later you would hear a recording of the same guy saying kill this guy, whack that guy" ("The Real Deal"). As storytellers themselves, the gangsters can play to their reporter audience with comic timing, and the crime reporters respond to their subjects as entertaining characters. It is when they are unaware of their audience—off-stage as it were (presumably on surveillance recordings)—that they are less entertaining than chilling.

Defining the "real deal" in a fictional gangster text is less interesting than looking at the ways in which the performativity and theatricality of real and fictional characters share the same role-playing space in media incarnations offered to an audience. One of the central traits of theatricality, Samuel Weber argues, is the staging of scenes or events on the presumption that they will be observed by an audience, without necessarily being able to contain them totally within the frame of that aesthetic (or even physical) space. Aware they were subjects of legal surveillance, often tools of that surveillance themselves ("He was a wiseguy wearing a wire" [Anastasia 304]),[1] real-life gangsters have always been conscious of themselves as having an audience, if not always a desired one. Rising to media prominence in the film and press in American culture from the early 1900s, gangsters have often been the unwilling subjects of media attention. *The Sopranos* notes the problems this makes for Tony: "How come every piss I take is a fuckin' news story?" ("Big Girls Don't Cry," 2.05). Tony is comically unaware of how his story is fodder for an insatiable public appetite for gangster narratives. The show itself satirizes how the interactive antics of the Mafia and law enforcement contribute to media industry and spectacle when the conflict to be generated by the "Mafia class of '04" is described as making "a good year for crime reporters" ("The Two Tonys," 5.01).

Crime bosses have also been conscious of the ways they could exploit the media for public relations purposes and, in turn, that attention has created an aesthetic space in which "the media gangster was an invention, much less an accurate reflection of reality than a projection" (Ruth 1) of the possibilities and excesses of the urban culture they sprang from and reflected.[2] As David E. Ruth describes, in his aptly named book *Inventing the Public Enemy*, the press and films chronicling and mythologizing the exploits of legendary figures like Al Capone were less interested in the factuality of the underworld than the "imagined gangster" (6) that was created in fascinating narratives of the dramatic rise and fall of an individual. "The Capone legend offered Americans a subversive set of metaphors for rethinking their business society" (130), often blurring the boundaries between criminality and respectability while chronicling the personal and economic success to be won and lost through violent masculinity. As Letizia Paoli notes in a comparison of the Sicilian and American Mafias, "For many people the Italian/American Mafia *is* and *behaves* as it is recounted in these romanticizing novels and films" (3). Where the boundary might be is not something the audience can easily determine. Even Dr. Melfi, Tony Soprano's reluctant therapist, as a non-mobster herself, only has media images to use to speculate about what his role as mob boss might be like outside their sessions: "Granted I get most of my information from movies and Bill Curtis" ("To Save Us All from Satan's Power," 3.10). Given the same could be said by any reader of stories in the press or viewer of Mafia stories on television or films, popular fascination with the gangster is more about responding to performance and theatricality than to representation. It may be, as Fred Gardaphé asserts, "The truth is that the fiction of the gangster is stronger than the facts, and the facts of American history will never be as attractive as the myths that have been created around the gangster" (98).

John McCarty trenchantly captures the blend of "reel" and "real" with his description of one gangster film (*Lepke*, 1975) as a movie "that plays like a filmed rap sheet" (214). McCarty sees that interaction as two-way when he notes that the actor George Raft replied to the question of why factual gangsters "sounded so much like their movie counterparts" by saying "that it was because gangster movies (his in particular, he noted) taught gangsters how to talk":

> America's gangsters have always been fascinated with the movies
> about them and their exploits. ... The story of Bugsy Siegel has special
> significance to this chronicle of bullets over Hollywood because Bugsy's
> rise and fall is not just a rattling good gangster story with all the genre's
> trimmings—money, power, violence—but a glitzy showbiz tale as well. That
> Robinson, Cagney, Raft, and other movie gangsters based their characters'
> styles of dress, their mannerisms, and other behavioral tics on the famous
> gangster personalities of their time we know. But the movie screen is a
> mirror with two sides, and gangsters, like children, are not immune from
> the desire to want to walk, talk, and be like their icons flickering back at
> them from the big screen. This may be why so many mobsters—from the
> big-time dons of New York to the street hoodlums we see on the nightly
> news—seem often like caricatures of their movie counterparts, acting out
> roles in their own real-life gangster melodramas. (241-2)

While performance theory supports the interrelatability of the social and the aesthetic, the degree to which cross-fertilization occurs is, ultimately, of less interest than the fact that there is a theatrical core to gangsterism that Hollywood can exploit, something even the gangsters themselves seem to be aware of. It is possible to find a "Mafia comfortable with the idea of a fictional representation of their activities" well before the FBI surveillance tapes of Mafia fans of

The Sopranos noted by Pattie (140). McCarty records that Bugsy Siegel was a childhood friend of Raft's from the Lower East Side of New York and that he even took a screen test to become an actor when he re-established his association with Raft in Hollywood while there on syndicate gambling business.

THE SOPRANOS AND PERFORMATIVITY

The intersection of the theatricality of actual mob events with narratives in fictional entertainment and public perceptions of the Mafia is highlighted in *The Sopranos* in "46 Long" (1.02), when Tony and his gang are listening to a television panel giving expert analysis for its viewers of the "situation on the ground today" in the Mafia. As Joseph S. Walker has pointed out, "the scene depends upon the audience's knowledge, or at least awareness, of a long tradition of stories about organized crime in America" (Walker 112). It is the easy acceptance by the gang that they and their business are a subject of media punditry that denotes the way the mob soap opera is integrated into the fabric of American culture. However, when Tony asks Silvio to role-play Al Pacino's line in the third *Godfather* movie ("Just when I thought I was out, they pull me back in"), the gang place themselves as more than consumers and subjects of gangster film history; they are performers of it: "Fuckin' spittin' image." When Silvio does the same line later in the episode while trying on an Italian suit and preening in front of a mirror, he is admiring the way he role-plays the theatrical image. When he reprises the line again in "Guy Walks into a Psychiatrist's Office," there is not just a sense that it is Silvio's role to be the repository of that film's lore for instant access as inspiration, comfort, and humor, as Pattie argues, but that the Mafia occupies the same theatrical stage as the movie and that Tony and his gang see themselves as actors sharing that stage. Thus, it is possible for Silvio to parody *The Godfather*'s theatricality, while *being* a parody—exaggerated curl of the lip, clipped speech and all—of the gangster stereotype.

Tony has "had offers" to be fictionalized, and *The Sopranos* may have had Bugsy Siegel in mind when the show gave Christopher Moltisanti, Tony's nephew and protégé, the same Hollywood crossover yearnings:

Christopher: You know my cousin Gregory's girlfriend is what they call a development girl out in Hollywood. She said I could sell my life story, make fucking millions. I didn't do that. I stuck it out with you.

Tony: I'll fucking kill you. What you gonna do, go Henry Hill on me now? You know how many mobsters are selling screen plays and screwing everything up?

Christopher: She said I could maybe even play myself...

("The Sopranos," 1.01)

Christopher's belief that he could play himself on screen articulates the theatricality available to storytelling when real-life gangsters live the violent rituals mined for screenplays in the gangster genre.

Christopher merges that theatricality and his own existence when he laments (in "The Legend of Tennessee Moltisanti" [1.08]) the lack of a story "arc" in his life that will give him respect, purpose, and celebrity. However, his failure to embody the charismatic wise-guy image of so many screen versions of the gangster is pointed out in "Guy Walks into a Psychiatrist's Office," as he gets high while Edward G. Robinson in a tough guy role appears on the television in front of him. As a drug addict, Christopher does not fit the romanticized stereotype of the movies he watches.

TONY PERFORMING TONY

The theatrics of role-playing is above all a symptom of self-delusion and deception in *The Sopranos'* narrative. As David Chase has noted: "Everything that everybody says is untrue: complete falsehoods, self-justifications, rationalizations, outright lies, fantasies and miscommunications" (Heffernan 5). Characters make use of theatrical imagery that implies deceptive role-playing—"Don't you think it's totally unfair what Mom's doing and now like making this little movie scene out of it?" says Meadow, referring to Carmela in "The Sopranos" (1.01)—and are called on the sincerity with which they do it: "Don't call me Godfather with that fuckin' cute smirk," Tony rebukes Feech La Manna in "All Happy Families" (5.04). The show also mines television and film imagery for epithets to typecast people, as when

A. J., Tony's son, is described as "Fredo Corleone" ("Sentimental Education," 5.06), or when there is a gap between characters and roles they may play, as when Pussy is irritated by playing detective to retrieve A. J.'s science teacher's stolen car: "I'm fuckin' Rockford over here" ("46 Long").

At one time or another, Tony, too, lies to almost everyone in his life, including his family, other members of the mob, his therapist, and to himself. Audience reaction to this deception and his violent, murderous gangsterism is complicated by the sympathy for the devil that has been noted in critical reception of his character[3]—sympathy that is a product of an aesthetic that appropriated the culture of organized crime and the sordidness of its subject matter to set its own ethical parameters. The "defining paradox" (Leitch 103) of the gangster narrative, after all, is that as characters gangsters both emulate and transgress social and moral norms. In Tony's case, "contemporary suburban life breeds both middle-class ennui and a complex tension with his mob world" (Fields 615). His contemporary frustrations, his appetites, his anger, his helplessness, his acquaintance with loss—to all forge audience solidarity with his predicament. As Leitch argues, this is not to say that gangster behavior is not condemned but that the audience is offered the contradiction between that condemnation and romanticism as theatrical entertainment.

While there are enough scenes of Tony acting brutally to counter the undoubted empathy the show encourages the audience to feel for him, it is his own performance of the sentimental, idealist mobster that underpins the audience's sense that Tony is a bit of a ham actor as much engaged in self-deception as deceiving others and in role-playing an idealized version of himself masking the criminal at the core. This is particularly so when his behavior references the sentimentality of *The Godfather* movie as his life strains to fit the theatrical parameters it offers him for making sense of personal experience. (He tries, for example, to emulate Vito Corleone and goes back to the mother country in "Commendatori" [2.04], only to learn that he is more of a tourist than a native son.)

Tony is, in his deceptiveness, a sentimental dramatist and mask wearer. While Tony can perceive the cloying overkill in playing *It's a*

Wonderful Life incessantly at Christmas ("Jeezus, enough already") in "To Save Us All From Satan's Power" (3.10) he is not above using that sentimentality for cynical public relations purposes in this episode when he role-plays community spirit and throws a Christmas party for the local children. In a plot moving back and forth between the gang's current search for someone to play Santa at the Christmas party and Pussy playing Santa in the past—while wired up by the FBI as a part of his betrayal prior to Tony ordering his murder—Tony realizes the ease with which he was deceived by Pussy's role-playing. Comically, at the same time, he wishes for better acting from a reluctant Bobby Baccalieri, who is the substitute Santa at the party. In a plethora of theatrical terms, Tony gives acting critique ("He's a method actor"); Silvio recommends theatrical training for Bobby ("Next year he goes to Santa school"); Bobby fights miscasting ("I don't wanna do this, shyness is a curse"); Paulie directs ("It would kill him to say Ho, ho, ho?"); and Tony realizes there is something to be said, at least, for an honest, if badly acted, performance: "I don't miss Pussy's fake, fuckin' good cheer, tell ya the truth."

The Christmas party is staged sentimentality, but Tony's desire for a compelling performance is not without reservations. Feeling a sense of loss over Pussy's execution, Tony sentimentally agrees with Silvio that Pussy was great in the role of Santa. However, he also recognizes that Pussy was a great actor as an FBI informant. As Pussy's friend and his murderer, Tony can distinguish between the two roles and regret Pussy's death with no guilt at having had him killed. When Paulie, still angry at Pussy's betrayal, rejects any sentimentalism—"In the end, fuck Santa Claus"—Tony still sighs, looks sad and, paradoxically, the audience is left feeling almost as maudlin as Tony over Pussy's loss, while reminded by the exaggerated comedy of it all that it *is* overly maudlin.

It is often his wife Carmela or Dr. Melfi who call Tony on his pretence. However, when Tony refuses to hand over his cousin Tony for execution to appease Johnny Sack in the middle of a gang war with Little Carmine and he justifies it to his own gang with rhetorical speechmaking—"We are a family and even in this fucked up day and age this means something" ("All Due Respect," 5.13)—it is his Consigliore,

Silvio, who does so: "With all due respect, you were ready to hand 'em your cousin a week ago, so it's not about standin' with the guys, or upholdin' some rules, not really." Silvio has known Tony since he was a kid and with clear-sightedness born of pretty close observation sees through his boss role-playing *The Godfather* myth:

> It's about you don't wanna eat shit from John. You don't wanna bow down. You told him to go fuck himself which, to be honest, wasn't exactly appropriate, considering.

As Silvio points out, even by Tony's own sentimentalized standards of mob protocol, thumbing his nose at the New York boss was not "appropriate" and, in what must be the most hilarious understatement in five seasons of the show, makes a diagnosis of Tony equal to anything Dr. Melfi has come up with: "I've known you since you were a kid Ton, frankly, you've got a problem with authority." With the comedy of that line, Silvio bursts the bubble of the romantic theatricality of Tony's gangster honor code as a self-justifying cover for having a tantrum at being told what to do.

The fact that the above insight is given by a character who is himself a gangster stereotype and the parodied repository of *The Godfather* lore in Tony's gang brings full circle the complex way in which the text of the show utilises and reflects on the theatrics and performativity of real and fictional gangster narratives. By the end of the episode, as Tony stumbles through the snow, running from the scene of the arrest of Johnny Sack and into the safety of home and hearth, Tony and the audience can breathe a sigh of relief that he is not named in the same indictment with the New York boss. In true show business style, an expectant audience is left rooting for Tony to be the last mob boss standing after his narrow escape—despite knowing he deserves a far darker fate.

New York seen from New Jersey. Photograph by Michael Prete.

11.

AESTHETICS AND AMMUNITION

ART IMITATING LIFE IMITATING ART
IN *THE SOPRANOS*

Franco Ricci

The TV screen frames a close-up of Christopher and Tony butting heads, locked together like brutal rams, eye to eye, chin to chin, breath to breath. Tony holds Christopher by the lapels, looming over the younger thug in menacing pose. A strident pale glow highlights their profiles, around them only darkness. The *chiaroscuro* effect is unmistakable—gripping, telling, above all *painterly*. Christopher has just boldly questioned both Tony's authority and motives; he has dismissed his affection for the boss by disrespectfully declaring, in past tense, "I loved you." An infuriated Tony lunges at the young man, the true weight of his agency expressed both in physical power and verbal precision. Paraphrasing Machiavelli ("it is much safer to be feared than to be loved when one of the two must be lacking" [Bondanella and Musa trans. 56]), he bellows: "Well you don't love me anymore. That breaks my heart ... but you don't gotta love me, but you will respect me!" ("Amour Fou," 3.12). Uncharacteristically—Tony's deep-seated love for his nephew has, until now, always triumphed in these situations—the tension does not dissipate. Christopher pulls away, exuding bravado. leaving the viewer to expect future ramifications. A glowering Tony remains alone in the frame. A painting hangs on the wall behind Tony. It looms large and acquires immediate significance, occupying the entire screen.

The scene finds pathos in the swirling mass of dark, brownish storm clouds that shrouds his figure. A brewing storm is an apt but facile analogy. Closer examination of the cloud formations, however, reveals two sneering tigers, nose to nose, eye to eye, chin to chin, revolving around a turbulent celestial vortex. One of the tigers is larger, his arched back poised in threatening stance, claws and teeth at the ready. He looms over the smaller tiger. As in the scene in which the frothing behemoth has just collared his younger nephew, here, too, further explosive action is anticipated.

The real pathos of the scene, however, is reserved for "the beast in me,"[1] the (un)willing but essential catalyst of the series that is Tony Soprano. The "beast," an image both real (in the painting) and imagined (in Tony's psyche), is part of the self that is ever-present, an interior psychological state *The Sopranos* seeks to display. Oblivious to the two swirling beasts behind him, Tony maintains his objective, intent on pursuing this plot line to its predestined end. Working within his own man-made constructs, Tony hopes to hold reality at bay by his threats. If he would only turn to see the approaching storm, but he does not. The future remains obscure, hidden like the snarling tiger tattoo he sports on his right bicep ("Guy Walks into a Psychiatrist's Office," 2.01). This painting signals impending doom for the viewer, but not for Tony. The imminent suicide of Gloria coupled with the attempted suicide of Artie Bucco ("Everybody Hurts," 4.06) will deeply affect him. Characteristically, Tony will change routes, rethink his strategies, and, relying on his own instincts, find the will to survive. At his camouflaged behest, Ralphie has taken out Jackie, Jr., symbol of Tony's own misguided youth and "suicide" into mob life. He will terminate his relationship to Gloria, recognizing in her aberrant behavior his own dysfunctional nature. The near equation of two painted tigers and the two raging beasts that are Tony and Christopher, Tony and Gloria, Tony and his mother, Tony and whomever, is a parallel process of equal importance to the actualization of the series. If Tony's drama is that of a patient attempting to lay to rest his own defamiliarized and dematerialized image of self, the insertion of the painted tigers into the series at this strategic moment helps to define his own literal presence.

The proliferation of artworks and artistic artifacts in *The Sopranos* helps to give the series its ironic bite, lends to its sardonic wit, and provides decorum and place. These strategically placed images subtly suggest that there is more to the action than what is occurring on screen. As metaphorical backdrops, they open up comparative spaces that serve to reinforce, if not reveal, the thoughts of the characters in a suggestive play of visual mimicry. Paintings and artifacts order both geographic and mental spaces. As the story ravels and is unraveled, a visual design emerges that tracks the developing plot and creates a concurrent visual commentary subtending the narrative. The juxtaposition of the main characters before these backdrops constitutes a subliminal drama that augments the series. Rather than mere visual tokens of no particular importance, images like Tony reminiscing before the stained glass in the old Newark Italian neighborhood, the paintings displayed in bedrooms, the posters in the backroom of the Bing, the artwork in Melfi's office speak of the depth of inspiration marking each story arc. A sign of the series' sublime writing and attention to detail, these signature visual moments in *The Sopranos* shadow its character moves. Though a secondary player, the viewer also plays an important role—as the appointed Ideal Observer, able to enhance the viewing experience and the series' message via visual interpretation of the artworks.

The tendency of the series is to fixate on specific backdrop images, especially either before or after specific acts have been committed. This trend begins in the first episode ("The Sopranos") where, amidst the hanging pig heads and hams of Centanni's (later Satriale's) Pork Store , hangs a collage of publicity photos of American film stars. (In his DVD commentary on the episode, Chase admits to having found the collage already hanging in the meat shop. Realizing that somehow "it worked," he moved it into the shot.) Reminiscent of the "Wall of Fame" hanging in Sal's Famous Pizzeria in Spike Lee's controversial *Do the Right Thing* (1989), they differ from Sal's "Wall of Fame" on two counts. First, where Sal privileged an "Italian Only" policy, this wall is multicultural. Second, it represents not a public display of ethnic pride but a piece of American film history nestled away in the back room of a butcher shop, a private gallery of public figures to be admired and remembered for their cultural influence. The camera lingers long enough to allow us to recognize such well-known screen stars as W. C. Fields, The Three Stooges, Beniamino Gigli, Telly Savalas, Laurel and Hardy, Fred Astaire, Humphrey Bogart, Ginger Rogers, Edward G. Robinson, Don Rickles, Marilyn Monroe, Sammy Davis, Jr., Frank Sinatra, John Wayne, Dean Martin, and James Cagney.

Christopher's remark about mixing cultures ("I thought the only sausages were Italian and Jimmy Dean's. See what you learn when you cross cultures and shit?") is relevant. Like the meat in sausage, these photos are minced, clippings combined to form an American mosaic (I'm tempted to substitute the word sausage!), but the lesson learned from the images is skewed. Christopher's remark may reflect the characteristically shallow knowledge of the information age, but these representations are not superficial. They are instead realistic representations of the public images of popular culture as perceived and acted-out by members of the New Age mob. These filmic images are real, even if they are misunderstood and inappropriately emulated by them. The power these images hold is manifest in the formal composition of the staring eyes of Bogart, Martin, and Robinson, the unflinching eyes of the pig heads, the lifeless body, the splattered blood. These sight lines establish a triangular perspective point between the viewer's eye, the "eyes" in the scene, and Christopher's eye that is both artistically transcendent and brutally realistic. Art and bullets collide to erase each other's influence. A seductive game of perverted myopia has begun.

The paradigm *seeing/being seen* is a significant and potent image that is carried through the entire arc of the series. One is an active stance, the other passive. The very first episode begins with Tony sitting in Dr. Melfi's anteroom woefully contemplating the message imparted by the statue before him. We see him not as a person but as an object among objects without meaning for himself. His passively impotent gaze is returned by the threateningly dark and deep-set eye sockets of the unflinching and unintimidated female statue. His man-centered world of objects has no draw here. This combination of the experience of meaninglessness (the introverted eye) and the courage to be oneself (the extroverted eye) is the key to the development of the entire series.

The real action thus opens with a Alfred Hitchcockian/David Lynchian cropped close-up of Tony's right eye. It is a thinking, penetrating, monocular eye. As the camera pulls back we note that Tony is lying in bed. A similar right eye advertising *Madame Marie, Reader and Adviser* surveys the Atlantic City boardwalk dreamscape in "Funhouse" (2.13). It foretells Tony's imminent epiphany regarding the furtive "looking" (spying) of Pussy. The same staring monocular eye reappears in the backroom of the Crazy Horse after Adriana has become the "eyes" of the FBI. It is ubiquitous on the dollar bills that are regularly collected and counted throughout the series. Dark ominous eyes stare out into the Soprano master bedroom from the mural behind the headboard; ancestral eyes probe his soul from family photographs; painted eyes fix Tony's eyes from the painting with Pie-O-My reminding him that the structures of reality have lost their meaning. Tony's spectator stance is exemplified, too, in the many dream sequences that punctuate the series. These few examples reinforce the notion that Tony is both a viewer and the viewed. Though he occupies center stage in his circumscribed world, he remains an onlooker, a divided self, haunted by futility.[2]

The use of artworks in *The Sopranos* is thus relevant towards an understanding of life in twenty-first-century America. *Sopranos* characters constantly ascribe erroneous features to the "reality" they perceive. They contemplate, but never truly understand, their surroundings. Tony, in particular, lives in abject confusion. Artworks, literature, and movies are, for Tony, windows onto this world. (Recall his addiction to the History Channel and movies about outlaws, be they cowboys or gangsters—because, as he tells Carmela in "The Test Dream" [5.11], "It's more interesting than life.") They reveal the premonitions of his soul while consolidating the distance between himself and the deep-seated fear of losing his own humanity. If he could only truly understand what he sees, but he won't allow himself, nor others. "Forget Hollywood screenplays, forget those distractions

... we've got work to do," he admonishes Christopher in the closing scene of the first episode. The tone is hammered and set. Fury and action will triumph over words and images, reality over fantasy, left-brain over right-brain. This is Tony's plight throughout the series, though he will migrate toward a softer position that contradicts this dictum while all the while resisting its redemptive potency.

Without exploring theoretical notions of interart analogies or comparisons,[3] suffice it to say that *The Sopranos* uses settings, but especially the placing of artwork within the scenes, as extensions of the storyline in time and space. Just as Francis Ford Coppola and Martin Scorsese are careful to pose their scenes before meticulously reconstructed and musically appointed settings, *The Sopranos*' attention to visual and aural detail—paintings, statues, movies, book covers, and music—places the series in the hallowed ground of art-house cinema.

One of the series' most painterly detailed moments arrives near the end of "The Strong, Silent Type" (4.10). The episode features portraits of strong, solitary men. A variety of pictorial images—shots of TV programs, the painting of Pie-O-My, the website Svetlana builds—proliferate throughout. Characters are mostly shot indoors, usually framed in window or door jambs, a *chiaroscuro* texture dominates the scenes. The last moments of the episode are especially salient. Furio and Tony share the same visual vocabulary: home, kitchen, cooking, eating. Furio prepares his own pasta from scratch and drinks wine. Tony microwaves cold rigatoni and drinks milk. The camera angles and slow pans emphasize their pairing. These portraits take for granted the presence of a viewer. Our informed interpretation (Furio's heartfelt fidelity to Carmela, Tony's nonchalant dalliance with Svetlana—does he make love to her or to the "image" of Greta Garbo?) adds solemnity and emotional depth to the private stories being painted before us. These are naturalistic representations, slices of life presented to the viewer with a bagful of moral judgment. Portraits of Christopher at the opening of the episode and of Paulie at its close serve as visual bookends that intensify the alchemy of the images of these four strong, silent men. The staccato marching drums that close the program further escalate the regimentation.

It is possible to construct similarities, in structure, color, framing, and meaning, between the artworks on the walls and the subject of the scene. This holistic approach permits a more complete appreciation of *Sopranos* aesthetic moments, creating a linkage that permits these visual systems to effectively dovetail, thus composing a design able to comment upon itself in often illuminating ways. One could ask the following questions: how do the artworks and their different styles influence viewer expectations? Are there underlying suppositions that favor the choice of one artwork over another? How does the viewer's stance correspond to the aesthetic perspective the artworks introduce to the series? Given the assumption that everything within camera range in any scene is judiciously placed, what are the connections between what is being acted and what is seen (scene)? These and other questions are both a means of eliciting specific responses and a method for opening and deepening our own perceptions, enabling visual interpretation, cultural appreciation, narrative analysis, and psychoanalytic approaches that may deepen the way we "read" the TV screen.

The artworks and artifacts of *The Sopranos* help set the mood and give the series credibility. These visual markers range from the kitschy—the pig on Satriale's Pork Store, the William Wegman poster of two dogs dressed in trench coats ("In Camelot," 5.07), the mural of the Bay of Naples in Vesuvio's;[4] to the weighty—the stained-glass windows of the church in the old neighborhood; to the sublime—the artwork in the Brooklyn Museum, original Picasso prints at Devon's mansion. Some are humorous: old neighborhood signs—about Italian Sausage, Fresh Pork Chops, Chicken Parts, Espresso—enshrine Tony's lifestyle and animate his preferred ambience. In the episode "House Arrest" (2.11), Tony and the gang enjoy an afternoon seated in front of Satriale's. As the naïf-style painted pigs look on from behind Tony's shoulders, the government "pig," FBI agent Harris, strolls the same streets (is he originally from the neighborhood?) enjoying the same neighborhood sights. He stops to talk about the Nets and Knicks with "the guys." The sign "Suckling Pigs, Any Size" takes on a new meaning. Some of the artwork is deadly serious: the photo wall in FBI headquarters, the photographs of dead mobsters, the original *Dr. Strangelove* framed poster used as a weapon by Christopher, smashing it over the head of his funds-delinquent friend ("In Camelot," 5.07).

If any one thing characterizes *Sopranos'* artworks, it is the way they sift the most important ideas of an episode. All of the works we see in the series are encoded with the private ethics of the characters deployed before them. The viewer perceives these scenes as a composite, watching the action on screen while noting the images that decorate the actions. Sometimes the two are self-referential, with the background art reflecting the action. For example, befuddled characters are often posed before abstract paintings (no qualitative comment intended). Tony's dalliances with his *goomahs* occur in motel rooms adorned with cheap abstract prints that resemble their inconsequential dialogue and confused emotions. This is an increasingly gray area for Tony. Sex is a "business" reality for Tony that used to be traditional and representational (like the Renaissance mural in his bedroom—more on this later) but which has become Modern, emotionally problematic, and open to psychological interpretation and spousal disapproval. An exception to this pattern is Gloria, Tony's dream woman. His initial relation with her is empowering and fulfilling. Their most sublime moment occurs beneath a traditional painting of a Venetian canal, that most romantic and timeless of places ("Amour Fou," 3.12). Confused visual patterns are reserved for a character where no love is lost: his nemesis Ralph Cifaretto. In "University" (3.06) we see him watching *Spartacus* on TV in his home, behind him a painting that is a splatter of color, a swirl of emotions and turbulence that reflects his demoniacal character and foreshadows the widening splash of blood that will encircle his body on the kitchen floor in "Whoever Did This" (4.09).

Often the art is revelatory, augmenting the action or dialogue. An example is the hospital scene in "Nobody Knows Anything" (1.11). Tony is in the hospital as a result of a botched mob hit. The FBI has offered him immunity and a new life in the Witness Protection Plan; Carmela is pushing for the move. As Tony derails her arguments with visions of selling Indian relics curbside ("maybe start a rattlesnake ranch") and eating tasteless tomatoes, he declares that her reasoning is faulty. The kids do have a father, he insists, "this one, me, Tony

Soprano, and all that comes with it." A. J.'s selfish concern about not being able to go to the dance is stifled by Meadow's telling comment on his (and by implication his father's) self-involvement. The poster behind Meadow and A. J. eavesdrops on their conversation as it declares: *Safe Families: Everybody Needs One.* Safe family indeed.[5] The scene cuts to a framed photo of Tony as a baby in a family portrait as a TV newscaster describes the attempted hit on him in the background. Livia and Junior watch the footage attentively and, concerned for their own safety from Tony's wrath, decide to visit him, again reiterating Soprano family values.

Most interesting, however, are those works that illuminate the scene by activating reflections in the viewer that lead to a deeper understanding of the characters. Such is the case with the artwork associated with Dr. Melfi's office. Much has been written concerning the opening shot of the series featuring Tony ensconced within the thighs of the nude female sculpture in Melfi's waiting room (see, especially, Gabbard 99–100). For our purposes she represents both the Mother (the placement of Tony between her legs suggests a birthing; the therapy sessions are meant to defamiliarize her influence) and the Medusa, the dangerous female who threatens to silence male discourse with her debilitating stare. Tony's apparent discomfort and verbal paralysis are the direct result of this double-fisted threat to his masculinity.

Carmela, too, is eventually positioned in a similar pose ("Second Opinion," 3.07) and expresses her own reading of the statue's possible (and threatening to her) message: "That statue is not my favorite." The typology of Melfi's office is ratiocinative and self-referential, communicating only itself and its own organization. Its visual logic is by necessity dualistic, emphasizing the conflict between the reasonable and the sensual, the female and the male principle. The potential signifiers in this system are therefore few yet fundamental. The inability to control the semiotics of this inner sanctum is painfully transparent to Tony. The statuary, the paintings, the books, create a synergy that remains beyond his threshold of articulation. A diploma from Tufts looms over his head, a reminder of his own never-fulfilled personal aspirations. A suite of four paintings of trees graces the wall behind Melfi's desk. While they represent the four seasons, they also allude to the real work of this place, that of growth and change. Tony is instead drawn to a painting in the anteroom ("Denial, Anger, Acceptance," 1.03). He stares, as do we, at the painting of a red barn. As he focuses on the door and the blackness beyond its threshold, we, along with him, contemplate the darkness. Tony goads Melfi smugly: "The painting ... it's a trick picture out there ... the barn and the old tree all rotted out inside." But there is no rotten tree. Instead, a healthy leaf-bearing oak dominates the serenity of the scene. Tony has projected his own anxiety and fear onto the painting. Attempting to familiarize the uncomfortable ambience, he calls the painting a "special made psychological picture like that waddyacallit test ... the Gorschach." Despite Melfi's claim to the painting's rural innocence and her own un-programmed intentions in its purchase, Tony is skeptical, threatened; he feels manipulated, not quite up to spec—a patsy in Melfi's psychological game. The painting, the office, Melfi and all her cohorts, according to his inner voice, cry out mockingly, "Hey asshole, we're from Harvard and what do you think of this spooky depressing barn and this tree we put here?" To Melfi's paradoxical query "How are things?" he says abruptly "Good, had a real good week. ..." The outburst, however, has proven otherwise. He is distraught. At his next session, trees are once again on his mind. He asks, "What happens to a tree when it is rotted out?" The same thing, we discover, that happens to a man with cancer: it dies. Tony has made the mighty oak a symbol of his friend Jackie Aprile's robust life, now withering, rotted out by cancer. The barn door, which we may have assumed led to his own subconscious, also leads inevitably to death.

Open doorways and enigmatic passages return in the next scene while Tony cavorts with Irena, his Russian girlfriend. Two paintings hang on the bedroom wall. One is an abstract: colorful arrows, lines, geometric figures, a Klee-like drawing of a head, a bull's-eye. The other, one of David Hockney's "Splash" paintings, depicts a swimming pool. Water, sand, and beach fronts are a recurring leitmotif of death in the series. From Tony's pool and the angst-provoking ducks, to the watery cemetery of his enemies, water images do not placate and appease Tony's existential condition. Instead, water is an entrapping, isolating element that circumscribes his existence and erects perimeters within which he moves as an automaton. He stares at the empty director's chair in front of two sliding doors and sees a barn-like structure in dark silhouette, a tree, and darkness looming menacingly. He asks Irena, "What's that paintin' mean to you?" She replies laconically, "Nothing, it just reminds me of David Hockey."

Tony's therapy and Jackie's impending death lead him to ponder the great mystery: Why are we here? Why do we question? "Do you feel like Frankenstein, lacking humanity?" asks Melfi. Tony remains silent. Yet, as if to posit an answer, Meadow's choir recital immediately follows. A cross hangs above the choir and lends solemnity to the event. As they sing of peace and gentle repose, two deaths are musically framed with *Godfather*-like precision. One is metaphorical: the irreverent Christopher is taken to the Jersey shore and "shot" in a ritual mock execution. From his soiled remains a dedicated family soldier will be resurrected. The other is literal: bragging Brendan is silenced, shot to death in his bathtub. Tony, meanwhile, has found solace and renewed faith in the lyrics of Meadow's hymn. As the words waft over him like a summer breeze, he regains his emotions, a momentary faith, able once again to look at trees without fear and make it through the night.

Yet even this token of liberation, we shall learn, hides ontological consequences that may disrupt his peace. The paintings juxtaposed at this early stage in the series present two distinctly salubrious worlds: country and shore. If only Tony could appreciate their qualities beyond surface value! Unfortunately, Tony's life has vowed to preserve and cultivate parallel worlds founded upon the illusion of redeeming activity and devoid of the potentiality for change. His engulfing and implosive experience of the world requires a transcendent self that allows a remote-control distancing of sensory experience. This is why he interprets these paintings as threats to his sense of self. The continued preservation of his false order cannot but produce feelings of unease and enmity that heighten his own detached inertia and will ultimately preclude escape, i.e. any real healing. Images of tranquility—of barns and pools—do not bring solace. Tony must live out his illusion by conniving his own deception, by distorting the images he regards. He must evoke evasion rather than reality and somehow protect his lamentably sequestered state in the hope he may maintain the game not for the ironic pleasure of ratiocinative play but for the assurance of his own survival.

Melfi's office mirrors this state as books and statuary change in subject and positions, in effect projecting the verbal drama of the scenes onto a visual plane. The first episodes of the series present an office devoid of statuary. In "Down Neck" (1.07), however, Tony speaks of his father for the first time. His account of seeing his father brutalize a delinquent client warrants a statue on the ledge behind Melfi of a man singing, its pose both contrasting and mimicking the vicious dance between the two men on the Jersey curbside. As well, a new book strategically placed to the right of Tony entitled *Future Youth* has materialized, an obvious allusion to the young Tony's future career path. Is this happenstance? Or can we map the changes of statuary as we follow Tony's intensifying sessions?

Subsequent changes on the two window ledges of Melfi's office suggest the moves are not arbitrary. Beansy's unfortunate loss of his legs in "Toodle-Fucking-Oo" (2.03) is echoed in a new statue of an armless and legless torso. This torso will reappear after Gloria's suicide. In "Proshai, Livushka" (3.02), the armless, legless bust becomes a dancing figure, a Chaplin-like statue of a clown, perhaps a Cagney-like hoofer, frozen in a tiptoe stance. Behind Melfi the sitting posture that has come to represent her remains poised, ever silent, like Melfi, and ready to listen. In this session it is Tony's turn to "dance," to speak of his feelings toward his mother. He talks of the duties of being a good son, yet he is troubled, cloven between such obligations, represented by the new statue of a figure frozen in a soldier's stance, and the irresponsible lightness of the prancing hoofer.

Statuary in the series thus comes to represent the stance Melfi and Tony solidify over the first two seasons and that, at the beginning of the third season, will either remain static, like the statues, or develop. Tony asks, "So we're probably done here, right? She's dead." Before these words the camera pulls back for a full shot of the office. Melfi and Tony sit on either side of a round glass table. The four windows on the far wall are a postmodern mirror of the four tree suite behind the analyst's desk. Three pieces of statuary sit on the far window ledge convincingly reflecting the doctor and patient seated directly before them. Tony and Melfi are at another crossroads, only now, with the mother dead, all positions are petrified.

The first session between Tony and Melfi in the very next episode, "Fortunate Son" (3.03), is dominated by close-ups. One statue is featured: the reclining listener over Melfi's left shoulder. During their second session of the episode, there are no statues behind Melfi. Tony is about to relive his first panic attack. The statues have been removed because doctor and patient are finally delving into the root cause of the attacks. Information overloads as images of father, meat, sex, mother, cold cuts, and violence converge in a stew of anxiety that produce the fainting spells. The statue of the passively reclining listener is not there because Melfi is finally able to assume an active role and verbalize a possible source for Tony's malaise and produce, in her own words, "good work, real progress." Yet, in "Employee of the Month" (3.04), the figure of the reclining statue has returned; the dancer is also back in its customary place. Tony and Melfi once again can only dance around the issues. In "Pine Barrens" (3.11) the statuary again changes. Next to Melfi stands a nude with head aright, proudly held upwardly outstretched arms, chest out, nipples upright, an expression of determination, striding confidently forward—a sharp contrast to the reclining listener behind Melfi. During this episode's first session, Tony is calm, serene, confident, but falsely so. He is indeed striding, but it's down the same old *cul de sac*. The last session of this episode begins with a close-up of the statue in Melfi's anteroom. We note a small replica of this same statue on the window ledge to Melfi's left, essentially placing it between her and Tony. If, as we have speculated, this statue is associated with his mother, it is noteworthy that the discussion returns to the "depressive personality, unstable, impossible-to-please women" to whom Tony is still attracted. Melfi asks: "Does that remind you of any other woman?" As in the opening shot of the very first episode, the small statue notes Tony's awkward silence.

As if to signal the increasing petrifaction of Tony's stance, the very next episode ("Amour Fou," 3.12) opens with statues of contorted figures. They are bent, furrowed, frozen in poses of pain, pensive, despairing. The same music that closed the last episode, Celia Bartoli's *Sposa Disprezzata* ("The Scorned Bride"), forms a bridge with this episode, connecting its artwork to the statuary in Melfi's office. Carmela and Meadow are visiting the Brooklyn Museum. Simultaneously inspired and depressed by the vision, Carmela cries before Giuseppe de Rivera's *The Mystical Marriage of St. Catherine*. To Meadow's naive comment "She's marrying a baby?" Carmela sarcastically confesses that we (women) all marry babies. The beauty, innocence, and peace the painting inspires are sorely missing in her life. The image of the child recalls Tony's heartfelt final query to Melfi in the preceding episode's last moments: "I do right by my family. Doesn't that count for anything?" Family, responsibility, angst, redemption. We are, at this juncture, midway through what is now a six-season series. Like an inveterate Dantesque voyager, Tony is finally asking the pertinent questions of himself. By this episode's end, he will receive the answer to his query of existential relevance. The answer will be no.

It is telling that statuary and paintings again assume primary importance in this particular episode. There is new statuary in the Melfi office. A long shot reveals that the statues of the dancer and the reclining listener are no longer behind her but have been placed on the far window ledge. Behind Melfi are two new statues. Both resemble Samurai warriors; one kneels, one stands stoically. The introduction of an Asian motif is revelatory. Tony may still quote Machiavelli to Christopher in this episode ("You don't gotta love me, but you will respect me"), but clearly the more practical *Art of War* by Sun Tzu is moving into Tony's line of thought and vision. He may compare Gloria's dark eyes to those of "a Spanish princess in one of those paintings by Goyam" ("Amour Fou," 3.12) but will succumb to the realization that those eyes are a "bottomless black hole." A hole equal in depth and profundity to the dark barn door before which they meet in Melfi's anteroom. Tony is achieving cognizance. He no longer remains conspicuously silent during his sessions or in his familial relations. From here on we will note both a more ruthless gangster and a more conventional—call him cynical for practical reasons—husband. He has indeed achieved a turning point. Yet he accepts the existential paradoxes of his choices. He questions the system but has adapted to its requisites and acknowledges his state as the logical consequence of a social routine that is neither better nor worse than any other. In essence, Tony is frozen in time and posture, much like the statues of this episode's opening sequence. His marriage is predicated on deceit and immoral dalliance; his family (both of them) has grown on the rotten stock of illegality. Is it any wonder that his tormented psyche is manifested in the contorted statues? Is it any wonder that a morally resurrected Carmela finds solace and pain in the unspoiled innocence of the naked Christ child? She too is deliberating the rationale for declining the total rejection of Tony (advised by her Jewish psychiatrist, Dr. Krakower, in "Second Opinion" [3.07]) for a more Catholic philosophy of living on the good part of Tony. Yet for Carmela there can be no cogent justification or redemptive human contact that will move her outside the box-like universe that underlines her self-imprisonment in an uncommunicative solitude.

The artworks that punctuate this episode clearly allow the viewer to collate the evolving subconscious verbal text in the visual images that subtend the characters. The gallery painting, Gloria and Tony's intense love sessions before tranquil scenes of Venetian canals, Tony and Christopher's unusually hostile argument before an equally dramatic painting of two sneering tigers, the pizzeria's trivial reminders of a mythical Italy amongst backward hanging Italian flags, the statuary of Melfi's office—all heighten the sense of detached inertia permeating everything and portending the debilitating consequences of Tony's deepening cynicism. A great deal of attention has been paid to the art in this episode because it forebodes the changing internal landscape of the characters. The "incessant self-regard" of which Melfi speaks has become the external *regard* of surrounding images that will portend either the resolution of conflict or its worsening.

In Melfi's office in Season Four we find two new statues gracing the far window ledge in "Everybody Hurts" (4.06). Both are of women: one reaches up to the heavens in a gesture of liberation; the other is of a woman cleaved in half, an allusion to Gloria's suicide. The analogy is reinforced in this episode's dream sequence, in which Gloria asks Tony which cloven part of her he wishes to see, her vagina or her neck. In Season Five, new statues again grace the window ledges. All have an African flavor and give the setting an air of primitive primal desire. Behind Melfi stands a happy dancer, stepping lightly, best foot forward, possibly signifying new beginnings, new journeys. On the far window ledge we note two statues; one a graceful dancer, the other, a reclining figure, hands and feet firmly rooted to the ground. The statues complement each other in their appositional placement and visual cues. Their postures resonate in the scene played-out before them. Tony has come to ask Melfi to take their relationship to an amorous (libidinous and thus primitive) level. The long camera shot places him between the two far statues. His slouching posture and size ape the statue behind him, while Melfi's crossed legs and pointing toe mirror the dancer's stance. Likewise, their conversation unveils similar contradictions and contrasts in the pain of living. Tony is upset and bewildered, resolved yet hesitant. Melfi, on the other hand, is resolute and firm. Both are frozen, like the statues, in their postures. They must maintain their familiar patterns if they are to survive. While Tony is trapped within a framework of erotic desire, Melfi's professionalism may only beget a standard, though painful, rejection of his entreaties. In this, their most private and intense moment to date, they look to each other for comfort and solace. But they must not allow their primal desire to unfold. They cannot, like the prancing statue, dance, but must remain reclining, seated and fettered to solid ground. Between them the tissue box holds an erect penis, Tony has a jones for Melfi and it is shown as paper thin and harmless.[6] A more blatant white tissue peeks out of the box in the anteroom. But Melfi continues to reject his entreaties. He returns home to his soul mate, to the only woman that has accepted him. As Carmela polishes a green apple, an obvious painterly illusion to images of the Fall of Adam and Eve, he sits alone in the dark, hunched and sullen like the statue on Melfi's ledge, cigar and gun at the phallic ready. He can only hope that the green apple ripens to red and that he be readmitted into Paradise.

If Melfi's office can be considered a psychological inner sanctum, Tony's other sanctums, his home and office, provide the opportunity to achieve a vividness of scene construction that utilizes a sort of visual thesaurus of recognizable and recurring icons. The bedrooms of Meadow and A. J. are youthful sanctums of evolving idiosyncrasies: A. J. with his band posters and action figures of ball players;[7] Meadow with her posters of poetic dictums as well as a symbol of her imminent transformation, the butterfly ("The Sopranos," 1.01). While the main house is typically void of ethnic mementos,[8] the master bedroom is replete with faux roman pedestals, Fontanini statues of angels that appear on the night stand on only one occasion ("From Where to Eternity," 2.09), and reproductions of Italian paintings.

These accouterments usually remain in the background, receiving scant attention while Tony and Carmela share their infrequent verbal and physical intimacy. In "Proshai, Livushka" (3.02), however, the camera lingers upon the large painting behind the headboard, a Renaissance-style canvas of four women. Two are seen from side view as they stand face to face. The commanding central figure, right shoulder towards us, wears a gown of regal lapis lazuli blue (a Renaissance style mark for the Virgin Mary) and a red kerchief (a symbolization of Christ). The obvious leader, her right hand rests upon the left shoulder of the woman confronting her as they gaze intently into each other's eyes. This is not an a-causal moment. The scene is wrapped in ominous silence yet it is evident that a secret has been, or is about to be, revealed. Their eyes meet with powerful intent. Bridging their gaze is the stolid, unflinching stare of a member of the sisterhood standing directly behind and between them; another woman stoically covers the central figure's back, looking out from behind her shoulders. Their deep-set dark eyes belie the foreboding knowledge of secular rites and rituals. Their presence is methodical, formal, necessary. They are the silent ministers of their master's purpose. The painting may be read as a female version of Tony's business praxis. Just as Tony is flanked by Silvio and Paulie during business negotiations, here the supporting duo provide physical security, communication safeguards, legitimacy, and honor. Before this public icon of private trust, power, fidelity, and secrecy, Tony and Carmela exchange their most intimate of moments in what amounts to a mob hideout. As if to finally acknowledge its presence and narrative importance as a signpost in the evolving dynamic, director Allen Coulter slowly pans down from the painting and onto the bodies of Tony and Carmela as they lie in bed. Sleepless and restless, Tony moves to the TV room where he comes to rest before another artistic icon, this time male, of the honored society: James Cagney in *Pubic Enemy*.

Tony's back offices at the Bada Bing and at Satriale's provide further evidence that wall coverings extend vicariously into the narrative. Satriale's back room is covered with a loose collection of pictures and postcards, a bit like Johnny Sack's usual hangout. The art is old and the posters are cheap, usually representing commercial images of the Italian peninsula. An interesting poster in Satriale's that dates the locale is a representation of a metaphorical "Italia" standing before an Italian flag. The Bing is much richer in both commercial and ethnic texture. Beside the requisite beer logos[9] and posters featuring girls in various stages of undress, the back room is a haven for pictures of Italian-American boxers. A poster of a young Sinatra in a line-up photo appears in Season Five.

The boss's inner sanctum at the Bing is walled in color-stained hammered glass. The glass lends a certain gravity to the place and reminds this viewer of the more opulent stained glass of Tony's old neighborhood church. During his visit to the church with Meadow in "The Sopranos" (1.01), Tony waxes proudly about her great grandfather and Brother Frank, immigrant masons who had helped build the church. The camera pans the main altar and its imagery of the Last Supper. The altar is back-dropped by large paintings of the Birth, Crucifixion, and Resurrection of Christ. Beyond the obvious symbolism and subliminal cultural pride the vision exudes,[10] our focus returns to the stained glass that both frames and colors our perception of the place. Tony and Meadow sit before scenes that represent "Jesus and the Elders" and "The Presentation of the Baby Jesus." All these church images are traditional, bedrock stories of Christianity. Their colored light imbues the scene with solemnity. If we compare these windows with the stained glass that decorates the church of Father Phil in "I Dream of Jeannie Cusamano" (1.13), we note that there are no biblical stories depicted. Instead, we find the abstract splotches of color, absent any redeeming message at all—much in character with the good priest himself!

If Melfi's office and the churches represent confessional havens rendering trust and honesty, their counterparts, Tony's home and offices, share the same metaphorical potential. But whereas the former inner sanctums can indeed be considered hallowed ground, the latter can only be termed sacristies of slime. An episode that confirms our reading occurs at the Bing the night Tony disposes of Ralph Cifaretto ("Whoever Did This," 4.09). After proper ablutions, a change of clothes, and sleep, Tony awakes at the Bada Bing. The night and the whiskey, however, have not erased the lingering presence of Ralph. Behind Tony is a poster of Tessa (read Tony) the Tease. The caption reads "She'll bring you to Hell." Topless Tessa holds a long black silk scarf behind her in a provocative dance pose. One end of the scarf hangs lower than the other. Its balled shape resembles that of a head and calls to mind the severed head of the now Hell-bound and decapitated Ralph held by Christopher as he placed it in a bowling bag. An adjacent poster features a kneeling stripper clad in white viewed from the rear. Only her legs and posterior are visible as she bends over, her tail end raised alluringly, a visual reference to Ralphie's latent sexual proclivity for being sodomized.

Yet perhaps the most obvious and intended connection with artwork is Tony's commissioned painting of the horse Pie-O-My. Not surprisingly, horses figure prominently in the life of these mob figures, present or alluded to throughout the series. "Horse," for example, is street rap for heroin, to which Adriana's club, the Crazy Horse, speaks facilely. Tony's fascination with horses, however, is of another nature. His relationship with Ralphie's horse begins in "Pie-O-My" (4.05). He is fascinated both by its beauty and earning power. More importantly, the horse brings to the fore Tony's unfettered love for animals, an emotion he finds difficult to bestow on humans.[11] His commissioned painting begins as a flirtation with the Gloria-clone Valentina but is soon wrapped in the anxious state of uncertainty and insecurity that inhabits his waking, and sleeping, hours. After the deaths of both Pie-O-My and Ralph, Tony simply cannot bear to view the painting. He orders it destroyed in a fit of self-serving logic.

His thoughts eventually lead him ("All Due Respect," 5.13) to Paulie's home where, to his surprise, the painting of Pie-O-My, altered with himself now in general's uniform, hangs over the mantel. Tony is furious as a spate of unavoidable memories swell to the fore. He complains of being dressed like a "lawn jockey," of being a laughing stock, disrespected by his men. Paulie retorts earnestly. The altered Tony is a leader, dressed as Napoleon. Its no joke: "Something that captures more of what you're really all about ... that's not a lawn jockey, it's a general ... not a real general from history. Its you!" But Tony cannot bear the analogy, nor does he truly want the responsibility those words portend. He tears down the painting and tosses it into a dumpster, thus placing himself, literally, in the trash. But he is haunted by the image before him: the clenched right fist, the saber. His life choices—all wrong, as he has just confided to Melfi—have brought him to this new juncture, this new image of self. Staring at the painting, Tony is offered a moment of conscious self-awareness. His spiritual introspection imbues the moment with profound solitude and despair. The episode cogently juxtaposes Tony's war with New York with World War Two as seen on the History Channel. Tony learns of Rommel's leadership qualities and of his "sixth sense of sizing up a situation." As a general in his own war, Tony appreciates tidbits of information on historical leaders that legitimize his own position. He is reeling from the weight of the dilemma he faces. The close-up of Tony gazing into his own painted eyes unleashes an interminable spate of thoughts about his existential drama. Should he kill his cousin Tony Blundetto? The entire series seems to revolve around this vortex of decision.

Appropriately, instead of a growing sense of moral responsibility and repugnance for the atrocities of war seen on the screen, his own personal war acquires a contorted physiognomy. Does he follow the neurotic inner self of the disembodied victim-hero doing his duty, or the projected self of morally unfettered confidence? Indeed, Tony is not an automata; he has choices. But, as he has just confessed to Melfi, "I'm very confused. All my choices were wrong." Nevertheless, the rule-laden performance of his duties is the only reality he knows. He must remain coherent; he must remain the good soldier.[12] This painting, like the image of the tigers, has given reality revelatory contours. It has become the mediating object of his fateful decision. The burden of responsibility (remember the earlier conversation with Silvio at the Bing in this episode) is ponderous and lonely. As the camera probes the inner black of his eye, he resolves to kill his cousin Tony. He'll do so for the pressing and barbed sake of family. After the deed, he returns to the Bing. His men pay him all due, perfunctory, respect.

Watching actors act and looking at artworks are obviously two different sensorial experiences. Seen within the context of this series, the artworks present in *The Sopranos* form a narrative design that wishes to augment spectator involvement both visually and intellectually. At times these artworks render problematic, or at the very least expose, the notion of stereotypical encoding and public interpretation. Most often they enhance spectator pleasure by stirring aesthetic emotions and generating personal impressions that produce the dynamic patterns that over the arc of the series have become the tempo, timbre, tension, tone, and signature of *The Sopranos*. As a definite nod to the spectator, the artworks are displayed for pure effect, in essence permitting the viewer to interpret the actions on screen against a backdrop of nonviolent images.

The use of artworks at strategic moments thus liberates the series from the narrative justification of violence. By presenting a static visual counterbalance, they legitimize the violence as an idiosyncratic act relevant only to the closed world of mobsters who often use misinterpretations of the public art that surrounds them to justify their actions.

The artworks also move beyond this circumscribed world and directly into the viewer's realm. They test memories, cultural knowledge, visual acuity. This new narrative grid is not a homogeneous world but a multidimensional and heterogeneous terrain, replete with personal impressions, sustained by an ongoing process of assemblage. At the least, the empowerment of spectators nurtured on TV and mob films creates a dense weave of metapictures that form our collective identity. Liberally salting episodes with artwork, *The Sopranos* subtly reminds the viewer of that space between reality and fiction, thought and expression, violent act and aesthetic deed, that permeates the series and which finds Tony at its nexus.

CRIMINAL JUSTICE, POWER, HOMOPHOBIA, RACE

12.

TASTING BRYLCREEM

LAW, DISORDER, AND THE FBI
IN *THE SOPRANOS*

Douglas L. Howard

If you are looking for justice, don't bother turning on your television, or, at the very least, be ready to adjust your expectations along with your satellite dish. Once upon a time, it was difficult if not impossible to change channels without, to politely paraphrase Tony Soprano's cantankerous Uncle Jun, "tasting Brylcreem."[1] Even if you did not get that raise and the paperboy threw your copy of the *Times* in the rhododendrons, you could still sleep tight knowing Eliot Ness had dealt yet another blow to Capone's racketeering, and Joe Friday had changed the names on his case file to protect the innocent. Those days are gone. The officers in Adam-12 have turned in their keys, Barnaby Jones has finally retired, and the Mod Squad is no longer fashionable. Oh, you still might be able to find a cop on television if you need one, and the CSIs and *Law and Orders* of the world might neatly solve all of their problems (and yours) in just under sixty minutes, but if you really want to find out what has happened to the law on television, you need to sing a different tune and turn to the federal agents on HBO's *The Sopranos*.

As David Chase now considers the conflict between the mob and the FBI, the moral supremacy of the law is no longer such a given. In fact, this fight is not even close. The FBI are out there in the wilds of New Jersey, but they are not the square-jawed superheroes that brought Capone to his knees, made fleeing bank robbers drop their guns and surrender, and inspired excited five-year-olds to collect box tops for their TV fan clubs. At best, these feds are just another competing family, a connection Chase and his writers have reinforced throughout the show's run. Many of the agents, including lead Agent Frank Cubitoso, Skip Lipari, Agent Grasso, and Deborah Ciccerone, are Italian-American. The FBI are organized; instead of meeting in the backroom of a strip joint, they meet around a conference table in the board room. They operate and conduct themselves within a structured hierarchy—the other agents typically take their cues from Cubitoso—although not always to the satisfaction of its members. During a telling scene in "Big Girls Don't Cry" (2.05), Big Pussy and Lipari complain about how poorly their respective organizations are run and how they fail to adequately reward their "employees." While Pussy gripes about being passed over for promotion by Paulie, Lipari asks him to imagine a greater indignity: "being passed over for a Samoan ... three years out of Quantico." If we did not know any better, we might well think that they worked for the same "organization."

The feds also distribute money from the top down. When the informant Ray Curto asks his FBI contact to "talk to the higher-ups" ("Rat Pack," 5.02) about getting him a raise, the plea sounds like it could have been directed as easily toward a capo as toward an FBI agent. Lipari similarly takes Pussy's mob earnings like a capo and rewards him with only a small portion of his overall take ("Funhouse," 2.13); he is just as beholden and just as pressured to "earn" for his superiors, however, and, as Pussy keenly realizes, only squeezes him so tightly for information because "somebody's leaning on [his] ass" ("Do Not Resuscitate," 2.02). Where *The Untouchables* and *The FBI* once portrayed federal agents as determined lawmen devoted to a cause, Tony's lawyer, Neil Mink, now tells him the Bureau is, essentially, "a business [with] millions of tax dollars invested in watching [his] ass" and warns that "sooner or later, just like [Tony], they're going to want a return on their investment" ("House Arrest," 2.11).

A rather unusual scene at the end of "House Arrest" seems to confirm the feds really are, as Mink says, a business or another family.

While Tony and his capos take in the sun outside of Satriale's, the ubiquitous Agent Harris stops by to introduce Tony to his new partner, Joe Marquez, and strikes up a conversation about the Nets and the Knicks. The conversation is civil, even friendly. Though we might be inclined to romanticize the FBI's investigation of the mob as "a war," a personal, moral, emotionally charged conflict, Harris and Tony do not seem like adversaries here at all. They are more like rival businessmen (or rival family members), working different sides of the street in the same industry. The competition is not personal, though. They are both just doing their jobs, and, at the end of the day, they can still shoot the breeze (as opposed to each other) and talk about basketball.

The feds and the mob, as *The Sopranos* portrays them, even use the same methods and techniques to accomplish their goals. Like Tony and his crew, the FBI work through intimidation, what Allen Rucker (through his Jeffrey Wernick persona) defines as "the main tool of the Mafia trade," and through veiled threats on the lives of potential informants. Following the failed attempt on Tony's life in "Isabella" (1.12), for example, Harris is quick to visit Tony in the hospital and use the threat of future assassination attempts to scare him into becoming a government witness. "We're the only option you have left," Harris warns, an ultimatum that could just as easily have come from one of Tony's underbosses under different circumstances. Along the same lines, Cubitoso brings Tony in for what could well be called "a sitdown" with a group of his agents in order to play a recording of Uncle Jun conspiring with Livia at the Green Grove nursing home. Hoping to shock Tony with the revelation that his mother and uncle plotted against him, Cubitoso similarly uses this evidence to "motivate [him] to testify" on behalf of the government ("I Dream of Jeannie Cusamano," 1.13). In the same episode, a federal agent leans on Junior after his arrest by asking him "How many years you got left?" Even in his dreams, Junior sees the feds making him promises and bargaining with his life. As he undergoes cancer surgery, he imagines that federal agents offer him a deal: giving up Tony in exchange for a "guaranteed cure" ("Second Opinion," 3.07).

Most notably and perhaps most successfully, the Bureau intimidates, coerces, and blackmails Big Pussy and Adriana La Cerva to get inside information about family activities and, in the process, impossibly forces both to serve two masters. Just as Tony berates Pussy for his extended absence before allowing him to go back to work at the start of Season Two, Lipari reminds him that he has "been on [their] tit since '98" and that, in exchange for medical attention and his return to the streets, Pussy owes the government "results" ("Do Not Resuscitate"). When Pussy, clearly torn between his loyalty to Tony and his involvement with the FBI, later fails to provide adequate information about a possible merger with Philadelphia, Skip threatens him with the alternative, noting that he certainly is not acting "like a guy that's facing thirty to life for selling H." (Federal agents also used this kind of sentence to turn Fabian Petrulio, who, as Tony tells Christopher, flipped because "he got busted for peddling H" ["College," 1.05].) In Season Four, after Christopher's advances toward her end Deborah Ciccerone's undercover operation,[2] she and Harris are moved to pick Adriana up and, as with Pussy, use a twenty-five-year drug sentence to make her "rat" on the family. Coldly taking advantage of her trust and her friendship, Ciccerone and her superiors use Adriana to further their own ends, risking and trading her life, in Adriana's words, "to find shit out." The feds are not that different from Tony in this regard either. Tony uses Detective Vin Makazian's gambling debts against him in order to keep tabs on Melfi and get information about the FBI and then bluntly tells him, "I don't give two shits about you, your family, or whether you take it up the ass!"[3] ("Nobody Knows Anything," 1.11). In "Watching Too Much Television" (4.07), the agents even contemplate their response to Adriana and Christopher's wedding only insomuch as it applies to their investigation of the family. When Adriana, who is also conflicted about her role as informant and breaks down during one of Carmela's movie night meetings in "Rat Pack" (5.02), later tries to cover up a murder in her nightclub, a frustrated Cubitoso increases the price of her freedom to include getting "Tony Soprano on tape" ("Long Term Parking," 5.12) and, finally, "flipping" Christopher over as a government witness.

And then there are those moments on the show where the feds make (or appear to make) some serious arrests and crack down on family activities. (Interestingly enough, these moments almost always come toward the end of the season, as if to remind us that the government has been working—and lurking—through the excitement of the earlier episodes and is now ready to contain—or punish—some of the immoral excesses that have taken place.) Breaking up Jimmy Altieri's card game, federal agents find guns hidden beneath his pool table. While Tony plans his revenge for the attempt on his life, Uncle Jun (the titular head of the family), "Larry Boy" Barese, and a number of other mob underbosses are all paraded before the television cameras and hauled off to prison, the end result, US attorney Gene Conigliaro proudly tells the public, "of an ongoing investigation stretching back nearly four years" ("I Dream of Jeannie Cusamano"). Tony himself is taken away in handcuffs at the end of Season Two—the day before Meadow's high school graduation, no less—for the stolen airline tickets he absent-mindedly gives to Livia. Unaware of the tip Pussy gave Skip about the tickets, Tony blames himself for the error and nervously believes the government will build a case against him that will include "that Egypt Air thing" (the pre-9/11 flight 990 tragedy) and lead to "thirty to life" ("Funhouse"). And, of course, there is the FBI's arrest of Johnny Sack, famously falling out in the snow, that ends Season Five ("All Due Respect," 5.13), an arrest that they were looking to make when they brought Junior in at the end of Season One—the agent interrogating Junior in prison mentions Johnny by name—and that they were able to make through the informant Jimmy Petrille.[1]

Indeed, the FBI are often "out there" in The Sopranos, like Mulder's aliens or Jack Bauer's terrorists, plotting, scheming, listening, waiting to strike, and, frequently, getting into the heads of their suspects. As Junior tells his capos, "You guys see indictments under your beds at night" ("The Legend of Tennessee Moltisanti," 1.08); ironically, he is indicted at the end of the season. While Junior holds meetings with Tony in his cardiologist's office because the "law says feds can't bug your doctor's office" ("Do Not Resuscitate"), an increasingly anxious Tony, in an attempt to stay ahead of the government, has the bathroom in his office at the Bada Bing swept for bugs ("The Legend of Tennessee Molitsanti"), finds new hiding places for his guns and his money, holds meetings at the Green Grove nursing home

("Boca," 1.09), uses caution during his poolside discussions because "he fears parabolics [microphones]" ("Mr. Ruggerio's Neighborhood," 3.01), and leaves sensitive conversations for secluded roadsides or his basement, which is temporarily bugged at the start of Season Three. Since the series specifically focuses on Tony and his family, Chase and his writers rarely flesh out the FBI, and, as a result, they often seem more like a "force" rather than like real people. When Junior and the underbosses are arrested, the camera only shows an arm, a badge, and the mobsters' discouraged reactions. Many of the agents, in fact, are little more than extras; some do not have first names and even the ones that do are usually addressed as "agent" anyway—"Agent Harris, Agent Grasso, Agent Driscoll," etc. (How many of you knew that Agent Harris's first name was Dwight?) Most of the FBI agents working on the surveillance of Tony's family and the bugging of his house in "Mr. Ruggerio's Neighborhood" are nameless faces, as are the agents that arrest Jimmy and Big Pussy during their card game and descend upon Johnny Sack's house in Season Five.

Tony and his crew also have some difficulty identifying undercover agents, who seem at times like the morphing "Agents" in *The Matrix*. They can be anyone, anywhere. The waiter at the dinner where Uncle Jun is named boss is really an agent taking pictures of the guests through a camera in his lapel ("Pax Soprano," 1.06). The nurse Junior shamelessly flirts with at the doctor's office is really an agent who has been working there, as Murf reports, "since January or D-Day or something" ("For All Debts Public and Private," 4.01). Adriana also has no idea "Danielle" is an agent, takes her to Tony's house, and even confides to her about a pre-Christopher abortion. The family is always on the lookout for FBI informers, a constant source of anxiety and paranoia. In Season One, Mikey P. is convinced "the leak is in Tony's boat," and, although Junior knows his nephew is not talking to the feds, he still mistrusts Tony because he is talking about family business and "spilling his guts" ("Boca") to a psychiatrist. Along the same lines, Junior thinks that Tony should "put [Christopher] out of his misery" ("The Strong Silent Type," 4.10) after his drug addiction is revealed because of the damage he *could do* if the FBI ever brought him in. Tony, on the other hand, has Jimmy Altieri killed for informing on the family and a rat stuffed in his mouth, a pointed commentary on the crime he has committed. When his underbosses attempt to discover the identity of the witness to the Bevilaqua murder, the best news that Paulie can give Tony is that "he is not a rat," a fact that, ironically, makes Pussy, one of the biggest rats in terms of both his size and his importance to Tony ("Bust-Out," 2.10).

Though Tony discovers Pussy's betrayal and finally kills him, he still winds up with more informants and more rats than he can exterminate. The second episode in Season Five, "Rat Pack," refers as much to Frank Sinatra and his celebrity cohorts and the picture Jack Massarone gives Tony as it does to all of the family members—Massarone, Adriana, and Ray Curto, who is still on their payroll—who are ratting to the FBI. As his lawyer tells Tony at the end of "All Due Respect," even the raid on Johnny Sack's home is the end result of an informant, Jimmy Petrille, who gave the feds "eighteen fucking years worth."

For all the FBI do on *The Sopranos*, for all the bugging and the wiretapping, for all the coercion and pressure, for all the family members they flip and the information they get, for all the undercover agents that get on the inside and for all the busts they make, their plans almost never work, or, at the very least, they never turn out the way they intended, and they never really make a dent in Tony's "family business." Although Harris tells him he has to come in for his own safety in Season One, Tony dismisses the offer, in the same way Christopher rejects the possibility of going with Adriana after seeing the impoverished family at the gas station ("Long Term Parking"), because living in Utah and "having some Mormons over for dinner" is clearly not an "option" for him. And Cubitoso's tape only gives Tony the proof he needs to move against his enemies: to shoot Chucky Signore at the marina and have Christopher and Paulie "whack" Mikey P. out in the woods. Agents arrest Junior, but he never talks, and the indictment Conigliaro claims the government has worked so long and hard for "sounds better for the feds," as Tony explains to Carmela, "than it really is" ("I Dream of Jeannie Cusamano"). For all of the protection they promise, they get almost all of their informants killed. Pussy rats for over a year and is killed (and, as they realize in "Mr. Ruggerio's Neighborhood," they get almost nothing about the

Bevilaqua murder from Pussy's wire). Adriana rats for over a year and is killed (and Christopher never turns). Jimmy Altieri is killed. Jack Massarone is killed (and, like Jimmy, his mouth is "stuffed," in this case with a golf club cover). Tony kills Fabian Petrulio ("College") for ratting after he gets kicked out of witness protection. When the witness who can place Tony at the Bevilaqua hit finds out he is involved in a mob investigation, he quickly recants for his own safety and dismisses the FBI agents that tried to get him to testify as "lying cocksuckers" ("Bust-Out"). And though Tony is arrested for passing the stolen airline tickets, he is still out in time for Meadow's graduation. For all of the trouble they go through to bug Tony's basement, Meadow takes the lamp off to her dorm room. For all of the trouble they go through to put the nurse in Junior's doctor's office, he still gets off. Even Johnny Sack's arrest, which includes charges of "gambling, homicides, [and] trafficking," never involves Tony, who physically and legally gets away clean and is encouraged, by his lawyer, to "consider laughing or [rubbing] a hunchback's hump" ("All Due Respect"). Perhaps the strongest commentary on the FBI's effectiveness takes place at the end of Season Two in "Funhouse." As the episode closes with shots of calling card sales, garbage trucks, adult movie houses, the Webistics trading office, and even the ocean, where Pussy now "sleeps with the fishes," it is clear the family and their business is the real "force" here, a force of nature not unlike the ocean itself, a force the FBI and all of its agents and informants are virtually powerless to stop.

At their worst, the FBI in *The Sopranos* are cartoon characters, voyeuristic outsiders trying to catch a brief glimpse of the immorality and intrigue they purport to restrain, self-righteous do-gooders who are laughably outmatched, inept bunglers who cannot build the case they need or make the one they have. As Yacowar points out, if they are "a gang like Tony's," they certainly are not "as effective or smart" (126). By the time the agents show up to search Tony's house in Season One, he has already moved his money and his guns; even A. J. has taken the porn off his computer. While Agent Harris ridiculously looks for incriminating evidence under Tony's couch cushions, Agent Grasso checks the kitchen and breaks Carmela's salad bowl, an accident that leads her to consider him "a klutz" ("The

Legend of Tennessee Molitsanti"). Even Big Pussy's work with the FBI takes a turn toward the absurd; in what Lipari calls "[the] worst case of Stockholm Syndrome since Patty Hearst," Pussy begins discussing RICO predicates, calling Lipari with the code name "fat man," and tailing family members, until an exasperated Lipari finally reminds him that he "is not an FBI employee" ("The Knight in White Satin Armor," 2.12). And as Cubitoso, Danielle, and Agent Harris attempt to frighten an already shaken Adriana into informing on the family ("No Show," 4.02), she horrifically throws up all over their conference table and all over them, an act that again only serves to make them look all the more foolish and all the more ridiculous.

Probably the strongest commentary on the FBI takes place at the beginning of Season Three in "Mr. Ruggerio's Neighborhood." As Yacowar explains in his finely detailed analysis of the episode, the title refers to Tony's plumber and comically "parodies *Mr. Rogers' Neighborhood*" (125), but in this neighborhood, the joke is on the FBI, who consistently "have everything wrong" (125). Skip, for example, suggests that they should "consider 16: Bompensiero compost," but his body was dumped in the ocean and another agent confidently asserts that "the cartel had [Richie Aprile] whacked," but Janice really killed him in a fit of rage at the end of Season Two. After viewing footage of the basement, Lipari also points out that Tony has "about six months left" on his water heater before it blows, a prediction he makes based on the fact his "dad was a plumber." Shortly thereafter, when Tony and Carmela come home early and thwart the Bureau's bugging plans, Harris thinks "there must be a crisis with one of the children," but both Harris and Lipari are wrong: the water heater has just blown and Tony's basement is flooded. "In their dealings with the Sopranos," Yacowar notes, "the FBI can't deal with even that leak" (126).

In addition, the agents have to follow the entire family around in order to scope out the basement and put the lamp in place without Tony knowing it, another joke considering how much time they waste and what they get out of it. One agent listens in as Meadow's roommate talks about her binge drinking in Manhattan. Another agent tracks A. J. as he ditches out of assembly. Another agent watches Tony's Polish housekeeper as she helps her husband Stasiu study for his citizenship exam. And another agent stakes out Carmela's tennis practice, but winds up gawking at the scantily clad Adriana and her tennis instructor's more than professional interest in her. When two agents actually do stumble upon a legitimate threat—a distraught Patsy Parisi considers killing Tony for the murder of his twin brother—they are not sure how to handle it and simply look on as Patsy urinates in Tony's pool. At the end of it all, the only "messy job" they hear about is the one Tony gives Stasiu, to create an overflow for his new water heater, and the only information they get on Tony is that he needs more roughage in his diet and should use a different dental floss. Four episodes later ("Another Toothpick"), after all the trouble they go through to get it in the basement, Meadow unknowingly "neutralizes" their bug when she takes the lamp off to her college dorm room. It is nice to know the government's money is so well spent.

And lest we somehow miss the intention here, even the choice of music in this episode, an important staple of the series in general, is significant. As the agents race around tailing the family and bugging the house, a combination of the "Peter Gunn" theme and the "I'll be watching you" refrain from the Police's "Every Breath You Take" plays in the background. As Blake Edwards imagined him, Gunn may have been a "cool" private eye, but these agents, "so absorbed," according to Kim Akass and Janet McCabe, "in being hip, cool detectives from classic television shows" (159), are anything but cool. They sweat. They jump. They screw up. Even the music is laughing at them. The Police refrain reminds us they will "be watching" the Sopranos (as will we), but given how badly they misinterpret what they see, Tony may not have so much to worry about after all.

To add insult to this injury, from the FBI's failure to contain their business and to crack down on the family's criminal activities, Tony and his crew frequently fail to take the feds seriously themselves and often flaunt their contempt for the law in the face of the FBI's ineffective authority, a fact that encourages the audience to view them in the same way. Counting out piles of money in the backroom of the Bada Bing, Tony's capos ironically watch a talk show on the decline of the mob and listen to US Attorney Braun discuss the success of "an aggressive government policy" ("46 Long," 1.02) while Silvio does his best Pacino *Godfather* impression. The "FBI Warning" blares out from the television as they watch an "advanced bootleg" of *The Godfather, Part II* ("Commendatori," 2.04) on a stolen DVD player.[5] Tony tells Harris that he "can keep" any quarters that he finds in the cushions of his couch during their search. When Harris gravely asks Tony to come down to talk about the Bevilaqua murder, Tony cannot resist asking him to "roll the garbages down the hill" ("Bust-Out") for pick-up day, in spite of the seriousness of his visit. And as a disguised Harris later attempts to look inconspicuous during the stakeout of Tony's house in "Mr. Ruggerio's Neighborhood," Tony gives him the finger as he and Furio drive by, leaving the disheartened agent to tell his team, "They fuckin' made me." When Cubitoso calls him in to hear his tape-recording of Junior and Livia, Tony wonders if they are instead going to play "the Springsteen box set." And as an agent pressures Junior, already in prison for his role as mob boss, to cooperate because the FBI wants to bring down Johnny Sack, Mangano, and Teresi, he caustically quips, "I want to fuck Angie Dickinson. See who gets lucky first" ("I Dream of Jeannie Cusamano"). Forget organization here; the feds cannot even match their comebacks.

As I mentioned earlier, we hardly learn anything about the FBI agents in *The Sopranos*, but the ones that we do learn something about only add to the caricature of the Bureau the show constructs. We find out that Deborah, the agent who is working undercover as Adriana's friend, is really married to another FBI agent and has a baby at home. She is wife and mother by day, FBI agent by night. In the wake of films like *Donnie Brasco* (1997) or television shows like *Wiseguy* (1987–1990), this sort of storyline is almost cliché and is certainly meant to be viewed in that light. Aside from the fact that the agent is a woman rather than a man, the writers do not do that much with Deborah's home life or with the struggles she might face having to balance her responsibilities as wife, mother, and agent. We have no reason to connect with her. She comes off coldly in all of her roles; instead, our feelings are largely for the conflicted Adriana. Similarly, when Adriana complains because she feels exploited by Sanseverino, the concerned agent decides to share some personal information with her troubled informant. Sanseverino's story about her ex-husband who left her for a pay rise and a better job clearly does not equal the drama of Adriana's situation. Adriana, in fact, searches for something as deep, and when she hears that Robyn's marriage failed, she immediately looks for some kind of intrigue. "Did he cheat on you?" she asks. As Robyn goes on to convince Adriana that she is doing the right thing, she argues that, with the FBI, "the line [is] clearer between the good guys and the bad guys" and that Adriana is "with the good guys now" ("Rat Pack").

Sanseverino's speech, though, simplistically divides the world into good and bad and is pure indoctrination. If *The Sopranos* does nothing else, it demands that viewers see this world more complexly and judge these characters by their backgrounds as well as by their circumstances and their motivations. Given all that we know about Tony's upbringing and about his psychological issues, it would be rather reductive to label him simply as "bad." Sanseverino tries to ease Adriana's guilt by offering her such absurd moral absolutes, but as Adriana tries to go back and forth between these two worlds, clearly, her choices and these "worlds" themselves are not so easily defined.

In fact, generally speaking, we never really identify with the FBI, a rather odd occurrence considering that they are, in Sanseverino's words, "the good guys," and that television and the media have essentially conditioned us to view them as such. *The Sopranos*, however, turns that image on its head. Where other portrayals of the mob, like *The Godfather* trilogy, *GoodFellas*, *Casino*, *The Untouchables*, and *Reservoir Dogs*, often present the Mafia as "Other" and offer viewers a glimpse of a life and a lifestyle that is more than likely foreign to them, *The Sopranos* instead works to make the family understandable and sympathetic, in spite of the horrific murders committed in the name of *la cosa nostra*. As Allen Rucker's Jeffrey Wernick explains, "Aside from their line of work, the Sopranos are not a whole heck of a lot different than you and me. They're a family with a secret. ... Doesn't your family have its own deep, dark, disgraceful secret?" In this light, the FBI and its agents do not become our protectors or our saviors. They become that aspect of the government that appears to work against the family, that encroaches on our freedoms and limits our lives. They become the government that raises our taxes and closes down our loopholes, that monitors our Internet searches and scans our e-mail, that keeps tabs on what we check out at the library, and that adds more toll plazas out on the parkway. When Harris searches Tony's house and the feds take his children's computers or when they attempt to bug his basement in "Mr. Ruggerio's Neighborhood," we do not feel that we are watching the law in action or justice at work. Knowing how successful the government will probably be in these endeavors, we can only feel the family's sense of violation. Yacowar agrees that "the FBI subverts their privacy" in this regard, and "Each time Tony wafts down the driveway for his morning paper, in his open robe, t-shirt, and boxer shorts [–a mundane commonplace act–] he seems open and vulnerable, a sympathetic figure" (128). As opposed to preventing some heinous crime by putting the lamp in Tony's basement, the FBI ultimately appears to intrude upon one of the last "sacred" places in his house, where he can speak freely without fear of recrimination, and, in the conversation about Tony's diet and his dental floss, we might well hear our own mundane day-to-day concerns, now spooling out as a matter of FBI record.

The FBI's use of informants and the pressure they put on their witnesses to cooperate also never seem like justice in action. Rather, they lead them to commit the ultimate betrayal of friends and family–a sin Dante punishes in his final circle of Hell–and to rat on Tony, who generally wants to believe the best of them. Following Matt Bompensiero's reference to Kierkegaard in "D-Girl" (2.07)–that "every duty is essentially a duty to God"–the feds ask Pussy to wear a wire to A. J.'s confirmation, but he hesitates because he does not want to be bugged "in God's house." While Lipari convinces Pussy to comply, Pussy realizes the enormity of his crime when he tells A. J. about what Tony had done for him and his family in the past and about what "a stand-up guy" he really is. As he is affected by his own speech and breaks down in the bathroom, Lipari is just as moved in listening as we are in watching him deal with this dilemma, while Emma Shaplin's heartrending "Vedi, Maria" plays in the background. The FBI have not so much cracked down on the mob here as they have tragically driven Big Pussy to turn away from his God. As an ailing Tony comes to grips with Pussy's treachery, we do not celebrate the government's infiltration of organized crime or rejoice in Tony's distress. We sympathize with him as he accepts the reality of what he must do. Moreover, though Tony, Paulie, and Silvio have difficulty putting Pussy out of his misery ("Funhouse")—Tony even yells at Silvio for being so upset—Lipari and the FBI are quick to write off "CW 16" as "compost" and to throw out his picture at the start of the next season, just as they are also ready to dismiss Jack Massarone and Adriana, who have both been forced to compromise their relationships with Tony and his inner circle to serve the Bureau's greater good, without a tear. Ironically, for the FBI, this is just business, but, for the Sopranos, it is family.

In order to evaluate *The Sopranos'* legacy and its place in television, in order to examine as well the show's portrayal of the FBI and of justice within that context, we certainly do need to consider it within the tradition of the law and order (and *Law and Order*) dramas, the cop shows, and the private detective thrillers, to place it alongside *Dragnet, Adam-12, Hawaii Five-O, The FBI, Police Story, Columbo, Hill Street Blues, Miami Vice, Wiseguy, Homicide, NYPD Blue, CSI, The Shield, The Wire,* and *Monk* and judge it and them accordingly. Creator David Chase was and is a product of this kind of television. He grew up with it, in fact. As David Lavery and Robert Thompson note, he was "a fan of *The Untouchables* (1959–1963), which he watched with his father" (Lavery 20), and, in his interview with Allen Rucker, Chase recalls that he "fell out of love with TV probably after *The Fugitive* went off the air." In many ways, these shows mark off the spectrum of television justice, and *The Sopranos* is born from the visions of society that they represent. So many of the police dramas we have come to know and love come from the tradition of Eliot Ness and his incorruptible G-Men, who struck fear into the hearts of the mob and made Capone's businesses bleed on a weekly basis. Crime does not pay, they sternly remind us, and the police detectives and private eyes in this world always believe in their missions and always get their suspects. Joe Friday and Bill Gannon can question every witness and arrest the perpetrator in half an hour, with commercial breaks. *Adam-12's* Reed and Malloy are within driving distance of nearly every crime. And Gil Grissom (*CSI*) and Adrian Monk track down and analyze every significant clue, proving there will always be a wealth of incriminating evidence to convict even the most calculating criminal. The system always works; no one ever gets away.

But Chase's reference to *The Fugitive* points to a different vision, one where the system breaks down, where the real criminal goes free, where the law refuses to acknowledge its own mistakes, where the innocent man must find his own justice because society cannot do it for him. The thrill of *The Fugitive* is also the thrill of watching a criminal, albeit a wrongly convicted one, on the run. Our belief in Richard Kimble's innocence exonerates us from the guilty pleasure of the experience, but that belief hides the shadow beneath nonetheless. In fact, we may well be watching *The Untouchables* and *Hawaii Five-O* as much for Capone and Wo-Fat as we are for Eliot Ness and Steve McGarrett. Chase appears to have learned this lesson from *The Fugitive* (and *Public Enemy* and his other inspirations) and to have recognized what the culture is only now beginning to accept: that the real drama lies not with the "perfect, incorruptible hero" but with the imperfect villain who struggles with human choices and falls prey to human desires. (Who knew that *Star Wars* was really about Darth Vader?) *The Sopranos* thus caters to this fascination with the criminal and his humanity, and to this belief in the failure of the system, that can hardly contain the mob within thirteen hours of television much less in one. Organized crime, as the series considers it, is simply too big, too involved, too complex, and the attempt to stop it and those who have futilely dedicated themselves to stopping it, like Cubitoso and Harris and the other feds in the tradition of *The Untouchables*, must be viewed as absurd. For *The Sopranos*, these so-called heroes may be no better (and are conceivably worse) than the criminals that they track.

But, in giving its viewers what they want, and letting them watch and like and even love its criminals, *The Sopranos* also shows them the complexity of justice itself. (In this regard, the series has paved the way for other more involved law and order dramas like *The Shield* and *The Wire*.) Absolute justice is clearly a fiction, and personal justice is relative at best. David Milch's *Deadwood* may be a place with "no law at all," but the Sopranos do have a law and a code and the line between right and wrong, between what Sanseverino calls "the good guys and the bad guys" is often not so clear cut. Even without her blindfold, Justice might have a tough time making things balance out here. I am reminded of Season Three's "Employee of the Month," when Melfi is brutally raped in a parking garage. The police botch the arrest, and, as a result, her assailant goes free. Melfi knows that she could tell Tony about what happened, and he would do for her what the law did not and punish her attacker. For Melfi, though, Tony's response would not necessarily be justice or at least the justice that she is looking for. He is, though, just as much a source of it as the police or the FBI themselves. Like Melfi, we are, through *The Sopranos*, encouraged to entertain this other morality, to enter this other world and to see the sense within it and the reasons behind the "crimes" that take place. Having done so, however, can we ever go back to those other shows, watch those anonymous extras getting arrested for armed robbery or homicide and suspend our disbelief again?

So change the channel if you want to and try to take comfort in the one-hour, four-act police drama, where the good guys always win and the snickering criminals leer out from behind prison bars, but don't be surprised if the characters and the plots are a little unsatisfying and the "Brylcreem" is a little hard to swallow. From his portrayal of the FBI to the gangsters themselves, David Chase's *The Sopranos* has provided the discerning viewer with a more palatable alternative. And justice on television may never taste the same again.

13.

THE PRINCE
OF NORTH JERSEY[1]

Dean DeFino

In "Calling All Cars" (4.11), mob boss Tony Soprano abruptly concludes four years of psychotherapy with Dr. Jennifer Melfi by demanding to know what all of his efforts at "self-knowledge" have gotten him. Though he admits that early sessions taught him some useful leadership strategies (anger management, impulse control), "Now," he complains, "all we do is sit around and shoot the breeze." He describes psychiatry as the self-indulgence of Americans spoiled by prosperity: a theme repeated since the pilot episode. Four years later, on the verge of losing a patient whose treatment has been a source of significant professional and personal danger to her, Dr. Melfi rebuts Tony very much as she did at their first meeting. She argues that, while Americans may be spoiled, freedom from material want offers one the opportunity to "delve into sources of emotional and spiritual pain, and to search for truth." "Pain and truth?" Tony asks, in a tone at once mocking and despairing, "C'mon, I'm a fat fuckin' crook from New Jersey."

Though Tony reluctantly returns to Dr. Melfi in Season Five, his therapy has and will always be framed by the paradox he identifies at this moment: how do you treat an unrepentant sociopathic criminal, whose primary goal—in and out of therapy—is to make himself a more effective mob boss? Over the sound of Melfi's wishful rhetoric, Tony repeatedly intones his answer: you cannot. He is a murderer and a thief for whom self-knowledge is a luxury and legitimacy a joke intoned by his consigliere Silvio Dante, in an oft-repeated parody of Michael Corleone's *Godfather III* lament: "Just when I thought I was out, *they pull me back in.*" With growing justification, Tony draws no distinction between organized crime and corporate culture other than scale, and any speculation that he will end up in the Witness Protection Program or "selling lawn furniture on the Interstate" (his own telling illustration of legitimacy) is our wishful thinking.

If *The Sopranos* is in part a walking tour through the mind of a postmodern gangster, the purpose of Tony's therapy, like the program's frequent dream sequences, is not prescriptive but expository and critical, allowing us unique insights into his past and his professional and personal trials. Although Dr. Melfi successfully exposes aspects of her patient's psyche, Tony's revelations never proceed past his image of himself as "the sad clown"—outwardly happy, inwardly suffering—which, from a professional killer, hardly constitutes insight. Audiences and television critics alike have sought in Tony an emblem of redeemable humanity, of the Oedipal male (seeking approval from a mother who plotted his murder), or of what Ellen Willis calls in "Our Mobsters, Ourselves" "the predatory lust and aggression in all of us" (30). But the desire of critics and audience to mythologize, sympathize with, and, in many cases, champion Tony obscures one immutable fact: *The Sopranos*, like most great gangster stories, is first and foremost a study in the achievement and maintenance of power.

Models of power abound in the program, from mob hierarchy and law enforcement to family and religion. In therapy, Tony and Dr. Melfi attempt to address these models from a series of psychoanalytic, then philosophical perspectives. When Tony's son A. J. begins to despair the meaninglessness of existence after reading "Nitch" (Nietzsche) in a high school English class ("D-Girl," 2.07), and Tony finds himself approving what he perceives as the German philosopher's existential pessimism, Melfi attempts to guide him toward the central concept of Nietzschean philosophy: the will to power. This is perhaps a dangerous approach when dealing with a criminal sociopath, but one intended to encourage Tony toward more constructive forms of agency. Tony also dabbles briefly in Eastern philosophy while involved with Gloria Trillo, the quasi-Buddhist Mercedes saleswoman from Season Three. He is particularly drawn to Sun Tzu, whose *Art of War* was recommended to him by Dr. Melfi prior to the appearance of Gloria. "Most of the guys I know read Prince Matchabelli," he tells Dr. Melfi ("University," 3.06), referring to the Florentine humanist Niccolo Machiavelli, author of that infamous guide to political expedience, *The Prince*. But according to Tony, Sun Tzu's text is "much better about strategy." Ironically, though Tony claims to dismiss Machiavelli after briefly skimming *Cliffs Notes* for *The Prince*, it is the Machiavellian aspect of Sun Tzu that attracts him. "If your opponent is of choleric temper, irritate him," he advises Silvio after their psychotic associate, Ralphie Cifaretto, beats a stripper to death outside of Silvio's strip club, the Bada Bing. Tony's response to this event is textbook Machiavelli: first to abuse, then to reward (a public thrashing and shunning, followed closely by a promotion).

Locating Machiavelli as an essential text in *any* mob story is a matter of course, given that *The Prince* advocates the use of cruelty and brutality in the acquisition and maintenance of power. But Machiavelli's commentary on sixteenth-century Florence in *The Prince* (as well as ancient Rome in *Discourses on Livy*) also serves as a thematic platform for the political commentary of *The Sopranos*, with its emphasis on leadership, the machinations of power and, most importantly, the effects of political change on social order. If Sun Tzu's *Art of War* is a study in military strategy, *The Prince*, like *The Sopranos*, describes not only the transfer of power, but also its transformation.

In a notorious chapter of *The Prince*, entitled "How Princes Should Honor Their Word," Machiavelli addresses what he calls the "two ways of fighting: by law or by force":

> The first way is natural to men, the second to beasts. But as the first way often proves inadequate one must needs have recourse to the second. So a prince must understand how to make a nice use of the beast and the man.
>
> (Bull trans. 99)

Although Machiavelli believed in behaving virtuously, he was deeply pessimistic about our ability to do so. A realist, he warned:

> [A] man who wants to act virtuously in every way necessarily comes to
> grief among so many who are not virtuous. Therefore if a prince wants to
> maintain his rule he must learn how not to be virtuous, and to make use
> of this or not according to need. (Bull trans. 91)

Machiavelli's words seem cynical because his argument was aimed at corrupt men (the Medici of Renaissance Florence), so he has gained the reputation among modern readers as the exemplar of the principle that might makes right. Mussolini read *The Prince* as a justification for totalitarianism, where the state is supreme, and therefore the domain of the supreme power at its head.

Indeed, Machiavelli did hold the view that the perpetuation of the state was more important than the life of the individual. He also believed that power must, at times, be absolute, though only to serve the greater good. Napoleon so honored these principles that he carried his annotated copy of *The Prince* with him at Waterloo. As a pre-Enlightenment humanist, Machiavelli worked from a political paradigm that favors the community over the individual, where liberty and freedom are contingent upon ones active participation in that community, not upon a set of "inalienable rights." Tom Paine found much to praise in Machiavelli's idea of civic virtue, fearing the corrupting influence of privatization and the free market (which, Paine argued to deaf ears, favored the elite). Still, history remembers Machiavelli as the progenitor of genocidal maniacs and mob bosses like Idi Amin and John Gotti (who read him with deep admiration), not to mention Joseph Conrad's Kurtz in *Heart of Darkness* or Keyser Soze from *The Usual Suspects* (1995): men willing to destroy the things they love most in order to maintain power.

Tony Soprano is no Kurtz or Keyser Soze, though his capos—Silvio and Paulie Walnuts—do occasionally compare him to Napoleon. If Kurtz embraces what he conceives as his essential brutality, Tony's fainting spells (in lieu of conscience) remind him that no beastly act finally makes a man into a beast. And this is the source of crisis: that a complete transformation from man to beast may not be possible. The pilot episode ends with the Nick Lowe's words "God help the beast in me"—a plaintive prayer for the strength to suppress one's better self. Unlike Keyser Soze, Tony is not going to destroy his family or himself to show a rival the extent of his power. And those unwilling to do anything for power will eventually lose it.

Circumscribing Tony's personal struggles are the political and social machinations of organized crime. And here Machiavelli's political critique offers particular insight. Though Machiavelli intended *The Prince* to define a functional civic order that served *all*, not a self-enclosed criminal hierarchy, and though his ideal republic (from *res publica*, "public thing") is far more inclusive than the American Mafia, each is intended to serve the good of the whole. In the case of the Mafia, that "whole" is simply more localized (*la cosa nostra* meaning, "our thing"). Boss of the principality known as the North Jersey mob, Tony derives his authority partly from his ability to execute where others stumble (hence his pre-eminence) but, more important, from his community—the opinions, loyalties and backing of his comrades. But loyalty is a tenuous thing, particularly when Tony confuses it with love. "They go around complimenting you on your new shoes, tell you you're not going bald," warns his wife, Carmela. "Do you think they really care? You're the boss. They're scared of you. They have to kiss your ass and laugh at your stupid jokes" ("All Happy Families," 5.04). That is, until Tony makes choices that affect their wellbeing. When his cousin, Tony Blundetto, murders several members of a New York crime family in Season Five, Tony's first instinct is to protect the cousin. But when it becomes clear that dissent from within and without his family is growing, Tony is forced to kill the cousin himself ("All Due Respect," 5.13). In so doing, he serves the greater good *and* proves himself once again able to act under extraordinary circumstances.

The gangster is often included among avatars of the American frontiersman or rugged individualist, models of self-actualization and freedom deified by nineteenth-century Romantics and Transcendentalists, and later by the American motion picture industry. Hollywood exemplars include the John Wayne cowboy, the Humphrey Bogart detective, and the James Cagney mobster, each a variation on the theme of individualism. And Tony identifies himself with many of these figures: the "cold hard captain of industry type" exemplified by Gary Cooper, the John Wayne cowboy/soldier leading the charge, and especially Cagney's ill-fated thug, Tom Powers, in Tony's favorite film, *The Public Enemy* (1931). But while the frontiersman, cowboy and soldier protect the values of a culture, like the confidence man in American frontier literature the mobster exploits freedom, corrupting "legitimate" cultural institutions (public services, unions), and redistributing power according to a monarchal/feudal model. As a confederation of small self-sustaining "families," the Mafia is modeled on old Italian principalities. And like any royal family, the mob is incestuous, achieving and maintaining power through heredity and self-enclosure. Each of the so-called "five families" bears a name, which might as easily be Stuart or Medici as Gambino or Perciso. And like all incestuous political organizations, at times the power of the mob falls into the hands of less-than-capable leaders. Christopher, Tony's hotheaded addict nephew, for example, has been chosen to succeed him because Tony has no other "made" relatives (and, significantly, because he considers his own son too weak to carry on the family business).

But if the future of the Soprano family is uncertain, Tony continues to fortify the fundamental structure of the organization. Season Four begins with him confronting his ill-performing capos. "This thing of ours is a pyramid," he explains in "For all Debts Public and Private" (4.01): "Shit runs downhill, money runs up." The system is designed to protect the power at the top, a model owing as much to corporate America as to Italian political philosophy, and having little to do with the romantic gangster image proposed by Hollywood. Unfortunately for Tony, his is the story of a leader who has "come in at the end," as he tells his therapist on their first meeting in "The Sopranos" (1.01). The mob pyramid in America is collapsing under its own weight, loyalists betrayed by mercenary opportunists. Mobsters have been reduced to brute goombah throwbacks doing the "perp walk" on the six o'clock news in their running suits. They are pop cultural simulacra: mere shadows of Cagney's tragic anti-hero and Marlon Brando's brooding Don. Like Ozzy Ozbourne, Tony Soprano has become an eccentric, if occasionally menacing, suburbanite ("How real is *The Godfather?*" his neighbor asks over a round of golf in "A Hit is a Hit" [1.10]). Or worse, he has become like the brown bear that stalks his suburban neighborhood throughout Season Five: anomalous, threatening, but in the end not worth the trouble to shoot. Of course, he is being hunted, but the FBI agents following his trail are themselves part of the grand simulation/diminution of cops and robbers: part Joe Friday, part Keystone Kops, who apparently have half of the Soprano family on their payroll, yet still seem incapable of making a case against them.

This diminution is best exemplified by the struggle for power within Tony's crime family. When the series begins, Tony's childhood friend Jackie Aprile is at the helm, following the recent incarceration of their aging boss. Jackie contracts cancer shortly after and, as he dies in his hospital bed, Tony and Uncle Junior jockey for position. Though no Fredo Corleone, Junior clearly does not have the will or resources of his young nephew, and finds himself the unwitting pawn to Tony's ambitions. He is, as Tony says when we first hear Junior mentioned in the pilot episode, "a good guy," who is unfortunately "getting old" in a business that respects age but favors youth. Junior's steady decline into senility in later seasons is merely the physical manifestation of a pre-existing political situation. Tony represents an emerging order, beholden to many of the old ways (especially the beleaguered vow of *omerta*—the code of silence) but more global and proactive. Junior makes the bulk of his income from traditional mob businesses like drugs and union rackets, but Tony sets up investment scams—bogus internet companies, defaulted HUD loans—and builds a stock portfolio. He is the new model mob boss standing on the precipice of an emerging economic and social order, part waste management consultant (a nod to the past), part cyber-criminal.

Cruel and ruthless when they need to be, both men are Machiavellian in the broadest sense of the term. In Season One, Junior joins Tony's mother, Livia, in a plot to murder Tony; later, Tony attempts to smother Livia with a pillow. But their leadership models could not be more different. Junior is miserly and bitter, harboring grudges against his younger brother and his nephew, both of whom advanced ahead of him in the mob. On the other hand, Tony is bold and forward thinking. As a teenager, we learn in "Amour Fou" (3.12), he organized the successful robbery of a card game run by Feech La Manna, capo under Tony's father, to gain the respect of his superiors, who could not help but admire his audacity. Following his attempt to assassinate Tony, Junior complains to his nephew that "it could have gone the other way," and that Tony was served by good fortune in this case, not planning or skill. But while this may be true in the short run, it is Tony's bravado and vision that have allowed him to succeed all along, and to dominate his uncle even as Junior wears the boss's stripes.

Like any good Machiavellian, Tony is a student of history, studying the past in an effort to avoid the traps of fickle, unrelenting *Fortuna*. A devotee of the History Channel, Tony's primary interests not surprisingly run to military campaigns and ancient Rome. With the latter he feels a particular connection. In "Denial, Anger, Acceptance" (1.03), an Hasidic Jew under threat of death boasts about the steadfastness of his people by recounting a revolt in the first century AD at Masada, where 900 Jews resisted 15,000 Roman soldiers for over two years. "They chose death before enslavement," he tells Tony and his crew, punctuating his defiance with a taunt: "And where are the Romans now?" To which the boss answers, "You're lookin' at 'em, asshole." For Tony, this is more than a joke. The pedigree of history constitutes both an identity and a worldview. After discovering that A. J. also suffers from panic attacks ("Fortunate Son," 3.03), Tony begins to revisit Soprano family lore, trying to locate the "putrid, rotten, fucking Soprano gene" ("Army of One," 3.13) that lay in wait for him and his son long before they were born. Melfi attempts to personalize the issue—to bring Tony's fatalism back to root psychological issues—arguing, "When you blame genetics, you are really blaming yourself." But if there is some truth in her assessment, she nevertheless misses his point. Tony is interested in history, not genetics: the deeds of men, not their DNA. He refuses to be "a fucking robot to my own pussy-ass weakness."

In "Pax Soprana" (1.06), Tony warns his uncle, recently made boss, about the dangers of miserly leadership using the example of the Roman Caesar Augustus Octavian. "Everybody loved him 'cause he never ate alone," Tony explains. Augustus learned from the mistakes of his predecessor Julius Caesar, who seized dictatorial powers to end decades of civil war but hesitated to relinquish those powers once the state was put into order again, so incurring the wrath of the Senate. In his *Discourses on Livy*, Machiavelli demonizes Julius for effectively ending the 500-year Roman republic. He even excuses Caesar's assassins, reasoning that they were serving the greater good by disposing of a potential tyrant. Machiavelli has much less to say about Augustus, who on the surface at least appears to have been an ideal Prince: willful, but well loved; ruthless, but eager for good counsel. An autocrat, he knew how to cloak his power, and had Augustus not used this deception to further erode the republic, Machiavelli might have admired his political expedience. Rome under Augustus was an empire, which Machiavelli considered the lowest form of government because it deifies the power at the head. Though Augustus cleverly refused all titles but *principate*, the Romans did make a god of him after death.

Like Augustus, Tony leads his family without taking the title of "boss," damning his uncle with an empty mantle of office. After Junior's botched assassination attempt, Tony reappraises the situation, executing revenge on his conspirators with Machiavellian swiftness, then beginning a careful analysis of his relationships. No mean feat, he is faced with the specter of a hateful mother, a weakened but jealous uncle, a sister who runs afoul of his authority at every turn, a disintegrating marriage, two children whose relationships with him are ambivalent at best, an addict successor, grumbling capos, and FBI informants within his organization. Clearly, things will have to change. But to what? Though Tony has successfully overturned the power structure within the organization while maintaining order, he has made only nascent gestures at setting an agenda for his reign, more concerned with insulating himself from legal and political threat. Following a trip to Italy, where he favorably renegotiates a deal for stolen SUVs ("Commendatori," 2.04), he imports some old-world muscle in the form of Furio Junta—a ruthless enforcer—and informs his capos of the new leadership structure. He will incrementally remove himself from day-to-day operations, and rely more upon them. Many of his leadership moves are conservative and defensive, avoiding messy investment schemes, laundering and hiding money, silencing opposition before it has an opportunity to flower. In Season Five, for example, Tony concludes a tenuous reconciliation with Feech La Manna (recently released from prison and still angry about the card game Tony robbed twenty-five years earlier) by framing the elder statesman and having him thrown back in jail for the rest of his life ("All Happy Families," 5.04).

But Tony is also an innovative and daring leader: branching out into real estate deals, pressing his capos to develop new income streams, showing defiance to the New York family (especially the power-mad John Sacramoni) and, perhaps boldest of all, seeking psychiatric help. At times, his decisions seem short-sighted (such as relying upon Christopher) or capricious (such as hitting on Christopher's fiancé ["Irregular Around the Margins," 5.05]), more akin to his uncle's philosophy: "Steer the ship the best way you know how, and take your pleasures where you can" ("He is Risen," 3.08). But Tony cannot maintain this relativist position with his freedom and his family to protect (it is easier for Uncle Junior, a bachelor). Tony's leadership is about a greater (if localized) good: "I'm a good provider," he likes to say, "I do right by my family" (meaning here *both* of his families). Tony understands that, while the mob thrives in a capitalist free market, it is a self-enclosed society built upon Machiavellian principles of solidarity and interdependence.

The truth is that Tony has not "come in at the end," as he first claimed, but that he is being challenged to revitalize or reform the existing order, building upon the old principles but adjusting for fundamental shifts: in the character of the Mafia, in the world economy, in surveillance methods, etc. It is this pressure, not guilt or unresolved mother issues, that propels and frustrates him. According to Machiavelli, "there is nothing more difficult to plan, more doubtful of success, nor more dangerous to manage, than the creation of a new system," because "the initiator has the enmity of all who would profit by the preservation of the old institutions and merely lukewarm defenders in those who would gain by the new ones": a lesson Julius Caesar learned at the cost of his life (51). In transitional times, it is the willful person who will best succeed. But more than will, it takes a patient understanding of the weaknesses in human nature, particularly self-interest and greed, and how they can be manipulated.

Power and leadership require an understanding of what Machiavelli called the mob: from the Latin, *mobile vulgus*, meaning vacillating/riotous crowd. He envisioned the populous as a changing and changeable thing, a living organism with appetites, emotions, and a will of its own. For Tony, the *mobile vulgus* is another kind of mob, equally temperamental and difficult to control. Like any successful leader, he maintains his authority by projecting an image of power and stability: an image undercut by the discovery (in "I Dream of Jeannie Cusamano," 1.13) that he has been seeing a psychiatrist, but Tony manages this crisis by decisively executing his foes. His allies are more troublesome. Because they bear witness to the machinations of his power and share a common history, those closest to Tony pose the biggest threat to his reign.

In his own blind pursuit of power and identity, Tony's nephew Christopher fluctuates between reverence and distain for the boss. Because the two men share certain traits—a sense of disappointment about what they have achieved, impatience for success, depressive tendencies—they frequently come into conflict. At the end of Season Three, Christopher defies Tony's decision regarding the punishment of Jackie Aprile, Jr., who killed a made man and attacked Christopher himself in a card game robbery meant to pay homage to Tony's youthful exploit ("Amour Fou"). When Tony does not retaliate immediately, Christopher expresses his hurt by renouncing his love for his uncle. He later apologizes, confessing that he's failed to see the big picture, but the boss's response is fierce, intended to throw his subordinate off balance: "You don't have to love me, but you *will* respect me." In typical Machiavellian fashion, Tony will spend much of Season Four "attaching" a now confused and despairing Christopher to him by promising power, by handing over his father's murderer, and by forcing him into drug rehabilitation. Their relations are again tested in Season Five, when Christopher rightly accuses Tony of making sexual advances at his fiancé, Adriana, in his absence. Tony's first tactic is to demean his nephew, making him dispose of dog feces off of his shoe and refusing even to explain himself, but as Christopher's threats manifest in violent acts toward his uncle, Tony responds first with his own threats and finally with evidence to corroborate his innocence. But it is not until Adriana is exposed as a government informer that the two find their bond again: as usual, over spilled blood (Adriana's in this case).

In some ways a more formidable challenge to Tony's patience and power is Paulie Walnuts, an old-school gangster and long-standing member of the Soprano crew whose obligatory rise in rank seems to be his undoing. As the series progresses and Paulie moves from soldier to capo, circumspection and loyalty give way to paranoia and something akin to madness. In the eyes of his peers, he simply lacks vision: too focused upon his own immediate needs (the same charge leveled against other old school types like Uncle Junior, Feech, and Richie Aprile), he fails to see the bigger picture. This is most apparent in "Pine Barrens" (3.11), where Paulie's petty impulsiveness strands him and Christopher overnight in a snowy wood without shoes or food. Over the course of that night Paulie's composure—outwardly manifest by his carefully coiffed helmet of gray-winged hair—is undone by bitter cold, hunger and, most potently, fear that Tony will learn of his miscalculations. At one point, he seriously contemplates murdering Christopher in order to avoid having to explain himself.

Paulie and Tony share a great deal of history (he worked for Tony's father when the senior Soprano ran the family), but while Tony has excelled, Paulie rests on his past accomplishments, expecting preferential treatment simply for having "put in my time." Again he misses the point: to quote Silvio, "In this thing of ours, you're only as good as your last envelope" ("Eloise," 4.12). Friend or not, as boss Tony expects Paulie to earn. But Paulie feels slighted when, for example, Tony makes business decisions that favor the more profitable Ralphie, and he begins to betray Tony to the seemingly sympathetic Johnnie Sack from the New York family. Terrified when he discovers that Johnny has been playing him for a fool, Paulie races back to Tony with tribute money stolen from an elderly woman's mattress in a desperate, brutal burglary. But if Paulie is a short-sighted fool, even in his small acts of betrayal he reveals his profound respect for Tony, whose favor he so craves that it drives him to truly beastly deeds: not least of which, smothering a senior citizen for a pathetic wad of bills ("Eloise"). In another bizarre, fetishistic show of reverence, he absconds with a discarded painting of Tony standing beside his racehorse and has Tony repainted to look like Napoleon, Paulie's absurd gesture at deifying power ("Whitecaps," 4.13). The painting, which Tony demanded be destroyed after Pie-O-My dies in a fire, hangs proudly over Paulie's mantle. When Tony discovers it on a visit to Paulie's home in "All Due Respect" (5.13), the level of his love for Tony is revealed in his nearly tearful explanation: "I'm sorry, T. But you don't never come here no more ... I didn't figure it would be a problem."

To date, the most significant test of Tony's leadership skills has been Ralphie Cifaretto, who looms large in Seasons Three and Four. Ralphie is the psychotic manifestation of Machiavelli's beast. His ruthlessness, incessant self-regard, and disdain for all others makes him dangerous to enemies and associates alike. Though Ralphie knows enough not to come to blows with the crowned prince (his ruthlessness has left him without allies), he obeys the rules only as they serve him. After beating a stripper to death in "University" (3.06), he demands an apology from Tony when the boss slaps him, exploiting the age-old precept that you don't hit a made man. Shortly after, he bashes Georgie, the dull-witted Bada-Bing bartender, across the face with a tow chain. We have seen characters like Ralphie in many mob stories, from Hawks's *Scarface* (1932) to Scorsese's *GoodFellas* (1990): the sado-masochistic psychopath who flaunts rank with impunity. But threatening as he is, Ralphie offers Tony an opportunity for self-critique.

When passing Ralphie over for promotion, Tony says he sympathizes with him because they "share certain tendencies." Though never named, we may assume that he means Machiavellian tendencies, and that he sees in Ralphie a potential enemy. Reminded of Godfather Vito Corleone's warning to "keep your friends close and your enemies closer," Tony maintains business relations with him. While keeping Ralphie in his good graces because he is an excellent earner, Tony never lets Ralphie find his balance: questioning his subordinate's decision to kill Jackie, Jr., taking possession of his racehorse and later his girlfriend. This seems to suit Ralphie's masochistic nature and, by the beginning of Season Four, they have developed a mutually agreeable arrangement. Though Tony continues to despise Ralphie, particularly as his bizarre sexual proclivities come to light, he is able to separate personal feelings from business. That is, until Tony's racehorse is killed in a fire he suspects Ralphie of setting to collect on an insurance policy ("Whoever Did This," 4.09). Though we never learn for sure whether Ralphie is responsible, his relative indifference to the horse's death, and his repeated assertion that, from an insurance standpoint, the fire is a boon, earn him a deadly beating at Tony's hands: a savage, relentless, and mindless death. In what ranks as one of the series' most brutal scenes, Tony is transformed fully into a beast. His eyes burning from roach killer that Ralphie sprays in self-defense, skin blistered by butter and eggs flung from a hot frying pan, he smashes Ralphie's head on the tile floor until blood begins to pool around the dead man's eyes.

Ironically, the beast here emerges not to serve Machiavellian power schemes, but as a manifestation of an as-yet-unresolved psychological response having to do with animals. In a sense, Tony is back where we first found him: suffering panic attacks because ducks that once occupied his backyard pool have migrated for winter. But with one important difference: the ducks produced a neurological response that Tony could no more understand than control. When medical procedures and his own attempts to deal with the attacks failed, he took to the path of psychiatric "self-awareness." But here, he allows the beast to speak for the man. In a bizarre way, this constitutes success for Tony, a proactive response to emotional stimuli. When it is over, he is flushed and wary of others' responses but he manages the situation well, attempting to pass the buck onto Johnny Sack, who has a grudge against Ralphie for making a fat joke about his wife ("The Weight," 4.04) and turning the butchery and disposal of Ralphie's body into a bonding ritual with his nephew, Christopher. Yet this impulsive murder only reiterates Tony's original problem. By following his beastly instinct, by not exercising "impulse control," he has destroyed a valuable asset, not because Ralphie posed a risk, but because he was allegedly doing his job, generating income. In the end, we are left to wonder whether Tony will ever achieve the Machiavellian ideal of power (a temperate model, compared to Tony's example), or "self-awareness," or if indeed they are for him one and the same. Perhaps what Tony has failed to recognize is the extent to which the beast prevents him from realizing his original goal: to be a better leader, a better Prince.

14.

"BLACK GUYS, MY ASS"

UNCOVERING THE QUEERNESS OF RACISM
IN *THE SOPRANOS*[1]

Brian Gibson

> Is the lynching of the Negro not a sexual revenge?
>
> *Frantz Fanon*

In a series set in a macho Italian-American mobster world dominated by plans for a new scam, whispers about another power play, or orders for the next hit, it may seem that *The Sopranos* largely ignores homosexuality and race. The show's seemingly uncomplicated homophobia has gone unexamined, while one critic has observed that the "problem so central to understanding the American condition that is almost never confronted on [the show] is racism" (Simon 227). In many episodes, however, concerns about effeminacy and African American males swirl around each other, and this implicit, connected fear of gays and blacks reveals the panicked masculinity at the heart of David Chase's series. In an "old school" Mafioso world where words explode into deadly action and base prejudices are expressed with a gun, "Unidentified Black Males" (5.09) darkly crystallizes the violent gay and racial panic that has always run through Tony's notion of his "fucking" masculinity and untangles the queer racism of *The Sopranos*' male-bonding patriarchy, a sexualized bigotry that fuelled a different mob of white males a century earlier and which lies at the festering heart of American black-white relations.

Lynching remains the ugliest symbol of race relations in the post-Civil War USA. From 1880 until 1930, more than 2,500 African American men were lynched in the South because their "purported desire for white women and white power threatened the moral and social order of the traditional, patriarchal South" (Wood 195). Generations "of Southern whites ... had it constantly dinned into their ears from pulpit and press, in the home and school and on the street, that Negroes are given to sex crimes, that only lynching can protect white women" (White 6). Although the vast majority of interracial rapes were committed by white men against black women, African American men were repeatedly hanged to death by white mobs for supposedly violating white women.[2] Lynchings became public, "elaborate, highly ritualized tortures" (Wood 195) during which the victims were often castrated; white men removed the testicles or cut off the penis of one in three lynching victims (Brundage 66). The castration of the victim "enabled a perverse ... physical intimacy between the white male aggressor and his captive ex-slave," and thus "one encounters a sadistic enactment of the homoerotic at the moment of its most extreme disavowal" (Wiegman 99). In their emasculation and visual consumption of the conquering of the virile African American victim's supposed sexual rapacity, "[l]ynching provided a queer satisfaction" for white mob killers, concludes William F. Pinar, but by insisting on the victim as both "'fiend' and 'rapist,' white men were also conferring upon him 'stud' status" (7). Pinar argues that white men placed white women above and black men below themselves in their imagination:

> Black men [were] not stripped of sexual desire; indeed they became saturated with it. In order to protect themselves from facing their desire for black male bodies, white men positioned the black man as rapaciously desiring the white woman ... both the "white woman" and the "black man" were dissociated but bonded and sexualized elements in the white male mind.
>
> (11–12)

This psycho-sexual dynamic of the most appalling spectacles of American race-relations—the man's simultaneous idealization and dismissal of women combined with a perverse, sexually violent hatred of the African American male, in order to suppress the man's feelings of effeminate weakness and homoerotic fascination with the hyper-virile African American male body—surfaces again and again in the mob world of *The Sopranos* and is the masculine crisis at the root of Tony's panic attacks.

THE DREAD OF EMASCULATION

Dr. Melfi:	You're not respectful of women. ... I couldn't bear witness to violence or—
Tony:	Fuck you! (*leaves office; heard through slammed door*) You're a fuckin' cunt!

("The Two Tonys," 5.01)

In a world of "faggots and crybabies runnin' around," as he tells his psychotherapist, Tony Soprano longs for the "old school" patriar-chy of his father's heyday in the mob and idolizes the Gary Cooper and John Wayne models of strong, silent manliness. But while Tony claims "in this house, it's 1954" ("Nobody Knows Anything," 1.11), he often defers to women outside his male mob world, where Carmela wields power as the woman of the house, the image of the loyal wife, and the profit-sharer in the marriage, Dr. Melfi allows Tony to vent his frustrations while unknowingly giving him strategic business tips, and even young, independent Meadow gets her way. Tony over-ideal-izes the women in his life, romancing Melfi and calling both Carmela and Meadow his Italian-American princesses (4.12), while telling his fellow mobsters that his father's callous, self-deluding mistress, too, is "like a princess" ("In Camelot," 5.07). Tony's and his fellow mobsters' upbringings taught them to honor mothers and wives, and like South-ern white men, who "had pedestalized white women in their minds ... they had violated the equal humanity of women and removed them, in some degree, from possibilities of real intimacy with themselves" (Williamson 306–7). Tony's infatuation with his psychiatrist blinds him to the realization that she would never be able to accept his crimi-nal lifestyle; his marriage is increasingly based on monetary negotia-tions, not love; and he finds it difficult to relate to his daughter.

But in the New Jersey godfather's all-male world, women are marginalized, sexualized figures, "viewed exclusively as commodities" (Donatelli and Alward 71). They are bored strippers dancing in the background at the Bada Bing club or a series of unnamed *goomahs* flitting in and out of the gangsters' beds. From his fantasies about Jeannie Cusamano ("I Dream of Jeannie Cusamano," 1.13) and Annalisa ("Commendatori," 2.04), to his actual screwing of the born-again secretary at Barone Sanitation ("House Arrest," 2.11), Tony has casual sex with women "doggie style," so that he has utter control of the act and does not have to look at their faces. Tony assaults every one of his long-time mistresses and has Patsy threaten to kill Gloria to keep her away from him ("Amour Fou," 3.12), but viewers never see him hit Carmela. Tony's toxic view of women only spills into his private world through his bawdy/body language, especially his references to Livia, his Machiavellian, malevolent mother who is the abiding reason for Tony's anger, his hang-ups, and his idealization/dismissal treatment of women in his family/women in his underworld.

Although Tony, as part of an Italian-American, Roman Catholic family, was raised to honor his mother, he blames scheming, mean Livia for much of the misery in his life and in his father's; while his mother was alive, Tony would often say, "She's dead to me," and, even after her death, describes her to Melfi as "that fucking miserable selfish cunt. She ruined my father's life" ("Proshai, Livushka," 3.02). Tony is caught between living up to his romanticized image of his tough-guy father, Johnny, who praised him for not "running like a little girl" out of the deli when he witnessed an act of violence against Mr. Satriale ("Fortunate Son," 3.03) but then called his son's first panic attack "fainting," and fleeing his emasculating mother, her dominance in her son's psyche epitomized by Tony's dream in the first episode of the series, where he imagines a bird flying off with his penis. Melfi interprets this image as Tony's fear of being unsexed by his powerful mother, whom Tony forever associates with betrayal after the dissimulating Livia tries to have him whacked. Tony's fear of being dominated and betrayed by his mother's emasculating effeminacy likely derives from an Oedipus complex, as Gabbard notes, in which "the attack on his manhood and his self-esteem ... comes from Livia

... Mom—not Dad—is the real threat to Tony, and on some level he has always known it but has deeply repressed it" (102). Tony is a sociopathic epitome of "'splitting,' which is the tendency to idealize someone and then furiously to demonize them when they reject or disappoint" (Siegel, "Attraction" 46).

Tony's demonizing of his mother and idealizing of his father is part of his attempted backlash, from a regressive criminal underworld, at a modern society "in which traditional notions of manhood are reeling from the challenges of feminism and gay liberation" (Gardaphé 100), not unlike the crisis perceived by Southern men a century earlier, when, confronted by the New Woman and black emancipation, they beat a retreat into "a world compensating for ruined white masculinity" (Pinar 5). Masculinity in Tony's mob world is sex-based, for sex in Tony's criminal world is "about the order of power," where the business hierarchy means that the "man who places himself below a woman threatens the superior place of every other man in the gender order" (Rotundo 63), and the mobsters' control of their wives reflects their power as male bread-winners and "family" men. The made men's "fucking" masculinity is based on who's on top in bed, so Tony and his crew often control the strippers, prostitutes, and mistresses in their world by verbally reducing them to "cunts," suggesting their only worth is sexual.

"Cunts" in *The Sopranos* are merely brief receptacles for a hard, phallic masculinity, and otherwise pose the danger of being potentially betraying givers or receivers of pleasure. When Christopher, still in shock from the just whacked Adriana's cooperation with the FBI, tells Tony, "I thought she loved me," he sums up her betrayal flatly: "She's a cunt" ("All Due Respect," 5.13). Weak men are "pussies" and mocking men or nagging women are "busting balls," trying to break down a man's toughness. In Tony's backward-looking, crudely sexual patriarchy, non-wives must not be respected and, above all, they can never be submitted to or trusted. In "Boca" (1.09), for instance, Uncle Junior is complimented by his mistress Bobbie on his skill at cunnilingus, but his ashamed reaction suggests that it is his masculinity which will be consumed if such news ever leaks out:

Bobbie: If only they knew the other side of you...

Junior: They'd eat me for breakfast ... they think if you'll suck pussy, you'll suck anything. It's a sign of weakness. And possibly a sign that you're a *fanook* [fag] ... What're you gonna do? I don't make the rules.

To the mob patriarchy, cunnilingus means not only subordinating yourself to a woman by satisfying her—a "privileging of the feminine, a muffling of the male" (Walker 117)—but signifies effeminacy. Worse still, a man who will go down on a woman could as easily go down on a man, meaning he could be gay, or take a man down with him, that is, betray him. Thus effeminacy and homosexuality, in Tony Soprano's world, mean an utter erasure of tough-guy, "made man" masculinity—it *is* death.

THE THREAT OF EFFEMINACY

Carmela (to Tony): And what do you care, anyway, if someone's gay? It must be some big fear of yours or you wouldn't talk about it so much.

"Sentimental Education" (5.05)

Homophobia in Tony's homosocial mob world, where "a social structure without women raises questions about homoerotic desire in organized crime" (Donatelli and Alward 70), is linked to his mother-based fear of women as disloyal or untrustworthy. In the mindset of Tony's "fucking" masculinity, a homosexual is a "pussy," a penetrating, phallic man turned inside out who will allow himself to be penetrated by another man as easily as by G-Men, and so cannot be trusted. Tony confuses his concern that his longtime colleague Pussy has been "flipped" by the FBI—that is, turned on his masculine loyalty to the mob and become a non-man, a literal pussy—with his sexual obsession with pussy, an "ambiguity [that] confirms Pussy [and pussy, i.e., domineering, untrustworthy women like Livia] as the unacknowledged source of Tony's anxiety, his uncertainty about his safety and identity" (Yacowar 121), an anxiety that announces itself in the show's title, where Tony's surname sings out the notion of turning "state's evidence" and that "it is unmanly to betray one's gang" (16), as well as the underpinning matriarchy of his family. After a dream in which a fish (commonly associated with female genitalia, as in "Boca") tells him of Pussy's treachery, Tony searches for proof "beneath the Cuban cigars in Pussy's bedroom. As if to indulge a Freudian analyst, Pussy hid his betrayal under his cigars" (122).

The most humiliating, demeaning terms used by Tony and his crew about other men are homosexual slurs against them which exaggerate the ball-busters' own virility.[3] Incensed by Ralph's joke about his obese wife, Johnny Sack tells the wise-ass Ralph to "shove it up your ass" when he tries to give him money for his daughter's graduation ("Christopher," 4.03) and calls Ralph a "cute cocksucker" ("The Weight," 4.04). Soon after, in "Mergers and Acquisitions" (4.08), in which Ralph calls his buddies "fucking sick, all of youse," Tony justifies his merger with and acquisition of Ralph's *goomah* Valentina by confirming Ralph's non-masculine sexual habits, which he sees as deviations from the narrowly defined norms of mobster sexual machismo; thus Tony considers Ralph truly "fucking sick" because he likes sick fucking. Yet Ralph's masochism, Dr. Melfi suggests, can be traced back to an uncomfortably familiar past:

Tony: I received regular beatings when I was a kid, but I'm not going around looking for some woman to hook up jumper cables to my private parts...

Melfi: More than likely, he had a controlling and punishing mother. She loved him, but showed it only in connection with some sort of violent or abusive act.

Ralph's sexuality is the result of having a Livia-like matriarch. After Janice explains to her brother that Ralph can't enjoy "plain old fucking," the camera cuts to a shot of Tony reaching orgasm with Valentina. Tony can now make her his regular *goomah*, for after getting "my head into a place where I felt that I could really commit" and, unlike Ralph, getting off on "plain old fucking" her, he asserts his "normal," dominant masculine sexuality over his subordinate's effeminate, mother-formed sexuality. Ralph's private sexual submission to women, exemplified by his queer gender-switching when he has Janice screw him from behind with a strap-on dildo ("Christopher"), makes him seem an impotent, passive liar to Tony and a traitor who, like the rat Pussy, is hiding his false male loyalty beneath an exaggerated hard-guy image. So when Ralph lies about burning down a stable to collect the insurance (the fire killed Tony's favorite filly, and he is always protective of what he regards as innocent, feminized nature), Tony kills him in a bloody brawl in that space of domesticated femininity, the kitchen ("Whoever Did This," 4.09). As with Junior's special skill, male softness in private (parts) affects the importance of public respect and keeping "face" in a business where, as Tony tells Chris and Chris reminds himself and Adriana, "we're soldiers" and, as Tony says to Janice when she asks him why he's looking into Ralph's sex life ("Mergers and Acquisitions"), "you know, like the army, it's got policies about this shit, on account of combat." Tony's world, a "paramilitary patriarchy" (Gabbard 158), reflects the nation-state's armed forces, where "enemy men [are seen] either as sexual demons, bent on raping nationalist women, or as ... incapable of manly virility" (Nagel 406), while, within the ranks, the mere suspicion of an unmanly sexuality threatens the soldiers' male-bonding world. The male bond intact, cousin-warriors Tony and Chris dispose of Ralph's disloyal body.[4]

For Tony, being able to define a male's sexuality is key to maintaining the patriarchal tradition and loyalty in his business, where phallic masculinity is one's only acceptable self-identity and "betrayal and the loss of identity are synonymous" (Walker, "Cunnilingus" 115). Un-masculinity/homosexuality means secrecy and treachery, as with Pussy—about whom Paulie says, "I loved that cocksucker like a brother and he fucked me in the ass" ("To Save Us All from Satan's Power," 3.10)—and "that cute cocksucker" Ralph. Tony's closed-mindedness about "fags" is a crucial, traditional male holdover from his childhood. It is a legacy he seems to have passed on to A. J., too, who calls Carmela's parents' good friend Russ Fegoli "Doctor Faggio" ("Marco Polo," 5.08) and says that Mr. Wegler put his "faggy hands" on him ("Irregular Around the Margins," 5.05).

When Carmela, in an argument with Tony sparked by his suggestion that her secret lover, Mr. Wegler, is gay, suggests that Tony has a "little secret" himself ("Irregular Around the Margins"), she touches on the dark truth of Tony's reason for originally subjecting himself to Dr. Melfi's probing. His panic attacks, that "putrid, rotten, fucking Soprano gene" ("Army of One," 3.13) which Tony thinks causes the effeminate "fainting" that Tony's father saw him suffer (3.03), plague A. J. as well. Tony associates his son with Mr. Wegler, whom they both later mock, when he sees him with his eyebrows shaved after a drunken prank: "If you've got some kind of sexual proclivity with that teacher or whatever..." ("All Happy Families," 5.04). When Tony learns that A. J. has shown an interest in "event planning," he says, "It's gay, isn't it?" and then lies down on the bed, befuddled ("All Due Respect"). Tony's homophobia is an attempt to mask his fear of mother-driven, castrating effeminacy and his anxiety about his sole patriarchal endowment of panic attacks in an effort to maintain the façade of his simplistic, phallic, mob boss masculinity.

THE FEAR OF A BLACK PENIS

"Fucking niggers. Well, who else, huh? Who else?"

A car-jacking victim in "Commendatori"

Another deep-seated prejudice formed in Tony's mother-dominated childhood (Livia calls her housekeeper a "*ditsoon*" in "46 Long," 1.02), and thus linked to his fear of effeminacy, is racism towards African Americans. Tony sees African Americans as having taken over his old home turf and, in "Watching Too Much Television" (4.07), a nostalgic Tony takes A. J. to see the old neighborhood in Newark, telling his son that "this neighborhood used to be beautiful, one hundred per cent Italian." Tony's adoption of a traditional, American WASP majority mindset about homosexuality and racism signifies his patriarchy's attempt to embrace a white masculinity and break away from an historical association with minority groups such as African Americans: "Immigrants from the *Mezzogiorno* had already experienced racist categorization by Northern Italians, and after coming to this country they again faced discourses like those directed at blacks to position them as 'lazy, criminal, sexually irresponsible, and emotionally volatile'" (Baker and Vitullo 215, quoting Orsi 314–15).

African American men are associated with trouble and crime in Tony's post-immigrant, neo-white world and often used as scapegoats and lackeys by the mob,[5] but they are primarily the target of racism because of a basic fear. African Americans threaten the mobsters because of the long-held stereotype of the black male as hyper-sexual predators. The made men in *The Sopranos* attempt to emasculate their perceived hyper-masculine, African American enemy through macho violence or homophobic slander, for "notions of black depravity rested on both the black man's emasculation and the white man's hypermasculine honor" (Wood 196). When Chris faces construction site protesters, he mocks the African American man who confronts him with a homophobic and then misogynistic taunt, "You wanna talk to the foreskin?" In response to being called a "motherfucker," Christopher replies, "Keep your mother off the streets and I won't fuck her" ("Do Not Resuscitate," 2.02). Carmela sits silently in the car as Tony, in "Another Toothpick" (3.05), curses Officer Willmore, an African American cop who writes him a ticket for speeding on their way home from Melfi's office, saying to his wife, "This fuckin' smoke's actually writin' me up—affirmative action cocksucker," and he later calls the cop "Shaft," combining the name of a blaxploitation film character with the anal sex-suggestive phrase "getting the shaft" in his efforts to invert the hyper-phallic masculinity of the stereotypical African American male by marking him as gay.

Any member of Tony's all-male second family, whose masculinity clearly operates, as racial psychoanalyst Frantz Fanon puts it, "on the genital level," hates African American men because "he is yielding to a feeling of impotence or sexual inferiority" (159). In "A Hit is a Hit" (1.10), gangsta rapper Massive Genius shows off his big silver gun to Chris, emphasizing that he's packing but Chris isn't. Later, Massive lasciviously eyes Adriana in front of Chris as she dances. The mobsters' fear of African American men stems from a panicked psycho-sexual neurosis, outlined in Fanon's chapter "The Negro and Psychopathology," that savage, cannibalistic black men will sexually devour their white women and, by extension, rape the mobsters by penetrating their women, who are reflections of their patriarchal power. As Fanon writes, from the perspective of the white male:

> As for the Negroes, they have tremendous sexual powers. ... They copulate at all times and in all places. They are really genital. They have so many children that they cannot even count them. Be careful, or they will flood us with little mulattoes ...
>
> Our women are at the mercy of the Negroes.
>
> (157)

Tony doesn't hesitate to voice this base fear, the root of his bigotry, when he meets Noah, Meadow's half-Jewish, half-African American boyfriend.

> Tony: You're a *ditsoon*. A charcoal briquette. A *mulignan*.
> Noah: What's your problem?
> Tony: I think you know what my problem is. You see, your little friend up there, she didn't do you any favors bringing you into this house. Now, I don't know what the fuck she was thinking. We'll get to that later. See, I got business associates who are black. And they don't want my son with their daughters and I don't want their sons with mine.
> Noah: Fuck you.
> Tony: See, that's the kind of thing I'm hoping to avoid.
>
> ("Proshai, Livushka," 3.04)

Tony, careful to call Meadow (an apt name considering that Tony often feels violently protective of nature *and* women) Noah's "friend," not girlfriend, cannot endure the thought of an African American having sex with his daughter and, by extension, "fucking" him. Tony, like many white male supremacists, sees the African American male as so hyper-masculine that, in having sex with the women who are a reflection of his power, they are penetrating him as well, feminizing him; Tony is worried, as the white Southern man was, that the black man might violate his masculinity by violating the women for whom he acts as a protective patriarch.

After talking to Noah, Tony walks to the fridge, gets out some cold cuts, starts to have a panic attack, opens a cupboard only to see the logo on Uncle Ben's Converted Rice (an image obviously suggesting miscegenation), and passes out. The incident is forgotten for a time, as Tony's mother dies, but in fact Livia is directly related to Tony's panic attacks, not just his bigotry. In the following episode, "Fortunate Son" (3.03), Dr. Melfi discovers that Tony's panic attacks began when he saw his father cut off the butcher Satriale's pinky and then collect free meat from him, licking blood from it off Livia's finger at home, saying to her, "You like it standing with the bone in, huh, Li?" and then grabbing her behind. Melfi concludes that Tony's first panic attack came when he realized how his father fed his family after seeing "not only your mother and father's sexuality, but also the violence and blood so closely connected to the food you were about to eat." Melfi overlooks, however, Tony's concern about Meadow's sexual relations with Noah. Tony internalized an association of meat with sex, too, and seeing an African American male—whom Tony the proud, frequent barbecuer associates with meat when he slurs Noah as a "charcoal briquette"—as Meadow's boyfriend made him anxious about the possible "bone in" the daughter whom he wishes to protect as the father who brings home the bacon. Tony justifies his racism to Carmela with an appeal to the patriarchal family: "Yeah, if one of my sisters ever brought home a fuckin' butterhead, you know what my old man would do?" As Wood notes, "within Southern conceptions of honor, a man's masculine reputation was signified by his wife's (or daughter's, or sister's) virtue—to protect her purity was to assert his own masculinity" (Wood 204). Indeed, in Tony's seminal memory, before his panic attack, his father complimented him on not "running away like a little girl," thus marking the moment as an instance of a father recognizing the manhood of his son, part of the "homophobic passage" of a boy (Plummer 304), but also the beginning of Tony's self-loathing for ever seeming effeminate. Melfi also fails to see that, in Tony's association of meat with the phallus (and an effeminate rump as a sexualized object), he is connecting homosexuality with a carnal appetite; after all, in his argument with Carmela about identifying gay men, he calls them "bologna-smokers" (5.05).[6] Tony's deep fear of being too weak a man to prevent miscegenation is the unconscious legacy of, and a basis for, violent systemic acts of black-white racism in the USA.

A LYNCH-MOB MENTALITY

"fucking jigaboo cocksucking motherfuckers"
Tony in *"Unidentified Black Males"* (5.09)

The mobsters' verbal emasculation and imaginative lynching of African American males in order to bolster their phallic hardness and mask their effeminate paranoia resurfaces when Meadow has to introduce her newest boyfriend to her family, a meeting which introduces undercurrents of homosocial anxiety, homophobia, and racism that violently coalesce in "Unidentified Black Males." To Tony, the Italian-American background of his daughter's new boyfriend, Finn DeTrolio, is a welcome change from Noah and his successor, the power-hungry, blustering Jackie, Jr.,[7] who tried to fast-track his way into the patriarchy by murderously robbing a mob poker game (3.12). The death of Jackie, Jr., who was clipped from behind by the then-closeted Vito Spatafore in the ghetto where he was holed up ("The Army of One," 3.13),[8] is blamed on African American drug dealers. Meadow is complicit with this scapegoating when, after Jackie, Jr.'s funeral, she turns on his sister and, in an echoing of her mother's ignorantly ironic chastisement of her earlier ("Like a lot of other people, you go around looking for bogeymen to blame. Bogeymen with Italian names"), she lights into Kelli Aprile for blaming their fathers' line of business for her brother's death, concluding, "some loyalty?"

Finn puts Tony at ease when, after Carmela frets about the security of Meadow's apartment, he puts his hand around hers and says, "I'll protect her. Don't worry." A protective, Italian-American man is what Tony wants for his daughter, though he is a little perturbed by the fact that roommate Colin lives there but Finn does not, a situation that Tony tries to brush off by thinking Colin is gay (when he realizes Colin is straight, he becomes anxious again). A. J. unconsciously alludes to the university Jackie, Jr. dropped out from, saying, "I'll go to Rutgers, I guess," and then talks about a book report he wrote on Herman Melville's *Billy Budd*,[9] in which Carmela sees a metaphor for innocent Furio (whom she desires) being bullied by her brutish husband. So she vociferously objects to A. J.'s teacher, then Mr. Wegler, saying "It's a gay book," an observation that Finn says he's "heard ...

before." When A. J. says, "I didn't even know they had fags [in the nineteenth century]," Finn jokes, "I read where they found gay cave drawings in Africa."

This conversation sets up the homosexuality of Mr. Wegler in Tony's and A. J.'s minds, while Finn's pseudo-racist joke linking homosexuality to primitive man in Africa touches on the notion of innate, age-old masculinities, whether gay or savagely sexual. Carmela's complaints about the constant talk of homosexuality—"this gay nonsense they're teaching"; "It's ridiculous how everything's being sold as homosexual nowadays"—utter a feeble complicity with Tony's vocal gay-bashing (and foreshadows the hypocrisy of Carmela's defense of Mr. Wegler's mocked sexuality when she is sleeping with him), a complicity that echoes Meadow's racial scapegoating at Jackie, Jr.'s wake or Carmela's silence during Tony's slurs against Officer Wilmore in "Another Toothpick" (3.05). In that same episode, Vito Spatafore's brother Bryan is badly beaten by a thug named Mustang Sally, and Vito tells Tony, "I want this cocksucker to bleed from his ass, skipper."

In "Unidentified Black Males," it is Vito who marks Finn's anxiety-ridden initiation into the Soprano crew's macho world. Tony angrily reimburses Finn when he tries to pay for dinner, explaining, "When you have your own family, you pay." Finn's confusion about Tony's patriarchal values increases when Tony gets him an easy job at a construction site where he watches Vito and his fellow mobsters sit around and talk about baseball, a constant phallic theme and symbol of guys' culture throughout this episode where "the male bonding at the heart of the homosocial flirt[s] at the possibility of homosexuality" (Wyatt 52). The made men treat Finn like a buddy and talk to him about sports, even asking his opinion about a fantasy match-up in boxing, that white-controlled exhibit of homoerotic, black male athleticism: "If they fought today, both in their prime, Ali or Tyson?" When Eugene Pontecorvo and Little Paulie start "breaking balls" about each other's girlfriends, Eugene smashes a glass into Paulie's face and beats him. One of the guys, worried about the police, is quickly calmed by Vito: "What? I think I seen a couple a niggers runnin' that way." When the sickened Finn recounts the episode to Meadow, asking her if she has seen such violence, she continues the self-delusion about her father's friends as nice family men that she showed after Jackie, Jr.'s death and again accuses another of scapegoating, telling Finn that her previous boyfriend was killed by "drug dealers ... African Americans, if that makes you feel any better." Meadow reacts to Finn's account with disbelief—"Eugene Pontecorvo? He's so sweet"—echoing Tony's words to Carmela when she suggests divorce: "First of all, we're Italian. We don't believe in divorce. We believe in the nuclear family." Meadow's defense of her father's two families against perceived African American and gay threats is a reflection of a white masculine world that sees African American males as criminals or potential rapists and "the homosexual as being opposed to the family" (Plummer 28).

When Finn shows up to work early one morning, he spies Vito fellating a security guard in a car. Later, stepping out of the porta-potty, "Mr. John" ("john," of course, can also refer to a gay prostitute's client), he finds Vito standing there, demanding that Finn call him by his first name and that they go to the Yankees game that night. Vito knows that being outed in Tony's world means death, because if he can hide his non-masculinity, he can't be trusted (a notion bolstered by Vito's treacherous suggestion in "All Due Respect" that Tony should be killed if he doesn't resolve the cold war with Johnny Sack quickly), but he cannot kill a civilian who is dating his boss's daughter, so he falls back on male-bonding, acts intimidating and macho, and exhorts Finn to be chummy with him. Vito has pretended to "break balls" with the other guys and talk up his male prowess—boasting about how Adriana "can suck this pipe any time she wants" ("Irregular Around the Margins," 5.05)—but such homosociality, symbolized by Vito waiting under the big, phallic bat symbol outside the stadium for Finn, is a thin veneer for his underlying homosexuality, a truth that will get you killed in the mob world.[10]

Finn realizes that Vito must cover up his homosexuality at all costs.[11] Finn equates Vito's homosexuality with murder, hesitantly adopting Tony's homophobia to mask his fear that to be propositioned by a gay man is tantamount to fatal penetration. He tells Meadow, "He came on to me. Either that or he wants to kill me." Meadow again defends her father's patriarchy: "Vito Spatafore is a married man, Finn. I seriously doubt he wants to kill you." But Finn is so afraid of Vito that he's packed a bag to leave. Once Meadow sees this, she is angered by how Finn quitting his job will look to her father and cries, "This whole thing, this fight, this stuff with Vito, it's all about you not wanting to commit!" Meadow aligns Finn's expressed fear of Vito's homosexuality with an inability to be her male protector and heterosexual lover (i.e., is he afraid of being fucked by Vito or afraid of fucking her?) and, like her father, sees Vito's gayness as "a threat to [the mobsters'] patriarchal power derived from a version of family founded on heterosexual relationships in which women are loyal to male authority" (Baker and Vitullo 225). By the end of their fight, Finn breaks down, asks Tony's loyal daughter to marry him, and, cowed by Meadow's insistent defense of a phallic, patriarchal masculinity and the displacement of homosocial white violence onto African Americans, enters the Soprano family.

"Unidentified Black Males" begins with two family men, Tony and his cousin, Tony Blundetto, drinking beer and watching the ballgame on TV outside. Tony B., covering up the truth about being run over by Joey Peeps' car after he went behind Tony's back and killed him for Little Carmine,[12] says that he is limping because "two black guys jumped me." When Johnny Sack later tells Tony that a witness saw the shooter limping off, he nearly passes out, and, as Tony later talks to Dr. Melfi, she unearths the reason for his latest bout of panic attacks. Tony, who has long been haunted by becoming boss while his cousin went to jail for seventeen years because Tony missed a hijacking where Tony B. was arrested, told everyone that he was mugged by some "black guys" whose macho virility he lamely tries to invert: "the fucking jigaboo cocksucking motherfuckers." But Tony now admits to Melfi that this story, like Tony B.'s alibi for the night of Joey Peeps' murder, was a lie. In fact, that night seventeen years ago, Tony had a panic attack after arguing with his mother and cut his head open on the car door after he left the house, the son, both afraid and bad, literally running away from and out on her. Tony's guilt comes not just from the lie but from blaming hyper-masculine, tough black guys for what was in fact an effeminate fainting spell caused by his domineering mother, a racist-homophobic mask that Tony reveals with his Freudian language: "Black guys, my ass. I had a fight with my mother and I had a fuckin' panic attack! ... What am I gonna tell [Tony B.]? What am I gonna tell all of 'em? I had a fight with my mother and I fainted? That's why I missed the job. Jesus fucking Christ! ... Turns out I'm just a robot to my own fuckin' pussy-ass weakness."

Tony finally acknowledges the true, twinned fear at the root of his panic attacks, that "little secret" which Carmela touched on. From the narrow perspective of Tony's phallic masculinity, he sees his panic attacks as both feminine ("pussy"), in that they stem from his mother's dominance, and gay ("ass"), in that they are effeminate "fainting" spells, signs of unmanliness. Dominated by his mother and mocked for it by his father, who called the fits "fainting," he cannot let his fellow mobsters know that he's so weak, so he blames his "ass"-like effeminacy[13] on "black guys." He can't be "straight" with his men because he fears he is not "straight" enough to be their boss, so instead he twists his fear of his "pussy-ass" weakness and displaces it onto African American criminals, the only segment of society stereotyped as more masculine and criminal than Italian-American mobsters; it is, in fact, Tony who fears that he is the "cocksucking motherfucker," a son who is weak because of his all-powerful mother. Tony also displaces his weakness onto his once wannabe straight (i.e. civilian) cousin, telling him to "be straight with me," that is, to be a truthful, loyal adherent to the phallic masculinity of the mob, unlike the back-stabbing Pussy and Ralph. Tony finally decides, after telling Tony B. the truth about that night seventeen years earlier, to make sure his secret dies with his cousin, whom he calls a "two-faced cocksucker," again connecting homosexuality with deceit ("Long Term Parking," 5.12), but only revealing his shallow, "ego-defensive violence," whereby men "affirm their heterosexuality or masculinity by attacking someone who symbolizes an unacceptable aspect of their own personalities (e.g., homoerotic feelings or tendencies towards effeminacy)" (Herek 348). By the end of "Unidentified Black Males," thanks to the containment of gay panic through violent homosocial bonding and the repression of the fear of effeminacy with the creation of racial bogeymen, the Sopranos gain a new member while Tony's mob family will lose a member because of the "pussy-ass" guilt Tony B. constantly reminds the patriarch of.

In "The Test Dream" (5.11), Tony realizes that he is propping up his tough-guy façade with racial scapegoating and masked gay panic. In the dream, as he goes to the men's room with Annette Bening's husband, Bening tells him, "I don't want my husband coming out of there with just his cock in his hand," an image reminiscent not only of Michael Corleone's murder of Sollozzo in *The Godfather* but also of his castration dream in the first episode. Standing at the urinals, that site of homosocial anxiety created by the part-public unveiling of private parts, a shot rings out, Tony finds himself looking at Tony B. after he has whacked someone, and then an African American man says to him, "Wasn't that Tony there the guy you were supposed to cap to prevent this from happening?" Tony Soprano, still reluctant to admit his effeminate guilt, is confronted with it by the object of his scapegoating, and he says, "I don't know; I guess not." The crowd then runs after him, trying to chase him down as though they wish to lynch him (and also evoking Tony's recurring fear of being a toxic, Frankenstein-like monster). Here is Tony's wish for queer lynching come undone and revealed for what it is—a deep repression and displacement of the panic surrounding his effeminate weaknesses onto un-masculine gays and hyper-masculine African Americans, all in order to uphold his guise as the protecting, money-making patriarch. Tony, a man whose castration anxiety "is both ever-present and eternally repressed, another aspect of the mysterious, hidden Tony the straightforward surface man cannot control or comprehend" (Walker, "Cunnilingus" 117), unconsciously realizes that it is he who should be strung up and emasculated for his fundamentally cowardly, bigoted scapegoating, underpinned by misogyny and homophobia masking a mother-inspired, castration fear of dominating, treacherous effeminacy penetrating the mobsters' ranks.

In fact, Tony's simultaneous idealizations/dismissals of women and racist scapegoating/effeminacy-denial is a displacement-repression split. This split is part of Tony's and the mobsters' "precariously balanced image of masculinity that must be fiercely maintained to fend off any hint of weakness or femininity that might suggest homosexuality" (Gabbard 161), while the demonization and emasculation of the sexually predatory African American male allows the mobsters to feel like protective, hyper-masculine patriarchs who merely, as Tony tells Johnny Sack, "put food on the table for our families, our sons, the future. That's what's important" ("All Due Respect"). Elisabeth Young-Bruehl argues that hysterical types "act violently on their prejudices, which implies acting outward and usually targets the sexuality of their victims" and tend to "externalize affects" when "they diminish the sexuality of the males ... to the point of castration, emasculation ... to keep the victims in their place" (226).

Tony's repressive, displacing, phallic masculinity, upheld through hysterical means and similar to his mother's "kind of compartmentalization" (Gabbard 114), inextricably links him to the effeminate in a mob world where "men [are] haunted by the unacknowledged feminine undertow of their machismo" (Siegel, "Attraction" 41) and "the hysteria continually suffered by the masculine characters at the possibility of any form of emasculation [is] a possibility continually raised and continually denied by their own discourse" (Walker, "Cunnilingus" 117). The mobsters' attempted emasculation of the "stud"-liness of the African American male necessitates a queer focus on the African American phallus, and the attempted disempowering of African American males through penetrating their masculinity and stripping them of their hyper-virility suggests "that the desire to penetrate might invert into the desire to be penetrated" (Ross 315), thereby implicitly voicing homosexual desire.

Tony's attempts to stick to rigid definitions of an all-consuming, delusional, phallic masculinity seem hopeless on a show where the "fugue of shifting meaning inside each character goes on and on" and "Tony's subconscious, certainly, is catching up with him" (Siegel, "Attraction" 46), out of place and time in a modern world where multiple sexualities and masculinities proliferate, and even go amiss in his insular, patriarchal underworld. Not only do Tony's cover-ups, repressions, and lies lead to the deaths of his fellow mobsters, such as Ralph and Tony B., rather than their false, projected enemies, but they make widows of the wives that the patriarchy is supposed to protect. Since, as Siegel argues, *The Sopranos* is about interiority and the "really real unreality that results when inner life and outer life converge" (47), and, as Santo contends, there has been a shift from "a notion of masculinity that was essentially inward-focused ... to one that was outwardly visible" (84), Tony's queer racism stems from a fear of marginalized outer forces in his life (homosexuality, race) invading him and exposing his true fears of being weak, inferior, and generally unable to live up to white masculine ideals. Tony's basic anxiety, like many white males, concerns the exposure of this innermost fear: "If Americans were not so terrified of their private selves, they would never have needed to invent and could never have become so dependent on what they still call 'the Negro problem'" (Baldwin 477). The queer racism of Tony and his crew is slowly self-destroying, and at a time when the media and politicians in the "real world" manufacture talk of a clash of civilizations, an us vs. them dichotomy, and a shadowy enemy who wishes to destroy "our" way of life, there is a crucial lesson in The Sopranos' deadly tunnel vision of a patriarchal world which projects its own problems onto others and feebly ignores the faults and rifts within.

Appendix A

EPISODES, WRITERS, AND DIRECTORS

SEASON ONE

by Season | Consec. # | Title | Written by | Director | Air Date

1.01 | 1 | Pilot: The Sopranos | David Chase | Chase | 10 January 1999

1.02 | 2 | 46 Long | Chase | Chase | 17 January 1999

1.03 | 3 | Denial, Anger, Acceptance | Mark Saraceni | Nick Gomez | 24 January 1999

1.04 | 4 | Meadowlands | Jason Cahill | John Patterson | 31 January 1999

1.05 | 5 | College | Jim Manos, Jr. & Chase | Allen Coulter | 7 February 1999

1.06 | 6 | Pax Soprana | Frank Renzulli | Alan Taylor | 14 February 1999

1.07| 7 | Down Neck | Robin Green & Mitchell Burgess | Lorraine Senna | 21 February 1999

1.08 | 8 | The Legend of Tennessee Moltisanti | Renzulli & Chase | Tim Van Patten | 28 February 1999

1.09 | 9 | Boca | Jason Cahill & Green & Burgess | Andy Wolk | 7 March 1999

1.10 | 10 | A Hit is a Hit | Joe Bosso & Renzulli | Matthew Penn | 14 March 1999

1.11 | 11 | Nobody Knows Anything | Renzulli | Henry J. Bronchtein | 21 March 1999

1.12 | 12 | Isabella | Green & Burgess | Coulter | 28 March 1999

1.13 | 13 | I Dream of Jeannie Cusamano | Chase | Patterson | 4 April 1999

SEASON TWO

by Season | Consec. # | Title | Written by | Director | Air Date

2.01 | 14 | Guy Walks into a Psychiatrist's Office | Cahill | Coulter | 16 January 2000

2.02 | 15 | Do Not Resuscitate | Green & Burgess & Renzulli | Martin Bruestle | 23 January 2000

2.03 | 16 | Toodle-Fucking-Oo | Renzulli | Lee Tamahori | 30 January 2000

2.04 | 17 | Commendatori | Chase | Van Patten | 6 February 2000

2.05 | 18 | Big Girls Don't Cry | Terence Winter | Van Patten | 13 February 2000

2.06 | 19 | The Happy Wanderer | Renzulli | Patterson | 20 February 2000

2.07 | 20 | D-Girl | Todd A. Kessler | Coulter | 27 February 2000

2.08 | 21 | Full Leather Jacket | Green & Burgess | Coulter | 5 March 2000

2.09 | 22 | From Where to Eternity | Michael Imperioli | Bronchtein | 12 March 2000

2.10 | 23 | Bust Out | Renzulli & Green & Burgess & Chase | Patterson | 19 March 2000

2.11 | 24 | House Arrest | Winter | Van Patten | 26 March 2000

2.12 | 25 | The Knight in White Satin Armor | Green & Burgess | Coulter | 2 April 2000

2.13 | 26 | Funhouse | Chase & Kessler | Patterson | 9 April 2000

SEASON THREE

by Season | Consec. # | Title | Written by | Director | Air Date

3.01 | 27 | Mr. Ruggerio's Neighborhood | Chase | Coulter | 4 March 2001

3.02 | 28 | Proshai, Livushka | Chase | Van Patten | 4 March 2001

3.03 | 29 | Fortunate Son | Kessler | Bronchtein | 11 March 2001

3.04 | 30 | Employee of the Month | Green & Burgess | Patterson | 18 March 2001

3.05 | 31 | Another Toothpick | Winter | Jack Bender | 25 March 2001

3.06 | 32 | University | Teleplay by Winter & Salvatore Stabile, Story by Chase & Winter & Kessler & Green & Mitchell Burgess | Coulter | 1 April 2001

3.07 | 33 | Second Opinion | Lawrence Konner | Van Patten | 8 April 2001

3.08 | 34 | He is Risen | Kessler | Coulter | 15 April 2001

3.09 | 35 | The Telltale Moozadell | Imperioli | Daniel Attias | 22 April 2001

3.10 | 36 | To Save Us All from Satan's Power | Green & Burgess | Jack Bender | 29 April 2001

3.11 | 37 | Pine Barrens | Winter | Steve Buscemi | 6 May 2001

3.12 | 38 | Amour Fou | Renzulli | Van Patten | 13 May 2001

3.13 | 39 | The Army of One | Chase & Konner | Patterson | 20 May 2001

SEASON FOUR

by Season | Consec. # | Title | Written by | Director | Air Date

4.01 | 40 | For All Debts Public and Private | Chase | Coulter | 15 September 2002

4.02 | 41 | No Show | Chase & Winter | Patterson | 22 September 2002

4.03 | 42 | Christopher | Imperioli & Maria Laurino | Van Patten | 29 September 2002

4.04 | 43 | The Weight | Winter | Jack Bender | 6 October 2002

4.05 | 44 | Pie-O-My | Green & Burgess | Bronchtein | 13 October 2002

4.06 | 45 | Everybody Hurts | Imperioli | Buscemi | 20 October 2002

4.07 | 46 | Watching Too Much Television | Chase & Green & Burgess & Winter | Patterson | 27 October 2002

4.08 | 47 | Mergers & Acquisitions | Chase, Green & Burgess & Winter | Daniel Attias | 3 November 2002

4.09 | 48 | Whoever Did This | Green & Burgess | Van Patten | 10 November 2002

SEASON FIVE

Appendix B

INTERTEXTUAL MOMENTS AND ALLUSIONS IN SEASONS FOUR AND FIVE

Intertext/Allusion	Annotation
54: Speaking of A. J.'s new career goal of becoming an event planner, Carmela notes that he watches that Mike Meyers film—54—about Steve Rubell all the time (5.13).	1998 film, directed by Mark Christopher, about the trendy Club 54 in New York.
Al-Qaeda: Johnny Sack blames a failed Vespa theft on increased port security because of it (5.10).	The shadowy Islamic terrorist network, lead by Osama Bid Laden, behind the 9/11 attacks.
Albinoni, Tomaso. Richard LaPenna suggests his music would make the perfect score for the clash between Native American and Italian protestors on Columbus Day (4.03).	(1671–1751) influential Italian composer.
Ali, Mohammed: At the construction site, the boys ask Finn to settle a debate about who would win in an in-their-prime fight between Ali and Tyson (5.09).	(1942–). American boxer, born Cassius Clay, one of the greatest heavyweight champions of the 20th Century and one of the most famous athletes in the world.
"All debts public and private": The title of the first episode of Season Four (4.01).	These words are to be found on US currency.
"All Happy Families." The title of a fifth season episode (5.04).	The first sentence of Tolstoy's *Anna Karenina* is: "All happy families resemble one another, each unhappy family is unhappy in its own way."
Animal Farm: Mr. Wexler explains to Carmela that A. J. has turned in a "surprisingly cogent" draft on it (5.06).	Anti-Stalinist allegory by British writer George Orwell, published in 1944.
A-Team, The: Adriana watches it on TV while she waits for Christopher to come home (4.07).	American television series (1983–1987), created by David Chase's friend and collaborator Stephen J. Cannell, starring George Peppard and Mr. T.
Bailey's Irish Cream: Christopher warns his mother to stay off it (4.01).	A popular liqueur.
Barrymore, John: At Uncle Junior's Feech greets Tony with "Hey, John Barrymore" (5.02).	(1882–1942) Distinguished American actor and ladies man, most famous for his portrayal of Hamlet.

"Bartleby": With Rosie Aprile's depression in mind, Janice laments, "Ah, Bartleby. Ah, humanity" (4.02).	These are the last words of an 1854 novella by Herman Melville about a depressed scrivener who "would prefer not to" do anything.
Batali, Mario: Carmela watches *Mario Eats Italy* on TV while she cooks (4.08).	The famous Italian chef Mario Batali hosts *Mario Eats Italy* on The Food Network.
Bay of Pigs, The: Fran Felstein tells Tony her affair with JFK began just before the Bay of Pigs (5.07). See also Kennedy, John Fitzgerald.	Botched, secret invasion of Cuba, intended to overthrow Fidel Castro's communist rule of the Island, and one of the major failure of the Kennedy presidency.
Beatles, The: Trying to find "common ground" with A. J., Carmela makes small talk about Ringo Starr and Pete Best (5.04).	British group whose music forever changed the face of rock and roll.
Beethoven: Bobby Bacala's children watch it on TV after Sunday dinner (5.07).	1992 movie about a St. Bernard, starring Charles Grodin and Bonnie Hunt.
Bening, Annette: In Tony's "test dream" she appears as Finn's mother (5.11).	(1958-). American film actress, star of such movies as *The Grifters*, *Bugsy*, and *American Beauty*, and wife of actor/director Warren Beatty.
Best, Pete: See Beatles, The (5.04).	The original drummer of the Beatles.
Billy Budd: A. J. has to write a paper on it which leads to a later discussion about its possible gay subtext (4.12).	Posthumously published novella by Herman Melville about the fatal clash between master-at-arms Claggart, a sinister ship's officer, and an innocent sailor.
Body by Jake: Adriana watches an infomercial for it while waiting for Christopher to come home (4.05).	A popular American line of home exercise equipment.
Bugsy: In Tony's "test dream" Annette Bening insists that "There's something Bugsy about [Tony]" (5.11).	1991 biopic about gangster Bugsy Siegel, directed by Warren Beatty, and starring Beatty and Annette Bening.
Bunche, Ralph: At a construction site Patsy Parisi attacks a bystander with a crow bar who is about to call the cops, asking the African American "Who do you think you are, Ralph Bunche or something?" (4.02).	(1904-1971). African American educator and diplomat who won the Nobel Peace Prize in 1950.
Bush, George W.: Being tested for mental competence, Uncle Junior correctly identifies the current President of the United States (4.09).	George Walker Bush became the 43rd President of the United States in 2001.
Caan, James: A Mohawk tells Silvio that Iron Eyes Cody's possible non-Indianness matters about as much as his not being Italian (4.03).	(1940-). Jewish American actor best known for his role as Sonny Corleone in *The Godfather*.

"Called the English teacher Daddio": Entering a meeting with Mr. Wegler, Tony says "Let me guess. He [A. J.] called the English teacher daddio?" (5.04).	Lyrics from the hit 1959 song "Charlie Brown" by The Coasters
Camelot: The title of a fifth season episode is "In Camelot" (5.07).	Originally the legendary palace of King Arthur, "Camelot" came to be a name for the presidency of John Fitzgerald Kennedy.
Cannon: In Tony's memory of his mother's miscarriage, and his father's infidelity with Fran Felstein he is watching it on TV (5.07).	The private detective drama *Cannon*, starring William Conrad, ran from 1971 to 1976.
Canon, The: Meadow tells her mother she read "half the canon" while lying by the pool (4.02).	The "official" list of acceptable/sanctioned writers in the Western tradition.
CCCY vs. Kentucky: When Bobby Bacala recalls, after his death, that Carmine was a great man who invented, point shaving, Uncle Junior names the game and year, "CCNY vs. Kentucky, 1951" (5.02).	A basketball game between City College of New York and the University of Kentucky was fixed by mob interference, the tip of the iceberg of a larger betting scandal stretching back several years and involving seven schools.
Chef Boyardee: Tony tells Silvio that Italian self-esteem doesn't come from "Columbus or The Godfather or fuckin' Chef-Boyardee" (4.03).	A popular line of low quality canned Italian food that introduced the cuisine to many Americans.
Children's Television Workshop: Dr. Freid's daughter is marrying one of their puppeteers (5.04).	The PBS-affiliated organization that produces the long-running children's television program *Sesame Street*.
Christmas Carol, A: In Tony's "test dream" it is playing on the TV in his kitchen (5.11).	The classic, often filmed, Charles Dickens novel about Ebeneezer Scrooge. The version in this episode appears to be the 1938 black and white film starring Reginald Owen as Scrooge.
Churchill, Sir Winston: Tony watches a History Channel documentary about him and asks Carmela if she saw "that TV movie about him" (4.05).	Albert Finney played Winston Churchill in *The Gathering Storm* (2002), an HBO movie about the run-up to World War II.
Citizen Kane: The first movie the mob wives watch in their new film club (5.02).	1941 film by first time director Orson Welles (who also starred as Kane), often considered the greatest film ever made.
Clark, Mary Higgins: Carmela comments sarcastically that her books have been Meadow's only summer reading after her first year at Columbia (4.02).	(1929–). Prolific American author of best-selling suspense novels.

Cleaver, Eldridge: Moe refers to him as the model for his own renunciation of violence (4.07).	(1935–1998). Black militant leader of the 1960s, later a pacifist Christian, author of the autobiography *Soul on Ice*.
CliffsNotes: A. J.'s English teacher Carmela tries to help A. J. understand *Lord of the Flies* using them. Later, Tom Fiske describes his latest paper as 10% effort and 90% CliffsNotes (5.06).	Academic study aids used by students since 1958.
Cody, Iron Eyes: Ralphie insists that the actor and Native American icon was not really an Indian (4.03).	(1907–1991). Actor and Native American activist, born Espera Oscar DeCorti.
Color Tile: Carmela and Furio make plans to meet at one of their stores (4.12).	American store chain selling flooring of all kinds.
Copa, The: Fran Felstein claims to have first met JFK there (5.07). See also Kennedy, John Fitzgerald.	A swanky New York night club, the Copacabana has been a prominent setting in both television (*I Love Lucy*) and film (*GoodFellas*).
Corleone, Don: A. J.'s friend wants to know why his dad doesn't have that "Don Coreleone money" (4.06). Feech calls Tony "Don Corleone" after he gives him a share of a big poker game (5.04).	The godfather of *The Godather*, played in the 1972 film by Marlon Brando and (as a young man) by Robert DeNiro in the 1974 film.
Corleone, Fredo: English teacher Tom Fiske compares A. J. to him (5.06).	The ineffectual, bumbling, traitorous Corleone son, played by John Cazale in both *The Godfather* and *The Godfather II*.
Course in Miracles, A: The receptionist at Eleuthera House is reading it when Christopher checks in (4.10).	A self-help manual published by The Foundation for Inner Peace.
Crane, Ichabod: Tony B. confessed to Christopher that "some very sorry people" once called him this (5.10).	The gangly, fearful school teacher in Washington Irving's "The Legend of Sleepy Hollow."
"Creeps in this petty pace": Johnny Sack refers to waiting for Carmine to die using this phrase (4.13).	From the famous "To be or not to be" soliloquy in Shakespeare's *Hamlet*.
Cuomo, Mario: A D'Angelis' relative visiting Hugh's 75th birthday party is considered very special because he once shook hands with him (5.08).	(1932–). Italian-American lawyer and politician, governor of New York from 1983–1994 and one-time Presidential candidate.
Curb Your Enthusiasm: Uncle Junior watches it on TV and, in his dementia, thinks Larry David is himself and Jeff Garlin is Tony (5.03).	HBO comedy series (2000–) created by and starring Seinfeld co-creator Larry David.

Dali, Salvatore: Paulie greets Salvatore Vito with "There he is, Salvatore, my dolly" (5.03).	(1904–1989). Eccentric, bizarre Spanish painter, the most notorious artist of the surrealist movement.
David, Larry: See *Curb Your Enthusiasm* (5.03).	(1947–). Acerbic American comic, co-creator of the hit sitcom *Seinfeld* (1989–1998) for NBC and, later, *Curb Your Enthusiasm* (2000–) for HBO, in which he also starred.
Death in Venice: A. J.'s next reading assignment after *Billy Budd* (4.12).	A 1930 novella by Thomas Mann about a writer who falls in love with a young boy.
DeWalt: Tony tells Tony B. that he can't find this tool (5.04).	An American company that makes power tools primarily for home use.
Dr. Phil: Tony quotes him to Dr. Melfi on the ethics of dating your psychiatrist (5.01).	Dr. Phillip C. McGraw (1950–) parlayed his appearances on the *Oprah Winfrey Show* into a role as one of the major self-help guru of the early 21st Century.
Dr. Strangelove: J. T. Dolan has a poster of it hanging in his apartment, which Little Paulie will later smash over his head (5.07).	1963 black comedy film about nuclear war, directed by Stanley Kubrick.
Earl Scheib: Tony wonders if Feech has already gone there since his release from prison (5.01).	A chain of American auto painting and collision stores.
Eloise and Abelard: In after-sex pillow talk, Mr. Wexler tells Carmela about them, after she finds their letters as bathroom reading material (5.06).	A 12th Century priest and a nun whose affair was circumvented by the church but continued in a famous, later published series of love letters.
Emmy Award: A pawn shop dealer won't give J. T. Dolan more than $15 for his (5.07).	The Emmies are the annual awards, TV's most prestigious, given by the National Association of Television Arts and Sciences.
Enron: Tony counters Carmela's investment plans by insisting he doesn't have connections of this type (4.01).	Energy-trading corporation, destroyed in the early 21st century by the largest ever American business scandal.
Enya: Alan Sapinsly claims he has no problem working with a mobster, having been involved in "that Neapolitan copyright thing" for her (4.13).	(1961–). Irish-born Celtic and New Age musician.
Estrada, Erik: Christopher refers to him when Little Paulie voices his concern over cops on their cigarette run to North Carolina (5.05).	Puerto Rican-American actor who starred in the police series *CHiPs* (1977–83).
Faces of Death: Janice and Ralphie watch this on video (4.02).	1978 "documentary" by John Allen Schwartz, a compilation of gruesome death scenes, many real.

Favreau, Jon: Christopher recalls his encounter with him in "D-Girl" (5.07).	(1966–). American actor and director.
Fiedler, Leslie: In the debate over *Billy Budd*'s gayness, Meadow cites his work, which leads Carmela to suggest that he might be gay as well (4.12).	(1917–2003). Iconoclastic American literary critic, best known for his against-the-grain readings of classic American literature, especially his suggestion that Huck and Jim, in Twain's great novel, have a "homoerotic" relationship.
Fields, W. C.: The first evening after Tony moves back into the house he watches his *It's a Gift* on TV (5.12).	(1880–1946). Legendary American comic actor and writer, first in vaudeville, then in film.
Fluffernutter: Christopher asks his mother to make him one during a surprise visit (4.01).	A sandwich made with peanut butter and marshmallows.
Frida: Finn and Meadow watch it on DVD (5.04).	2002 Julie Taymor film about Mexican artist Frida Kahlo.
Fugitive, The: Tony and the installer watch it on his new home theatre system (4.08).	1993 Harrison Ford movie, based on a popular 1963–1967 television program, about a doctor on the run after being falsely accused of murder.
Garbo, Greta: Tony tells Svetlana she reminds him of her (4.10).	(1905–1990). Swedish-born film star of the 1920s and 1930s.
Garlin, Jeff: See *Curb Your Enthusiasm* (5.03).	American comic who plays Larry David's agent on *Curb Your Enthusiasm*.
Gleason, Jackie: Little Tony quotes Reginald van Gleason the Third to Tony: "Boy are you fat" (5.02). Tony B. does an imitation of one of his characters again in 5.08.	(1916–1987). Rotund American film and television comic and variety show host, best known for *The Honeymooners* and *The Jackie Gleason Show*.
Godfather, The: A. J.'s friend suggests he will never be drafted because his father will make an unrefuseable offer as in *The Godfather*.	Francis Ford Coppola's 1972 classic gangster film starring Marlon Brando.
Godfather II, The: Drawing comparisons to it, A. J.'s friend asks if he's worried about his house being attacked. Devin Pillsbury wants to know if the Sopranos also have a place in Tahoe (4.06).	Francis Ford Coppola's 1974 sequel to *The Godfather*, starring Al Pacino and Robert DeNiro.
Google: Adriana tells Tony that she used it to find information on Irritable Bowel Syndrome (5.05).	Internet search engine; its tremendous turn-of-the-century success made its name a synonym for searching the Web.

Harpie: Janice claims she didn't want to seem like one by complaining about Bobby Bacala's continued obsession with his dead wife (4.11).	According to the Internet Encyclopedia Mythica, "Harpies were described as beautiful, winged maidens. Later they became winged monsters with the face of an ugly old woman and equipped with crooked, sharp talons. They were represented carrying off persons to the underworld and inflicting punishment or tormenting them. Those persons were never seen again."
"Harpo's Song": The inspiration for Janice's son's name, Tony brings it up at a Sunday dinner in order to bate her into anger (5.10).	A 1973 song by Phoebe Snow.
Harry Potter books: Raymond Curto comments, enviously, that these are a "gold mine" (4.02).	The phenomenally successful Harry Potter books (six so far, beginning in 1997), written by J. K. Rowling, have made their author the richest woman in the UK.
Helgenberger, Marg: Bobby Bacala responds to Janice's sleuthing–she deduces that he's been to the cemetery by the dirt on his shoes–by saying "What are you Marg Higinbrenner now" (4.11).	(1958). American actress best known for her role as a Las Vegas police forensic expert in the hit television drama *C.S.I.: Crime Scene Investigation* (2000-).
High Noon: In Tony's "test dream" it is playing on the TV at Vesuvio's (5.11).	Classic 1952 Fred Zinnemann Western starring Gary Cooper as a sheriff who must face a gang of revengeful outlaws on his own
"The Highway was jammed with broken heroes on a last chance power drive"· Christopher explains his being late for a meeting by saying this (5.12).	Christopher quotes from the Bruce Springsteen song "Born to Run," the title song from a 1975 album.
Hitler, Adolf: Ruben insists, in a remark that angers Hesh, that Columbus "was no better than Hitler" (4.03).	(1889-1945). Founder of the National Socialist Party (the Nazis) and Führer and chancellor of Germany (1933-1945), whose dreams of a Third Reich provoked World War II.
Honeymooners, The: Tony, A. J., and Artie watch it on TV (5.04).	Classic 1950s television sitcom starring Jackie Gleason and Art Carney.
Horse Whisperer, The: Ralphie tells Tony, who is talking to Pie-Oh-My, to stop this "horse-whispering shit" (4.08).	*The Horse Whisperer* was a 1998 film directed by (and starring) Robert Redford, based on the best-selling book by Nicholas Evans.
How to Marry a Millionaire: Carmela watches it on TV while waiting for Tony to come home (4.12).	1953 film directed by Jean Negulesco and starring Betty Grable, Lauren Bacall, and Marilyn Monroe.

Hunchback of Notre Dame: See Quasimodo (4.01).	Novel by Victor Hugo (1802–1885), published in 1831.
"I don't want my husband coming out of there with just a cock in his hand": In Tony's "test dream" Finn's mother/Annette Bening uses these words when her husband and Tony go to the restroom (5.11).	This line recalls a similar one uttered in *The Godfather* (1972) by Sonny Corleone (James Caan) prior to the fateful meeting between Michael (Al Pacino) and Sollozzo and Captain McCluskey in an Italian restaurant.
"I Got you Babe": Bobby Bacala and Janice sing it after returning home after Uncle Junior's mistrial is declared (4.13).	A 1965 hit song by Sonny and Cher.
"I Shot the Sheriff": Tony listens to it in the kitchen (4.11).	A 1974 hit song by Eric Clapton, written by Bob Marley.
"Impossible Dream, The": See *Man of La Mancha* (4.12).	The most famous song from the musical *Man of La Mancha*, sung by Don Quixote.
James, Henry: Meadow recommends her parents read him to learn more about "the restorative nature of travel" (4.02). See also Robbins, Anthony.	(1843–1916). Incomparable American-born, expatriate (in the UK) fiction writer, many of whose novels are about Americans abroad.
Jehovah's Witnesses: Tony claims that they are more interesting than Jack Massarone (4.02).	An apocalyptic Christian denomination that uses the Hebrew name for the divine being and actively proselytizes worldwide.
Johnny Mnemonic: Christopher describes Uncle Pat's ability to remember where the Johnson brothers are buried being like him (5.10).	The titular character in a 1995 science fiction film, directed by Robert Longo, based on a short story by cyberpunk founder William Gibson.
Judas: After comparing Big Pussy to him, Rosie Aprile then adds that at least he didn't go into any "Apostle Protection Program" (5.02).	The infamous apostle who betrayed Jesus after the Last Supper, making his whereabouts known to the Roman authorities.
Kennedy, Jackie: Tony claims that she "thought the marriage was over" (5.07) because of Fran Felstein's affair with her husband.	(1929–1994). Jacqueline Lee Bouvier Kennedy Onassis was the wife of John Fitzgerald Kennedy, First Lady of the United States, and later the wife and widow of Greek shipping tycoon Aristotle Onassis.
Kennedy, John Fitzgerald: Being tested for mental competence, Uncle Junior incorrectly (but purposefully) identifies him as the POTUS preceding Bush (4.09). Fran Felstein claims to have an affair with him (5.07).	(1917–1963). 35th President of the United States (1961–1963), he had numerous affairs during his political career. He was assassinated in Dallas, Texas in November 1963.
Kiley, Richard: See *Man of La Mancha* (4.12).	(1922–1999). Stage and screen performer, whose performance in *Man of La Mancha* was one of his signature roles.

King of New York, The: Tony greets Johnny Sack in their first meeting after his becoming boss with this appelation (5.12).	1990 gangster film, directed by Abel Ferrara, and starring Christopher Walken.
Kreskin, The Amazing: Tony angrily insists he is not him (4.01).	(1935-). Psychic, mind reader, and entertainer, who made frequent appearances on American television in the 1960s and 1970s.
La Dolce Vita: Uncle Junior watches (but falls asleep during) a TV screening of it. He is not impressed by the fake Christ hanging from a helicopter (5.08).	Watershed (1960) Italian film, directed by Federico Fellini and starring Marcello Mastroianni.
LaRosa, Julius: Nucci and her "friends" remember him on a shopping trip (4.12).	(1930-). Handsome Italian-American singer and performer, best known for his appearance on television's *Arthur Godfrey Show*.
Lauren, Ralph: Janice cites Ralphie's wearing of his clothes as proof he has "a sense of style" Tony lacks (4.02).	(1939-). American fashion designer of high-end ready-to-wear clothing.
Law and Order: See Wolf, Dick (5.07).	A long-running (1990-) crime drama on American television set in New York, the flagship series of a variety of spinoffs.
Lawford, Peter: Fran Felstein mentions him being present when she first met JFK (5.07). See also Kennedy, John Fitzgerald, Rat Pack.	(1923-1984). American actor, a fellow traveler of The Rat Pack.
"Legend of Sleepy Hollow": Headed for upstate New York, Tony B. tells Christopher that the Disney cartoon version of this story scared "the piss out of me" when he was a child (5.10). See also Crane, Icahbod.	Washington Irving's famous short story about a school teacher's encounter with frightening "headless horseman."
Lemon, Jack: When Christopher returns from rehab, Tony greets him by asking "Hey Jack Lemon, where's Lee Remick" (4.13).	(1925-2001). Great American stage and screen actor, who starred with Remick in Blake Edwards' *Days of Wine and Roses* (1962)
LexisNexis: Uncle Junior laments how much he is paying his lawyer for "fuckin' lexus fees" (4.01).	A search service providing case-law information for the legal professional.
Little Rascals, The: Christopher watches an episode (with a guerrilla) while injecting himself with heroin (4.10).	"Our Gang, also known as The Little Rascals or Hal Roach's Rascals, was a long-lived series of comedy short films about a troupe of poor neighborhood children and the adventures they had together" (from Wikipedia.com)

Lord of the Flies: A. J. buys a paper on it on the Internet (5.06).	1954 novel by the British Nobel Prize winner William Golding (1911–1983) about school boys stranded on a desert island.
Lord of the Rings, The: Ralphie's son is seriously injured by an arrow as he and another boy act out scenes from it (4.09).	Peter Jackson's trilogy of films (*The Fellowship of the Ring* [2001], *The Two Towers* [2002], *The Return of the King* [2003]), based on J. R. R. Tolkien's classic fantasy novels, were a cultural sensation in the early twenty-first century.
Madame Bovary: Mr. Wexler recommends that Carmela read it (5.05, 5.06).	Classic 1857 novel by Gustave Flaubert (1821–1880) about a woman whose infatuation with Romance novels leads her to a tragic end.
Magnum, P.I.: On the television set as Christopher kills Barry Haydu, the cop who supposedly killed his father (4.01).	Popular American television show (1980–88) about an Hawaii-based private investigator played by Tom Selleck.
Malden, Karl: Paulie mentions him because his nose hair shows up very prominently in his new DVD version of On the Waterfront (4.10).	(1912–). American character actor, known for his strikingly unattractive face. In On the Waterfront he plays a priest who ministers to longshoremen.
Maltin, Leonard: At the mob wife movie club, Carmela reads his description of *Citzen Kane* (5.02).	(1950–). American movie critic and commentator, known for his video and DVD movie guides.
Man of La Mancha: At dinner after The Producers Paulie and Nucci recall it, and Paulie claims Richard Kiley sang "Impossible Dream" directly to his mother (4.12).	1960s musical version of the story of Don Quixote by Dale Wasserman, Mitch Leigh, and Joe Darion.
Meet the Press: Aunt Concheta dies of a heart attack while watching it (5.07).	Long-running (1947–) NBC Sunday morning news program, featuring interviews with major political figures.
Monroe, Marilyn: Fran Felstein mentions being aware that JKF had other women, including her (5.07). Later Fran does a disturbing version of her infamous "Happy Birthday" serenade of JKF. See also Kennedy, John Fitzgerald.	(1926–1962). American actress, the greatest sex symbol of the 1950s.
Morning Edition: FBI Agent Sanseverino is listening to it on NPR (5.12).	National Public Radio's morning news show, hosted, at the time, by Bob Edwards.
Mr. Clean: Tony greets laundry delivery man Tony B.'s entrance into the Bada Bing with "There he is, Mr. Clean" (5.03).	Eponymous 1950s and 60s American advertising icon—a bald, muscular man in a t-shirt—the spokesperson for a cleaning liquid.

Murder One: Adriana watches it on TV and gets the idea that she won't have to testify against Christopher if she marries him (4.07).	High concept, short-lived television drama (1995–1997) that devoted an entire season to a single murder trial.
Nash Bridges: J . T. Dolan talks about how his heroin addiction caused him to miss a deadline for it (5.07).	1996–2001 television detective show, set in San Francisco and starring Don Johnson and Cheech Marin.
New Jersey Nets: Carmela criticizes Tony for taking A. J. to one of their games on a school night (5.04).	National Basketball Association professional basketball team, playing at Continental Airlines Arena in The Meadowlands.
New York Jets: Adriana's friend mentions selling paperweights as Christmas gifts to the New York Jets front office (4.02).	NFL professional football team.
New York Mets: Tony asks Svetlana (prior to sleeping with the one-legged woman) "How about those Mets?" (4.10).	National League major league baseball team.
News Hour, The: At Uncle Pat's farm, Tony watches it (5.10).	60 minute PBS evening news program hosted by Jim Lehrer.
Nolte, Nick: See *Prince of Tides* (5.01).	(1941–). American movie actor, known for his tough guy persona.
Nostradamus: See Quasimodo (4.01).	"Nostradamus (1503–1566), born Michel de Nostredame, is one of the world's most famous authors of prophecies. He is most famous for his book *Les Prophéties*, which consists of rhymed quatrains . . . grouped into sets of 100, called Centuries" (from Wikipedia.com).
On the Waterfront: Paulie tells Silvio about watching it on a new DVD (4.10).	1954 film by Elia Kazan set on the New York docks, starring Marlon Brando as a has-been boxer.
"Once, Twice, Three Times a Lady": In Tony's "test dream" Vin Makasian, playing Finn's father, unaccountably sings it (5.11).	A hit song by The Commodores.
Opus Dei: Little Carmine is upset at his father's funeral arrangements and blames this "New Jersey housewife fundamentalist shit" on Ginny Sack, who is in Opus Dei (5.02).	A conservative Catholic organization.

Ouija Board: A. J. uses one to pretend to contact the dead (4.11).	"Ouija (pronounced wee-juh or wee-jee) refers to the belief that one can receive messages during a séance by the use of a Ouija board (also called a talking board or spirit board) and planchette. The fingers of the participants are placed on the planchette which then moves about a board covered with numbers, letters and symbols so as to spell out messages" (from Wikipedia.com).
People's History of the United States, A: A. J.'s required-for-class reading of it leads to a breakfast table argument about whether Columbus committed crimes against humanity (4.03).	This radical history of America was written by Marxist historian Howard Zinn.
Picasso, Pablo: Uncle Junior recalls that the late Karen Baccalieri had once told him he looked like him (4.03). In 4.06, A. J. discovers that his rich girlfriend's father collects work from his later period.	(1881–1973). Spanish painter and sculptor, who spent most of his life in Paris. One of the titanic figures of 20th Century art.
Pocahontas: Paulie claims the dealer at the Mohawk Casino, who he calls Pocahontas, is "scalping us" (5.06).	"(1595–1617) was an Algonquian Indian whose life has formed the basis of highly romanticized legends" (from Wikipedia. com).
Pre-Raphaelite: Vito Spatafore refers to Janice as having a "pre-Raphaelite quality" (4.02).	School of Victorian poets and painters that rebelled against modernity by seeking to return to a painterly aesthetic that predates Raphael (1483–1520).
Prince of Tides, The: Tony makes his mistress stop her TV grazing to watch it, because he likes Nolte (5.01).	1991 film, directed by Barbra Streisand, about the relationship between a psychiatrist (Streisand) and her patient (Nick Nolte).
Priscilla Queen of the Desert: As evidence that Billy Budd might be gay, Finn cites the fact that the actor who played him in the film, Terence Stamp, was also in this film (4.12).	1994 Stephan Elliott film about two drag queens and a transsexual on an epic journey across the Australian outback.
Producers, The: Paulie's mother Nucci and her "friends" have tickets to it (4.12)	Incredibly successful Broadway musical by Mel Brooks, a theatricalization of his earlier film *The Producers* (1968).
Protestant Ethic: Carmela tells A. J. that bribery is the Italian version of it (4.01).	In *The Protestant Ethic and the Spirit of Capitalism*, German sociologist Max Weber presents a theory of the origin of the work ethic of western societies in the Protestant concept of salvation.

Quasimodo: Bobby Bacala insists that he predicted 9/11 (4.01).	The hunchback bell ringer in Victor Hugo's *The Hunchback of Notre Dame* (1831).
Rap: At an anger management meeting, Janice fulminates against "that rap shit" (5.10).	About.com defines Rap as "[a] form of popular music developed especially in African-American urban communities and characterized by spoken or chanted rhyming lyrics with a syncopated, repetitive rhythmic accompaniment."
Rastafarian: Tony B. recalls the habits of a Rastafarian inmate in prison (5.09).	A follower of the religion founded by His Imperial Majesty Haile Selassie, Emperor of Ethiopia. Rastafarianism became well known at the turn of the century due to the influence of the music of the Jamaican singer Bob Marley.
Rat Pack, The: Jack Massarone gives Tony a painting of them (5.02).	A group of American entertainers, including Frank Sinatra, Dean Martin, Sammy Davis, Jr., Joey Bishop, and Peter Lawford, who frequently performed together, especially in Las Vegas.
Remick, Lee: See Lemon, Jack (4.13).	(1935-1991). American film actress.
"Revenge is a dish best served cold": Tony quotes this famous line to Dr. Melfi but mangles it as "Revenge is like serving cold cuts" (5.10).	The original use of the aphorism— "Revenge is a dish best served cold"— appears to be in the eighteenth-century novel *Les Liaisons Dangereuses* by Choderlos De Laclos.
"Ride of the Valkires": A very drunk Brian Cammarata hums it when he learns that he is going to get a ride on a helicopter (4.12).	Orchestral music from Wagner's Ring Cycle, made famous in its use by Lieutenant Colonel Bill Kilgore (Robert Duval) to "scare the Gooks" in *Apocalypse Now* (1979).
Rio Bravo: Tony watches Dean Martin sing in a scene from it (4.01).	1959 Howard Hawks' western, starring John Wayne.
Robbins, Anthony: Uncle Junior watches his infomercial on TV, which includes the title (attributed to Henry James) "It's time to start living the life you imagined" (5.03).	(1960-). American motivational speaker and success guru.
Rommel, Field Marshall Erwin: Tony watches a History Channel documentary about him (5.13).	1891-1944). German general, one of Hitler's most dependable military leaders in France and Africa. By the end of the war he had turned on Hitler and backed attempts to overthrow him.

Rosebud: Janice announces on movie night after watching *Citizen Kane*, "Six months [of marriage] and Bobby still hasn't found my rosebud" (5.02).	In Welles' film, "Rosebud" is Kane's last word, and only at the end of the film do we learn that it was the name of a sled he played with as a boy.
Rubenesque: Adjective Johnny Sack uses to refers to his wife's figure in a conversation with Tony (4.04).	(1577–1640). Flemish painter, famous for his nudes of voluptuous women.
Sanford and Son: Told that Angelo Garepe's son is in "architectural salvage," Tony B. asks "Like Sanford and Son" (5.11).	1972–1977 television series about a junk dealer played by Red Foxx.
Seabiscuit: Hesh refers to him as he visits Pie-Oh-My at the stable (4.05).	Famous underdog race horse who became a national hero during The Great Depression.
Seattle, Chief: A native American speaker at an anti-Columbus Day rally quotes from his famous speech (4.03).	(1786–1866). Suquamish Indian leader famous for a speech he supposedly delivered in 1854. Seattle, Washington was named after him.
"Second Coming, The": Melfi quotes "The center cannot hold" and "the falcon cannot hear the falconer," both lines from it, to a non-comprehending Tony (5.10).	Famous poem by the great Irish poet William Butler Yeats.
Sentimental Education: The title of a fifth season episode (5.06).	*Sentimental Education* is a novel by Gustave Flaubert, whose *Madame Bovary* Carmela reads in the episode.
Seven Deadly Sins: Silvio tells Tony that "There's seven deadly sins, and yours is pride" (5.13).	In Medieval Catholic tradition the seven deadly sins were: gluttony, lust, avarice, sadness, anger, acedia, vainglory, and pride.
Shylock: Christopher calls Lorraine Calluzzo by her nickname, "Lady Shylock" (5.02).	Shylock is, of course, the money lender in Shakespeare's *Merchant of Venice*.
Simmons, Richard: Johnny Sack mentions that Ginny has sought weight loss help from him (4.04).	American weight loss guru, most famous for his "Sweating to the Oldies" tapes.
Sinatra, Frank: Trying on the new sport coat Christopher brings him, Feech insists that he "looks better than" him (5.04).	(1915–1998). Italian-American singer and actor, one of the great vocalists of the twentieth century.
Sondheim, Stephen: Cookie Cirillo claims she prefers his work to *The Producers* or *Man of La Mancha* (4.12).	(1930–). American composer and lyricist, best known for such musicals as *West Side Story*, *Into the Woods*, and *Sweeney Todd*.
Sorvino, Paul: Christopher mentions his role in *That's Life* (5.07).	(1939–). American television and film actor, best known for his role in *GoodFellas*.

Spears, Britney: A Muslim woman at Columbia tells Meadow about someone punished for having a photo of her (4.04).	(1981–). Louisiana-born singer and actress, a major turn-of-the-century pop star.
Spielberg, Steven: Johnny Sack insists Ralphie is "more creative than Spielberg" (4.04).	American film director, one of the most important figures in film in the last quarter of the 20th century, best known for *Jaws, E. T., Raiders of the Lost Ark,* and *Schindler's List.*
Starr, Ringo: See Beatles, The (5.04).	The Beatles' drummer.
Stella: Ralphie shouts "Stella" when he arrives at Janice's house to announce he has ditched Rosie Aprile (4.03).	Stanley Kowalski screams out his wife's name "Stella" in Tennessee Williams' *A Streetcar Named Desire*–a line made famous by Marlon Brando in Elia Kazan's movie of *Streetcar.*
"Surfin' USA": After Tony awakes from a frightening dream of his mother, he hears it playing in the distance as he stands on his Miami Beach hotel balcony (4.11).	1963 hit song by The Beach Boys.
Taliban: Silvio claims to be using a technique for blocking interception of a cell phone conference call perfected by them (4.04).	Ultra-orthodox Muslim sect that in the 1990s ruled Afghanistan with an iron hand and harbored terrorists, including Osama Bin Laden.
That's Life: J. T. Dolan speaks of a friend who is making a lot in residuals off it (5.07).	Television series (2000–2002), starring Ellen Burstyn and Paul Sorvino.
Three Amigos, The: Christopher watches it on TV at the Bing after Adriana has been whacked (5.12).	1986 comic film directed by John Landis and starring Steve Martin, Chevy Chase, and Martin Short.
Tracy and Hepburn: In the middle of a big shouting match with Tony, Carmela exclaims, "Who knew all these years that you wanted Tracy and Hepburn" (4.13).	Spencer Tracy (1900–1967) and Katherine Hepburn (1907–2003) were American film stars who appeared together in numerous films and were intimate friends/lovers from the 1940s on.
Trompe L'oeil: Little Carmine shows off his art knowledge by pointing out his tacky Venetian-view wallpaper (5.08).	A painting intended to be so authentic as to deceive the viewer into mistaking it for reality.
Tyson, Mike: See Ali, Mohammed (5.09).	(1966–). Former heavyweight champion of the world (1987–1990).
Valli, Frankie: A Mohunk coerces Tony into asking him to perform at his Delaware casino (4.03).	Popular Italian singer of the 1960s, the lead vocalist for The Four Seasons. Plays Rusty Millio in Season Five.
Varsailles: Little Carmine refers to "Versales" and "Lewis" in a meeting in Miami with Tony (4.11).	The unofficial capital city and palace of France at the turn of the 18th century, founded as such by Louis (not Lewis) XIV.

"Wall, The": Tony sings it in the shower (4.08).	1979 album by Pink Floyd, the inspiration for a 1982 film of the same name.
Wegman, William: While making love, Tony is distracted by one of his photographs on the wall (5.07).	American photograph famous for his photographs of his usually clothed dogs posed in human situations.
Weight Watchers: Johnny Sack mentions that Ginny has sought weight loss help from them (4.04).	American commercial weight loss organization sponsoring 12 step style meetings and selling dieting advice and food.
Who Wants to Be a Millionaire?: Uncle Junior watches it while discussing a hit on Johnny Sack with Tony (4.04).	Popular ABC game show (1999–2002, 2002–), hosted by Regis Philbin (and later Meredith Viera).
Wolf, Dick: J. T. Dolan talks to Christopher about how wealthy he must be from "that *Law and Order* money" and hopes (but does not succeed) to become a writer for the show (5.07).	(1946–). American TV producer, most famous for *Law and Order* and all its spinoffs.

Appendix C

CHARACTERS

The following list of characters, the actors/actresses who play them (in parenthesis), and the season/seasons in which they played a role is far from complete. It does include all the major characters from Seasons 4 and 5 as well as characters discussed in the essays in this volume.

Jimmy Altieri (Joseph Badalucco, Jr.): Season 1

Giacomo (Jackie) Aprile (Michael Rispoli): Season 1

Giacomo (Jackie, Jr.) Aprile, Jr. (Jason Cerbone): Seasons 2 and 3

Richie Aprile (David Proval): Season 2

Rosalie Aprile (Sharon Angela): Seasons 1-5

Bobby Baccilieri, Jr. (Steven R. Schirripa): Seasons 2-5

Bobby Baccilieri, Sr. (Burt Young): Season 2

Karen Baccalieri (Christine Pedi): Season 5

Larry (Larry Boy) Barese (Tony Darrow): Seasons 1-5

Matt Bevilaqua (Lillo Brancato, Jr.): Season 2

Angie Bonpensiaro (Toni Kalem): Seasons 2-5

Salvatore (Big Pussy) Bonpensiero (Vincent Pastore): Seasons 1 and 2

Artie Bucco (John Ventimiglia): Seasons 1-5

Charmaine Bucco (Kathrine Narducci): Seasons 1-5

Lorraine Calluzzo (Patti D'Arbanville): Season 5

Brian Caminarata (Matthew Del Negro): Season 4

Ralph Cifaretto (Joe Pantoliano): Seasons 3 and 4

Agent Frank Cubitoso (Frank Pellegrino): Seasons 1-5

Raymond Curto (George Loros): Seasons 1-5

Gabriella Dante (Maureen Van Zandt): Seasons 1-5

Silvio Dante (Steven Van Zandt): Seasons 1-5

Hugh DeAngelis (Tom Aldredge): Seasons 2-5

Mary DeAngelis (Suzanne Sheperd): Seasons 2-5

Finn DeTrolio (Will Janowitz): Season 5

J. T. Dolan (Timothy Daly): Season 5

Fran Felstein (Polly Bergen): Season 5

Angelo Garepe (Joe Santos): Season 5

Georgie (Frank Santorelli): Seasons 1–5

Furio Giunta (Federico Castelluccio): Seasons 2–4

Agent Harris (Matt Servitto): Seasons 1–5

Detective Lieutenant Barry Haydu (Tom Mason): Season 4

Father Phil Intintola (Paul Schulze): Seasons 1–5

Svetlana Kirilenko (Alla Kliouka): Seasons 2–4

Dr. Elliot Kupferberg (Peter Bogdanovich): Seasons 2–5

Adriana La Cerva (Drew De Meteo): Seasons 1–5

Feech La Manna (Robert Loggia): Season 5

Valentina La Paz (Leslie Bega): Seasons 4 and 5

Dr Richard La Penna (Richard Romanus): Seasons 1, 3, 4

Phil Leotardo (Frank Vincent): Season 5

Skip Lipari (Louis Lombardi): Season 2 and 3

Professor Longo-Murphy (Roma Maffia): Season 4

Carmine Lupertazzi (Tony Lip): Seasons 3–5

'Little' Carmine Lupertazzi, Jr. (Ray Abruzzo): Season 5

Vin Makazian (John Heard): Seasons 1 and 5

Jack Massarone (Robert Desiderio): Season 5

Dr. Jennifer Melfi (Lorraine Bracco): Seasons 1–5

Harold Melvoin (Richard Portnow): Seasons 1–5

Rusty Millio (Frankie Valli): Season 5

Neil Mink (David Margulies): Seasons 2 and 5

Coach Molinaro (Charley Scalies): Season 5

Christopher Moltisanti (Michael Imperioli): Seasons 1–5

Patsy Parisi (Dan Grimaldi): Season 2–5

Joe Peeps (Joe Maruzzo): Season 5

Irina Peltsin (Oksana Babiy): Seasons 1–4

Fabian (Febby) Petrullo; aka Fred Peters (Tony Ray Rossi): Season 1

Devin Pillsbury (Jessica Dunphy): Season 5

Herman (Hesh) Rabkin (Jerry Adler): Seasons 1–5

Professor Del Redclay (Larry Sellers): Season 4

Reuben 'The Cuban' (Yul Vazquez): Season 4

Jesus Rossi (Mario Polit): Season 3

Ginny Sacrimoni (Denise Borino): Seasons 3–5

Johnny (Johnny Sack) Sacramoni (Vincent Curatola): Seasons 1–5

Agent Robyn Sanseverino (Karen Young): Season 5

Alan Sapinsly (Bruce Altman): Season 4

Charles (Chucky) Signore (Sal Ruffino): Season 1

Chief Doug Smith (Nick Chinlund): Season 5

Anthony (A. J.) Soprano, Jr. (Robert Iler): Seasons 1–5

Barbara Soprano (Nicole Burdette): Seasons 2 and 3

Carmela Soprano (Edie Falco): Seasons 1–5

Carrado (Uncle Junior) Soprano (Dominic Chianese): Seasons 1–5

Janice (Parvati) Soprano (Aida Turturro): Seasons 2–5

John (Johnny Boy) Soprano (Joseph Siravo): Seasons 1, 3, and 5

Livia Soprano (Nancy Marchand): Seasons 1–3

Meadow Soprano (Jamie-Lynn Sigler): Seasons 1–5

Tony Soprano (James Gandolfini): Seasons 1–5

Vito Spatafore (Joseph R. Gannascoli): Season 2–5

Stasiu (Albert Makhtsier): Season 3

Noah Tannenbaum (Patrick Tully): Season 3

Maurice Tiffen (Vondie Curtis-Hall): Season 4

Gloria Trillo (Annabella Sciorra): Seasons 3 and 5

Paulie Walnuts (Tony Sirico): Seasons 1–5

Robert Wegler (David Strathairn): Season 5

Jeffrey Wernick (Timothy Nolen): Season 1

Leon Wilmore (Charles S. Dutton): Season 3

State Assemblyman Zellman (Peter Reigert): Seasons 3 and 4

NOTES

INTRODUCTION

1. These remarks echo Chase's observations in a foreword to a volume collecting the best *Sopranos* screenplays, summarized by me elsewhere: "Although the major American television networks, all of which passed on the show, have attributed the tremendous success of *The Sopranos* to HBO's cable TV freedom to air nudity and profanity, Chase finds that explanation superficial. It is not bare breasts and obscenities that have set *The Sopranos* apart but, according to its creator, a variety of other factors: the narrative possibilities granted by the absence of commercial interruption, the freedom to allow characters to develop slowly over time, the series' insistence on treating its audience as highly intelligent." Lavery, "The Sopranos" 191.

2. Not surprisingly, the "Jesus Lady" of American television, Martha Williamson, creator of *Touched by an Angel*, speaks with envy of Chase's premium cable luxury in her interview with James Longworth and suggests she could produce a higher-quality product under similar circumstances. Then again, she also proclaims in the same interview, far less believably, that, if put in charge of *Oz*, HBO's highly profane prison drama, she would have taken the show in precisely the same direction as Tom Fontana.

3. This list does not include the late John Patterson (1940–2005), director of thirteen of the sixty-five existing *Sopranos* episodes, who died in February of last year from prostate cancer.

4. Gilbert misidentifies Warshow's classic work on gangster films as a product of the 1990s and not the 1950s (18–19), as I had already established earlier in the essay.

5. Though I will not consider them here, a number of paratexts have been inspired by *The Sopranos*. Such lesser efforts as Chris Seay's *The Gospel According to Tony Soprano* or Anthony Schneider's *Tony Soprano on Management* are easily dismissed. The official *Sopranos* books, however, are must-reads. *The Sopranos: Selected Scripts from Three Seasons* offers, in addition to an introduction by David Chase, the text of "The Sopranos" (1.01), "College" (1.05), "The Happy Wanderer" (2.06), "The Knight in White Satin Armor" (2.12), and "Pine Barrens" (3.11). Though its premise and organization are more than dubious,

The Tao of Bada Bing: Words of Wisdom from The Sopranos does put in print almost 200 pages of *Sopranos* dialogue. And Allen Rucker's *The Sopranos: A Family History* and *The Sopranos Family Cookbook* might be the most inspired commodity intertexts ever published in the USA (see Lavery, Review Essay). A third book—on "Entertaining with the Sopranos" is promised.

6. Despite its misleading title, Simon's book has virtually nothing to say about the series itself. Written by a criminologist, its concerns are almost wholly sociological and not critical.

7. Whatever the fate of *The Sopranos* and the Sopranos, it seems likely that *Sopranos Studies* will go on for quite some time. In his interview with Peter Bogdanovich on the Season One DVDs, Chase explains that the show's writers, himself included, never planned all the buried significance, the hidden meanings, eventually to be discovered in Melfi's office. They trusted their "instincts" in order to create enigmas, implant unknowables, pose questions and then set out to find plausible solutions, credible answers. *Sopranos* scholar-critics have responded in kind and found its open text richly provocative, and they're not done yet. We have so much more work to do.

8. In a special *TV Guide Sopranos Companion* published in the fall of 2002, Chase responded to the question of whether the show's fifth season would be its last by insisting: "That is it. For sure. Definitely. No more. People don't believe me because I've said that before. I mean, they may choose to keep doing it. It's just that I don't want to. I just think, Tony Soprano, guys of his ilk, they're not very reflective people, they don't do a lot, in reality. So there's only so many stories, so much depth, that you can impart to a character like that and still stay true to realism. Plus, it's just my personality. I can't stand solving the same problem over and over again" (11).

2. Homeward Bound

1. As Lavery and Thompson report, Chase's initial conception of the show's opening was quite different: "In a discussion of the opening credit sequence with Bogdanovich, Chase recalls that it had been his wish to use a different song every week and had protested unsuccessfully HBO's insistence that Tony's drive from New York to New Jersey always be choreographed to A5's 'Woke Up This Morning'. He admits that he originally considered a single theme song—a staple of television programs for decades—'bourgeois'" (22).

4. Disciplining the Masculine

1. Some might remember that the first appearances of Janice are in Tony's flashbacks to his childhood, one of which includes little Janice giving Tony the finger as she drives away with her father to "Ride Land" ("Down Neck," 1.07).

2. Adriana is eventually murdered by Silvio Dante (Steven Van Zandt), one of Tony's men, for being an informant to the FBI. Adriana tells Christopher that she had been in dialogue with the FBI, and asks him to enter the Witness Protection Program with her. Instead of going with Adriana into the program, Christopher tells Tony, who arranges her murder.

3. For $3000 dollars, Janice will later reveal to Tony that Ralph "bottoms from the top"—that he "likes to control things and pretend he doesn't" ("Mergers and Acquisitions," 4.08).

6. Bloodlust for the Common Man

1. See David Lavery's introduction to *This Thing of Ours*, particularly pages xi–xii, for a survey of both positive and negative responses to the show in a broad range of media.

2. Also see the beginning of Akass and MaCabe for an overview of women's negative representations in the more general category of the "gangster" film.

3. In "Denial, Anger, Acceptance" (1.03), Tony had identified himself—and more generally the Mafia—as the last of the Romans to an Hasidic Jew motel owner he has been hired to strong-arm, and the audience, if not Melfi, is likely to recall this moment in her description of the Rottweiler's ancestry.

4. While *The Sopranos* has enticed a number of scholars of Italian American heritage (including myself) into its discussion, and raised some dubious arguments that Italian Americans might somehow have more authority on the show, such studies tend to favor examinations of glamour and nostalgia while glossing over the very serious issue of racism in Italian American heritage. Since the show itself addresses this racism as unflinchingly as issues of violence, it's surprising how few articles address race at all, and how, as far as I know, none has made race its central subject.

5. Fred Gardaphé develops the show's Old World/New World dichotomy more thoroughly in his article "Fresh Garbage."

8. From Columbus to Gary Cooper

1. Pattie argues that Scorsese's work plays the role of the repressed unconscious for Tony Soprano and crew. According to Creeber, Tony's longing for a "golden age" refers "as much to the *dramatic universe* Tony inhabits as it does to the reality of the Mob itself" (126). For Auster, "*The Sopranos* underscores the continued validity and contemporary relevance of the gangster genre" (15). And Nochimson reads *The Sopranos* as "the unmasking of the heretofore thickly disguised emotional subtext of gangster stories" (3) that extends as far back as *Little Caesar* (1930) and *Public Enemy* (1931).

2. Paglia's complaints about stereotypical depictions of Italian-Americans in *The Sopranos* can be found in the online articles cited in the bibliography. For an

account of Italian-Canadian reactions to the series, see Johnston. Orban and Wise offer the most detailed analyses of stereotyping in the show.

3. An important early example of such a character is Jennifer's ex-husband, Richard LaPenna, who rails against gangster films as stereotyping vehicles in "The Legend of Tennessee Moltisanti" (1.08).

4. Jacobson identifies the civil rights era as that in which the whiteness of groups like Italian-Americans (previously thought to inhabit a "middle ground in the racial order" (62)) is most firmly established. According to Jacobson, "non-Anglo-Saxon immigrants and their children were perhaps the first beneficiaries of the modern civil rights movement, in that the movement helped confer upon them a newly consolidated status as Caucasians in a political setting where that meant—and continues to mean—a great deal" (Jacobson 272). The white "ethnic revival" which follows the civil rights movement is thus the clearest symptom of historical amnesia about the process of becoming-Caucasian.

5. Thomas Guglielmo's chapter in the same book arrives at the following conclusion: "Italian Americans' whiteness ... was their single most powerful asset in the 'New World'; it gave them countless advantages over 'nonwhites' in housing, jobs, schools, politics, and virtually every other meaningful area of life. Without appreciating this fact, one has no hope of fully understanding Italian American history" (42–3). Another text that makes a similar argument is Joseph P. Cosco's *Imagining Italians*, which concludes with a chapter entitled "The Fight for Whiteness."

6. Commenting on the assimilated status of the Soprano family, Chris Messenger reads Tony's drive in the opening credits as a simulation of "the long march (but short distance) earlier immigrants took from the now grim, older factory towns in new migration to a suburban frontier" (283). And Maurice Yacowar describes the Soprano house and its furnishings as bland and characterless, indicative of their assimilated status (45).

7. Similarly, Tony tells Meadow in "College" (1.05), "You know there was a time, Mead, when the Italian people didn't have a lot of options." Meadow isn't buying it, however. She replies, "You mean like Mario Cuomo?"

8. The only on-screen appearance of Gary Cooper in *The Sopranos* to date occurs during the long dream sequence of "The Test Dream" (5.11). As Tony enters the restaurant at which he and Carmela are to meet Meadow, her fiancé Fin, and Fin's parents, Tony sees *High Noon* playing on the television above the bar. Cooper appears on the TV screen briefly as Tony and Carmela walk past the bar to their table.

9. I have argued elsewhere ("Unmade Men") that Tony's recurring panic attacks are the result of his racial anxiety.

10. In a case of life imitating art imitating life, New York Mayor Michael Bloomberg was harshly criticized, in the days following the airing of "Christopher" on 29 September 2002, for inviting *Sopranos* regulars Lorraine Bracco (Jennifer Melfi)

and Dominic Chianese (Uncle Junior) to march with him at the New York Columbus Day parade on 14 October. The Columbus Citizens Foundation, which organizes the annual parade and has frequently accused *The Sopranos* of portraying Italian-Americans in a negative light, actually obtained a temporary restraining order that prohibited Mayor Bloomberg from marching with the actors. Bloomberg elected not to attend the parade and instead spent the afternoon with Bracco and Chianese at an Italian restaurant in the Bronx.

11.   In "The Legend of Tennessee Moltisanti," we do hear a comment (made by Dr. Melfi's father in a dinner-table conversation): "You never saw the Scotch-Irish pissing and moaning about always being portrayed as rustlers and gunslingers." Gary Cooper is not specifically mentioned.

10. Show Business of Dirty Business?

1.   This book is one of the countless biographies of crime lords or families available detailing Mob dealings and selling to a public whose interest remains unsated.

2.   This contemporary media urge to romanticize the gangster is not confined to urban contexts, of course, and has much in common with what has been called social banditry in peasant communities. See Blik.

3.   For three responses that epitomize discussion of the issue see articles by Carroll, Harold, and Lippman.

11. Aesthetics and Ammunition

1.   Nick Lowe's song "The Beast in Me" plays over the final credits in "The Sopranos" (1.01).

2.   See Laing's *The Divided Self* and *Self and Others* and Tillich.

3.   An abundance of literature is available on the topic of interarts comparisons: Aristotle's *De Anima II*, Leonardo's *Paragone*, Alberti, Lessing, Bryson, Mitchell, Manguel.

4.   Gaudy paintings and commemorative statuary (Jesus Christ, Columbus, Lou Costello) abound. From Vesuvio's views of Naples and the Roman Forum to the mural of a Venetian gondola in Carmine's restaurant, these pieces place the action within definite ethnic parameters. Perhaps the most self-conscious moment of kitsch appears in the episode "Marco Polo" (5.08). The episode opens upon a gold gilded Venetian chandelier. A huge Renaissance-style painting is slowly panned. A bare-bosomed, partially clad maiden looks on with vicarious interest onto the unfolding scene, one hand partially covering her breast, the other timidly touching her chin. Two naked male angels attend to her needs. The modesty of the maiden contrasts sharply with the topless dancers that closed the preceding episode. The camera follows her line of vision into the room, falling upon another painting of a faux window with

balcony and accompanying view of the Bay of Naples. Little Carmine, who has entered the room with his guests, gives critical commentary. He speaks of "trompay le oil" (trompe l'œil), "fool the eye," adding that it was done by an artist in West Hampstead.

5. During another hospital visit, Janice attempts to discuss inheritance money matters with Livia. An *In Case of Fire, Use Stairs* sign looms behind Livia. It features a stylized figure running down the stairs. At obvious loggerheads, Janice imagines Livia tumbling down the stairs. Livia is wicked in her posturing, Janice disarming in her treachery. ("Guy Walks into a Psychiatrist's Office," 2.01).

6. Tony's true physical and emotional feelings for Melfi can never manifest themselves. In "Funhouse" (2.13) he arrives at a session with a very obvious "friend" (in a delightful play on words, Melfi asks a confused Tony if his "friend" is Pussy). The indecorum of their sexual encounter is skirted by making this a dream sequence.

7. In the episode "Big Girls Don't Cry" (2.05), Tony enters A. J.'s room to apologize to his son and after being told to control his anger and "grow the fuck up!" by Carmela. His penitent child-like eyes linger on the ball player figurines as he exits. A more mature Tony makes love to his wife before figurines of angels in "From Where to Eternity" (2.09).

8. Apart from Livia's home and its requisite portraits of popes and presidents, and mementos from the old country, the Soprano home is emblematic of what Fred Gadarphe terms ethnic "basement culture." As ethnic families assimilated and became more affluent, material legacies of their roots found their way to the privacy of the basement. As a means of further distancing Tony from his true ethnic roots, Chase gives the home an unfinished basement with no ethnic regalia whatsoever.

9. An interesting logo is the neon Z that appears, in Season One, over Tony's head when he sits at his desk. A Lacanian symbol for censure, a paradigm for mirror images, the verge of antithesis, it disappears in the second season. Perhaps the psychological overtones were too apparent!

10. In "A Hit is a Hit" (1.10) even Melfi, in a prideful outburst that rails against the deprecatory remarks of the Cusumanos with respect to typical ethnic trappings, states, "I like Murano glass!" An obvious nod to her luminous heritage.

11. Tony's externalization of his own self-contempt takes the form of despising others while idealizing a rapport with non-psychologically threatening agents, in his case, animals. Ducks, bears, indeed all animals hold special sway over him. It is not until an episode appropriately named "In Camelot" (5.07) that we understand why. Once again, it is a visual image that jogs a conscious awakening. The idealization of his father (the reason for Tony's subsequent career path) to the detriment of his mother reaches a climax. Confronted with a photograph of his childhood pet Tippy (long assumed dead but in reality

given as a present by his father to his mistress), the dynamite of his inner frictions explode. All the hopelessness of his neurotic self comes into clear relief. He realizes he is powerless to change the past and is trapped in the crosscurrents of his chosen profession.

12.   In an interview with the *Star Ledger*, Chase comments on Tony's maturation in Season Five: "I don't want to say 'lion in winter,' because it isn't winter for him, but he's been doing this for quite a while now and it's about what it takes to be a leader despite your feelings."

12. TASTING BRYLCREEM

1.   In one of the most memorable lines ever to come out of the series (and there have been quite a few), Junior complains, "The federal marshals are so far up my ass I can taste Brylcreem" ("Toodle-Fucking-oo," 2.03). Unless otherwise noted, all of *The Sopranos* quotes in this essay come from either *The Sopranos* DVD or VHS collections. I am also indebted to HBO's *The Sopranos* website for providing episode synopses and to *Sopranoland.com*, for providing complete transcripts of the first two seasons.

2.   Even the agents themselves are not above the same desires. In the wake of Christopher's advances toward Deborah, Cubitoso admits to Harris, "I had a dream about her the other night" ("No-Show," 4.02). Along the same lines, Yacowar points out that the overheated agent who stakes out Carmela's tennis practice "even sounds like a wiseguy" (126) as he instead ogles Adriana and is moved to exclaim, "How green was my fuckin' valley," and "Sweet fuckin' Jesus" ("Mr. Ruggerio's Neighborhood," 3.01).

3.   As Tony describes him, the troubled Makazian, who commits suicide after his arrest in a whore house, is "a degenerate fuckin' gambler with a badge" ("Nobody Knows Anything," 1.11) and another example of how badly "the law" comes off in the show.

4.   Johnny Sack's arrest is another scene in the series that may well connect the FBI and the mob. Inasmuch as the figures initially appear blurry and Tony's response to them is simply panic, they could just as easily be confused for hitmen. The viewer does not really get a sense of who they are and what they are there for until they get closer and Johnny also makes a run for it.

5.   A similar scene takes place in Season Five's "Rat Pack," as Adriana and the mob wives watch *Citizen Kane* (a film that Leonard Maltin praises for "breaking the rules") at Carmela's "movie night." When the "FBI Warning" comes up large on the screen, they all sit quietly, suddenly semi-conscious, despite their forced efforts at obliviousness, that the excesses they enjoy are ironically a product of their husbands' FBI violations.

13. THE PRINCE OF NORTH JERSEY

1. An earlier version of this essay appeared in *The Journal of Popular Film and Television* 32.2 (Summer 2004).

14. "BLACK GUYS, MY ASS"

1. My thanks to Robin Durnford, whose discussions with me on gender issues in *The Sopranos* influenced the writing of this paper.

2. Such disproportionate punishment had changed little one hundred years after the Civil War. Staples notes, citing a 1974 source, that "the most severe penalties for rape are reserved for black males accused of raping white women. Although 50% of those convicted for rape in the South were white males, over 90% of those executed for this crime in that region were black. Most of their alleged victims were white. No white male has ever been executed for raping a black woman" (378).

3. See Santo 89–90 for an analysis of moments in the series where men's (usually inadvertent) display of their bodies to other men produces effeminacy-denouncing moments or provoke homophobic reactions.

4. In "The Two Tonys" (5.01), Tony explains to Chris that he has to keep picking up tabs and kicking up money to Paulie because the system is like that of "the samurai," who had pages; Tony thinks he is making an analogy between proud, manly warrior cultures, but in fact the samurai-page relationship often involved homosexuality, so Tony's example merely voices the homosexual masquerading as homosocial in the mobsters' world.

5. Junior hires two African-American men to whack Tony, but they fail ("Isabella," 1.12); African-American youths jack cars from the streets for Tony's crew, vehicles they will then strip and sell to Italy, their Old World homeland ("Commendatori," 2.04); Tony co-opts African-American Reverend Herman James Jr. in a construction job scam ("Do Not Resuscitate," 2.02) and African-American social housing co-ordinator Maurice Tiffen in a scam that involves selling off ghetto properties at a huge profit ("Watching Too Much Television," 4.07). In "Whitecaps" (4.13), when Chris hires two African-American drug dealers to whack Carmine, telling them to make it look like a "carjacking," the pair point out the mob's racial profiling to him: "that's some stereotypin' shit." The hit is called off and Chris has two lackeys mortally silence the hired killers.

6. Tony's psychological and verbal connections of meat with sexuality are in keeping with the "mobspeak" of the series, in which many of the sexual and racist Italian-American words, such as *"fanook"* (from "finocchio," or fennel) and *"mulignan"* (eggplant) have their origins in Italian words for food. His association of violent and/or sexual revenge is expressed in his Freudian malapropism "revenge is like cold cuts" ("Cold Cuts," 5.10). Meat, of course, is often already carved from the insides or intestines of other animals and connected with the male victims whose bodies Tony and his associates cut up,

and is consumed orally but excreted anally, so the connection of consuming male flesh with the two orifices on the male body that Tony associates with giving or receiving unmasculine sex lends meat homoerotic overtones.

7. For an elaboration on Jackie Jr.'s "attempt to match his father's 'balls'" instead of becoming a "pussy," see Yacowar 164. Jackie Jr. suggests that his mother's lover, Ralph, is a latent homosexual (3.12), a supposition that becomes not far from the truth in Tony's eyes. Jackie Jr. was also the young man whom uncle Richie Aprile wished his own, effeminate-seeming, ballroom-dancing son would be more like, in a discussion about Richie's "*disgraziata*" of a son that led him to punch Janice in the mouth and Janice, the natural heir of her mother's emasculating matriarchal power, to shoot him to death ("The Knight in White Satin Armor," 2.12).

8. Interestingly, the actor Michael K. Williams, who plays Ray Ray, the man who takes Jackie Jr. into his housing project apartment in the episode, went on to star the next year as Omar in the HBO series *The Wire*, where he plays a homosexual African-American who robs drug dealers in the projects.

9. Some literary critics argue that miscegenation and homosexuality are the two great taboos of nineteenth-century American literature and that Melville broke them both with the inter-racial homoeroticism in *Moby-Dick* (1851).

10. As Michele McPhee reported, shortly after "Unidentified Black Males" first aired:

    Vincent (Vinny Ocean) Palermo, former boss of New Jersey's DeCalvacante family, said to be the model for "The Sopranos," testified last week there is one way to handle gay gangsters: kill them.

    "What's the rule ... about this?" federal prosecutor John Hillebrecht asked the mob turncoat on Wednesday.

    "You die," Palermo replied.

    That was the punishment meted out to DeCalvacante wiseguy John D'Amato in 1992, whom Palermo ordered whacked after being told his underling had rendezvoused with another man at a swingers club.

11. Joe Gannascoli, who plays Vito Spatafore, simultaneously expresses pride in and attempts to keep an anxious distance from the role on his self-promoting website, <http://www.josephrgannascoli.com>, where he includes news items about the episode. In an interview with the *Daily News* that shows how men's gay tolerance is a thin mask for gay panic, Gannascoli notes that it was his idea to make Vito homosexual, but "[takes] pains to point out he is not gay—adding just as quickly, 'Not that there is anything wrong with it.'" Gannascoli says that Tony Sirico, who plays Paulie Walnuts, asked him, "'You okay with this? You want me to have a talk with David Chase?'" and adds that his pretend coming out will still, in the real world, mean that he'll "'have to deal with a lot of grief in the neighborhood.'" A *Star* article included on the website reported that James Gandolfini, expressing consolation in Tony's phallic terms, told Gannascoli,

"'"You've got balls" (Rozdeba). Gannascoli reiterates that he is "'very straight'" and even hopes to turn his fictional homosexuality into landing women: "'The guys have been saying hello,' he says. 'But I'm definitely meeting more women. I'm hoping the women will think they can make me straight.'"

12. This assassination, which starts the chain of events leading to Tony B.'s death and the brief cold war between Johnny Sack and Tony, was provoked by the killing of Little Carmine's lover and second cousin, Lorraine Calluzzo. Lorraine, in "Where's Johnny?" (5.03), connects homophobia and racism when she comes to collect a payment and tells the back-talking guy, "Say I'm some big nigger—you gonna treat me like that?" Then Phil Leotardo comes in and doubly emphasizes her effeminacy by scaring her so much that she offers to "suck your cock," to which he replies that her boyfriend "probably showed her how" to fellate. In the next episode, Lorraine, running out of the shower naked, is killed along with her boyfriend, thus eliminating these two unacceptable weak links in a tough-guy world.

13. After his sweat-drenched, heavy-breathing admission, Tony notes, "You know, sometimes what happens in here is like taking a shit," significantly relating the cathartic confession to a purging of gay panic from his anus, which, to someone of Tony's genital-fixated masculinity, is also associated with gay sex. The anus is also that "bottomless black hole" that Tony likens to his mother ("Amur Fou," 3.12), linking maternally emasculating effeminacy to deadly, masculine-devouring homosexuality; see Bersani for an elaboration on the idea that homophobes' fear of anal sex is linked to notions of "the suicidal ecstasy of being a woman" (212). Livia's successor, her scheming daughter Janice, is also likened to homosexuality when Tony tells her to shove the love seat he helped her to move "up her ass" ("The Knight in White Satin Armor," 2.12).

BIBLIOGRAPHY

"50 Greatest Shows of All Time." *TV Guide* 4 May 2002: 18-55.

"A&E Pays Big Bucks for 'Sopranos' Reruns." *Pittsburgh Post-Gazette* 1 Mar. 2005, Arts & Entertainment: B4.

Adalian, Josef, and Michael Schneider. "20th in a 'Family' Way." *Daily Variety* 25 Mar. 2004, news: 1.

Akass, Kim and Janet McCabe. "Beyond the Bada Bing!: Negotiating Female Narrative Authority in *The Sopranos*." Lavery, *This Thing* 146-161.

Alberti, Leon Battista. *On Painting.* Trans. John R. Spencer. New Haven: Yale UP, 1966.

Anastasia, George. "If Shakespeare were Alive Today, He'd be Writing for *The Sopranos*." Barreca 149-66.

___. *The Last Gangster: From Cop to Wiseguy to FBI Informant: Big Ron Previte and the Fall of the American Mob.* New York: Regan Books, Harper Collins, 2004.

Aristotle, *De Anima II.* Trans. W. W. Hett. Cambridge: Harvard UP, 1957.

Atkinson, Claire. "HBO's Playbook: Playing Hard to Get; Pushes hard, but quietly to ensure 'Deadwood,' 'Entourage' get their due." *Advertising Age* 28 Feb. 2005, 3.

Auster, Albert. "*The Sopranos*: The Gangster Redux." Lavery, *This Thing* 10-15.

Baker, Aaron, and Juliann Vitullo. "Screening the Italian-American Male." *Masculinity: Bodies, Movies, Culture.* Ed. Peter Lehman. New York: Routledge, 2001. 213-26.

Baker, Jennifer. "The Unhappiness of Tony Soprano: An Ancient Analysis." Greene and Vernezze 28-36.

Baldwin, James. *The Price of the Ticket.* 1963. London: Michael Joseph, 1985.

Barreca, Regina. "Why I like the Women in *The Sopranos* Even though I'm Not Supposed to." Barreca 27-46.

___, ed. *A Sitdown with the Sopranos: Watching Italian American Culture on TV's Most Talked-About Series.* New York: Palgrave Macmillan, 2002.

Barthes, Roland. *Image-Music-Text.* London: Fontana P, 1977.

Baudrillard, Jean. "The Ecstasy of Communication." *The Anti-Aesthetic.* Ed. Hal Foster. Seattle: Bay Press, 1983. 126-134.

Bellah, Robert. *Habits of the Heart: Individualism and Commitment in American Life.* Berkeley: U California P, 1996.

Bersani, Leo. "Is the Rectum a Grave?" *AIDS: Cultural Analysis, Cultural Activism*. Ed. Douglas Crimp. Cambridge, MA: MIT, 1988. 197-222.

Blik, Anton. *Honor and Violence*. Cambridge: Polity, 2001.

Booth, Wayne C. *The Rhetoric of Fiction*. Chicago: U of Chicago P, 1961.

Braun, Stephen, and Michael Goodman. "Mobsters Finger Mates Who Made Others Swim with the Fishes." *The Sydney Morning Herald* 30 April-1 May, 2005, Weekend ed., sec. News: 18.

Brownfield, Paul. "At HBO, the bonfire of the vanity projects: Shows with a wry peek inside Hollywood just keep coming, partly because the network so attracts the showbiz player." *Los Angeles Times* 10 Jul. 2005, Sunday home ed., Calendar: E1.

___. "Call It Must-Buy TV: At the Home of 'The Sopranos,' the Payoff Isn't Huge and Neither Are the Ratings. But HBO Sure Has Cachet. Can It Hold onto That and Add New Series?" *Los Angeles Times* 25 Feb. 2001, Calendar: 8.

___. "The Nation: 'Sopranos' Staying Hip Amid Hype." *Los Angeles Times* 15 Sept. 2002, part 1: 1.

Brundage, W. Fitzhugh. *Lynching in the New South: Georgia and Virginia, 1880-1930*. Chicago: U of Illinois P, 1993.

Bryson, Norman. *Vision and Painting: The Logic of the Gaze*. New Haven: Yale UP, 1983.

Butler, Judith. *Bodies that Matter: On the Discursive Limits of "Sex."* New York: Routledge, 1993.

Canfield, Jack and Mark Victor Hansen. *Chicken Soup for the Soul: 101 Stories to Open the Heart and Rekindle the Spirit*. Santa Barbara: Health Communications, 1993.

Carroll, Noel. "Sympathy for the Devil." Greene and Vernezze 121-36.

Carter, Bill. "He Lit Up HBO. Now He Must Run It." *The New York Times* 29 Dec. 2002, final, sec. 3: 1.

___. "'Sopranos' Draws Record Viewers to HBO." *The New York Times* 18 Sept. 2002, late ed.: C6.

___. "Tony Soprano and Crew Will Return for '07 Season." *The New York Times* 12 Aug. 2005, nat. ed.: C5.

___. "TV Notes; Bada-Bing Go the Ratings." *The New York Times* 7 Mar. 2001, final late ed.: E6.

Cassidy, Lisa. "Is Carmela Soprano a Feminist? Carmela's Care Ethics." Greene and Vernezze 97-107.

Cavellero's, Jonathan J. "Gangsters, Fessos, Tricksters, and Sopranos: The Historical Roots of Italian American Stereotype Anxiety." *Journal of Popular Film and Television* 32.2 (2004): 50-63.

Chandler, Raymond. *The Simple Art of Murder*. Vintage Crime. New York: Vintage Books: Random House, 1988.

Combs, Steven C. ""Tony Soprano and the Art of War: New Jersey Meets the East." Greene and Vernezze 17-27.

Corliss, Richard, and Simon Crittle. "The Last Don." *Time,* March 4th, 2004: 44-50.

Cosco, Joseph P. *Imagining Italians: The Clash of Romance and Race in American Perceptions, 1880-1910.* Albany: State U of New York P, 2003.

Creeber, Glen. "TV Ruined the Movies" Television, Tarantino, and The Intimate World of *The Sopranos.*" Lavery, *This Thing* 124-134.

Creedon, Jeremiah. "The Greening of Tony Soprano: Even Mobsters Feel the Pain of Ecological Alienation." *Utne Review* May/June 2003.

Da Vinci, Leonardo. *Paragone: Poetry and Painting.* Ed. A. Phillip McMahon. Princeton: Princeton UP, 1956.

Damsky, Lee, ed. *Sex and Single Girls: Straight and Queer Women on Sexuality.* Seattle: Seal Press, 2000.

de Moraes, Lisa. "Deadwood' Saddles Up for a Third Season." *The Washington Post* 31 March 2005, Style: C07.

DeFino, Dean. "The Prince of North Jersey." Journal of Popular Film and Television 32.2 (2004): 83-89.

Dempsey, John. "Cablers Raise Syndie Stakes." *Variety* 15 Sept.–21 Sept. 2003, television: 15.

___. It's Lonely At The Top." *Variety* 10 Sept.–16 Sept. 2001, news: 1.

Denfeld, Rene. *The New Victorians: A Young Women's Challenge To The Old Feminist Order.* New York: Warner Books, 1995.

Doane, Mary Ann. "Film and the Masquerade: Theorizing the Female Spectator." *Feminism and Film.* Ed. Ann Kaplan. Oxford: Oxford UP, 2000. 418-36.

Bellah, Robert. *Habits of the Heart.* Berkeley: U of California P, 1985.

Dolan, Marc. "The Peaks and Valleys of Serial Creativity: What Happened to/on *Twin Peaks.*" *Full of Secrets: Critical Approaches to Twin Peaks.* Ed. David Lavery. Detroit: Wayne State UP, 1995. 30-50.

Donatelli, Cindy and Sharon Alward. "I Dread You"? Married to the Mob in *The Godfather, GoodFellas,* and *The Sopranos.*" Lavery, *This Thing* 60-71.

Douglas, Susan and Meredith W. Michaels. *The Mommy Myth: The Idealisation of Motherhood and How It Has Undermined Women.* New York: Free Press, 2004.

Douglas, Susan. *Where The Girls Are: Growing Up Female in the Mass Media.* New York: Random, 1995.

Dunne, Sara Lewis. "'The Brutality of Meat' and 'the Abruptness of Seafood': Food, Violence, and Family in *The Sopranos.*" Lavery, *This Thing* 215-26.

Dutka, Elaine. "On DVD; This just in: Kerry still trailing Bush; The satiric 'Daily Show' bets it's not too late for repackaged coverage of 'Indecision 2004.'" *Los Angeles Times* 28 June 2005, home ed.: E1.

Echols, Alice. "The Taming of the Id: Feminist Sexual Politics, 1968-1983." *Pleasure and Danger: Exploring Female Sexuality.* Ed. Carol Vance. London: Pandora, 1992. 50-72.

Fanon, Frantz. *Black Skin, White Masks.* New York: Grove, 1967.

"Fast Track." *Broadcasting and Cable* 1 Mar. 2004, Top of the Week: 31.

Fellezs, Kevin "Wiseguy Opera: Music for *Sopranos*." Lavery, *This Thing* 162-75.

Feuer, Jane. "Melodrama, Serial Form and Television Today." *Screen* 25 (1984): 1, 4-15.

Fields, Ingrid Walker. "Family Values and Feudal Codes: The Social Politics of America's Twenty-First Century Gangster." *The Journal of Popular Culture* 37.4 (2004): 611-33.

Findlen, Barbara, ed. *Listen Up: Voices From the Next Feminist Generation*. Seattle: Seal Press, 1995.

Fish, Stanley. *Surprised by Sin: The Reader in Paradise Lost*. Berkeley: U of California P, 1971.

Flamini, Michael. "'Pa cent' anni, Dr. Melfi': Psychotherapy in the Italian American Community." Barreca 113-127.

Foucault, Michel. *Discipline and Punish: The Birth of the Prison*. Trans. Alan Sheridan. London: Penguin, 1991.

___. *The Will to Knowledge. The History of Sexuality*, Vol. 1. Trans. Robert Hurley. London: Penguin, 1998.

Friedan, Betty. *The Second Stage*. New York: Summit Books, 1981.

Friedman, Susan Stanford. "Making History: Reflections on Feminism, Narrative and Desire." *Feminism Beside Itself*. Eds. Diane Elam and Robyn Wiegman. New York: Routledge, 1995. 11-54.

Gabbard, Glen O. *The Psychology of The Sopranos: Love, Death, Desire, and Betrayal in America's Favorite Gangster Family*. New York: Basic, 2002.

Gardaphé, Fred. "Fresh Garbage: The Gangster as Suburban Trickster." Barreca 89-111.

Gettings, Michael E. "This Thing of Ours: Language Use in *The Sopranos*." Greene and Vernezze 159-70.

Gilbert, David. *Behind the Scenes 1: The Godfather Family: A Look Inside*. Bonus Materials, *The Godfather* DVD Collection, Paramount Pictures, U.S.A., 2001.

Gilbert, Sandra M. "Life with (God)father." Barreca 11-25.

Gini, Al. "Bada-Being and Nothingness: Murderous Melodrama or Morality Play?" Greene and Vernezze 7-14.

Gledhill, Christine (1992), "Speculations on the Relationship Between Soap Opera and Melodrama," *Quarterly Review of Film and Video* 14.1-2 (1992): 103-124.

Golden, Arthur. *Memoirs of a Geisha*.

Gordon, Linda (1990), Debate with Joan Wallach Scott. *Signs* 15 (Summer 1990): 4.

Green, Robin. Conf. On "The Sopranos: Behind the Hit." Centre for Communication, New York. 10 May 2004.

Green, Ronald M. "'I Dunno About Morals, but I Do Got Rules': Tony Soprano as Ethical Manager." Greene and Vernezze 59-71.

Greene, Richard. "Is Tony Soprano Self-Blind?." Greene and Vernezze 171-81.

___ and Peter Vernezze, eds. *The Sopranos and Philosophy: I Kill Therefore I Am*. Popular Culture and Philosophy. Chicago and LaSalle, Illinois: Open Court, 2004.

Guglielmo, Jennifer and Salvatore Salerno, eds. *Are Italians White? How Race is Made in America*. Routledge: New York and London, 2003.

Hahn, David. "The Prince and I: Some Musings on Machiavelli." Greene and Vernezze 48-56.

Hare, Peter H. "'What Kind of God Does This . . .'?" Greene and Vernezze 195-206.

Harold, James. "A Moral Never-Never Land: Identifying with Tony Soprano." Greene and Vernezze 137-46.

Hartley, Cecilia. "Letting Ourselves Go: Making Room for the Fat Body in Feminist Scholarship." *Bodies Out of Bounds: Fatness and Transgression*. Ed. Jana Evans Braziel and Kathleen LeBesco. Berkeley, CA: U of California P, 2001. 60-73.

Hayward, Steven and Andrew Biro. "The Eighteenth Brumaire of Tony Soprano." Lavery, *This Thing* 203-14.

HBO: The Sopranos (official website). 2005. Home Box Office. July 2005 <http://www. hbo.com/sopranos/index.shtml>.

Heffernan, Virginia. "Cut to the Chase." *The Sydney Morning Herald* May 3rd, 2004, sec. The Guide: 5.

Hendin, J. Gattuso. "tony and Meadow: *The Sopranos* as Father-Daughter Drama." *LIT: Literature Interpretation Theory* (Jan-March 2003).

Henry, Astrid (2004). *Not My Mother's Sister: Generational Conflict and Third-Wave Feminism*, Indiana UP, 2004.

Herek, Gregory M. "Psychological Heterosexism and Anti-Gay Violence: The Social Psychology of Bigotry and Bashing." *Men's Lives*. Eds. Michael S. Kimmel and Michael A. Messner. 3rd ed. Needham Heights, MA: Allyn & Bacon, 1995. 341-53.

Heywood, Leslie and Jennifer Drake, eds. *Third Wave Agenda: Being Feminist, Doing Feminism*. Minneapolis: U Minnesota P, 2003.

___. "Introduction." Heywood and Drake, *Third Wave Agenda* 1-24.

Higgins, John M., and Allison Romano. "The Family Business: It became a cultural phenomenon, but now *The Sopranos* is a money-making machine beyond Tony's wildest dreams." *Broadcasting and Cable* 1 Mar. 2004, Top of the Week: 1.

Hill, Lee Alan. "'Sex and the City'." *Television Week* 20 June 2005: 48.

hooks, bell. *Outlaw Culture: Resisting Representation*. New York: Routledge, 1994.

Howard, Douglas L. "'Soprano-speak': Language and Silence in *The Sopranos*." Lavery, *This Thing* 195-202.

"An Interview with David Chase." *The Sopranos: A Family History*. Ed. Allen Rucker. New York: New American Library, 2000: n.p. [referred to in the text as the Rucker interview].

Jacobson, Matthew Frye. *Whiteness of a Different Color: European Immigrants and the Alchemy of Race*. Cambridge, MA and London: Harvard UP, 1998.

Johnson, Merri Lisa, ed. *Jane Sexes It Up: True Confessions of Feminist Desire*. New York: Four Wall Eight Windows, 2002.

Johnston, Dawn Elizabeth B. "Way North of New Jersey: A Canadian Experience of *The Sopranos*." Lavery, *This Thing* 32-41.

Kocela, Christopher. "Unmade Men: *The Sopranos* After Whiteness." *Postmodern Culture* 15.2 (2005): http://www3.iath.virginia.edu/pmc/current.issue/15.2kocela.html.

Lacey, Joanne. "One for the Boys? *The Sopranos* and Its Male, British Audience." Lavery, *This Thing* 95-108.

Laing, R. D. *The Divided Self.* New York: Pantheon, 1965.

___. *Self and Others.* New York: Pantheon, 1968.

Lavery, David. "Apocalyptic Apocalypses: The Narrative Eschatology of *Buffy the Vampire Slayer.*" *Slayage: The Online International Journal of Buffy Studies* 3.1 (August 2003). http://www.slayage.tv/essays/slayage9/Lavery.htm.

___. "'Coming Heavy': The Significance of *The Sopranos*." Lavery, *This Thing* xi-xviii.

___. "Coming Heavy: Intertextuality, Genre, and *The Sopranos*." *PopPolitics.com* (March 2001): http://www.poppolitics.com/articles/2001-03-03-heavy.shtml.

___. "'I wrote my thesis on you': *Buffy* Studies as an Academic Cult." *Slayage: The Online International Journal of Buffy Studies* 4.1-2 (October 2004): http://www.slayage.tv/essays/slayage13_14/Lavery.htm.

___. Review Essay of *Buffy the Vampire Slayer: The Monster Book* by Golden, Bissette, and Sniegoski, *Buffy the Vampire Slayer: The Watcher's Guide*, Vol. 2 by Holder, Mariotte, and Hart, and *The Sopranos: A Family History* by Alan Rucker. *Television Quarterly* 31.4 (Winter 2001): 89-92.

___. "*The Sopranos*." *50 Key Television Programmes.* Ed. Glen Creeber. London: Arnold, 2004. 188-92.

___, with Robert J. Thompson. "David Chase, *The Sopranos*, and Television Creativity." Lavery, *This Thing* 18-25.

___, ed. *This Thing of Ours: Investigating the Sopranos.* New York: Columbia UP, 2002.

Laware, Margaret L. "Circling the Missiles and Staining Them Red: Feminist Rhetorical Invention and Strategies of Resistance at the Women's Peace Camp." *National Women's Studies Journal* 16.3 (2004): 18-41.

Learmonth, Michael. "'Sopranos' Chief Singing New Tune." *Daily Variety* 25 May 2005, news: 1.

Leitch, Thomas. *Crime Films.* Genres in American Cinema. Cambridge: Cambridge UP, 2002.

Levin, Gary. "HBO met its match in itself." *USA Today* 28 Sept. 2004, final ed., life: 1D.

Lessing, G. E. *Laocoon: An Essay upon the Limits of Poetry and Painting.* Trans. Ellen Frothingham. New York: Farrar, Straus and Giroux, 1969.

Levinson, Paul. "Naked Bodies, Three Showings a Week, and No Commercials: *The Sopranos* as a Nuts-and-Bolts Triumph of Non-Network TV." Lavery, *This Thing* 26-31.

Lintott, Sheila. "Tony Soprano's Moral Sympathy (or Lack Thereof): *The Sopranos* and Subjectivist Ethics." Greene and Vernezze 72-85.

Lippman, Mike. "Know Thyself, Asshole: Tony Soprano as an Aristotelian Tragic Hero." Greene and Vernezze 147-56.

Littleton, Cynthia. "'Sopranos' creator nets $15 mil deal." *BPI Entertainment News Wire*, 17 Jul. 2001, entertainment news.

Longworth, James L. "David Chase: 'Hit' Man." *TV Creators: Conversations with America's Top Producers of Television Drama*. The Television Series. Syracuse: Syracuse UP, 2000: 20-36.

Lumby, Catherine. *Bad Girls: The Media, Sex and Feminism in the 90s*. St Leonards (NWS): Allen & Unwin, 1997.

Machiavelli, Niccolo. *The Prince*. Trans. George Bull. New York: Penguin, 1961.

___. *The Prince*. Trans. Peter Bondanella and Mark Musa. New York: Oxford UP, 1998.

Maltby, Richard. "The Spectacle of Criminality." *Violence and American Cinema*. Ed. J. David Slocum. New York and London: Routledge, 2001.

Manguel, Alberto. *Reading Pictures*. Toronto: Vintage, 2002.

Martin, Denise. "Tony and his henchmen go artsy." *Daily Variety* 1 Feb. 2005, news: 1.

___. "HBO moves 'Feet' back to Sunday" *Daily Variety* 28 June 2005, news: 4.

Mattessi, Peter. "The strong, silent type: psychoanalysis in The Sopranos." *Metro Magazine* 138 (Fall 2003): 136-38.

McCarty, John. *Bullets over Hollywood: The American Gangster Picture from the Silents to "the Sopranos."* Cambridge, MA.: Da Capo Press, 2004.

McCourt, Frank. *'Tis: A Memoir.* New York: Scribner's 2000.

McPhee, Michele. "TV wisegay 'Sopranos' fella hits the other way." *New York Daily News* 3 May 2004: 2-I.

Messenger, Chris. *The Godfather and American Culture: How the Corleones Became "Our Gang."* Albany: State U of New York P, 2002.

___. *"The Godfather* Sung by *The Sopranos."* The Godfather *and American Culture* 253-90.

Miller, John. *The Real Deal, Documentaries, Special Features, the Sopranos: The Complete Second Season, Disc 3.* HBO Home Video, 2000.

Millman, Joyce. "We are Family: You Don't Have to Be Italian for *The Sopranos* to Hit Home." *Salon.com* 14 January 2000: http://dir.salon.com/ent/col/mill/2000/01/14/sopranos/index.html?sid=569901.

Milton, John. *Complete Poems and Major Prose.* Ed. Merritt Y. Hughes. Indianapolis: Bobbs-Merrill, 1957.

Mitchell, W. J. T. *Picture Theory.* Chicago: Chicago UP, 1994.

Modleski, Tania (1994) *Loving with a Vengeance: Mass Produced Fantasies for Women.* London and New York: Routledge, 1994.

___. *Old Wives' Tales: Feminist Re-Visions of Film and Other Fictions.* London: I.B.Tauris, 1999.

Morreale, Joanne. "Sitcoms Say Goodbye: The Cultural Spectacle of *Seinfeld*'s Last Episode." *Critiquing the Sitcom: A Reader.* Ed. Joanne Morreale. The Television Series. Syracuse: Syracuse UP, 2003. 274-85.

Nagel, Joane. "Nation." *Handbook of Studies on Men and Masculinities*. Eds. Michael S. Kimmel, Jeff Hearn, and R. W. Connell. Thousand Oaks, CA: Sage, 2005. 397-413.

New York Times on The Sopranos, The. New York: Ibooks, 2000.

Nochimson, Martha P. "Tony's Options: *The Sopranos* and the Televisuality of the Gangster Genre." *Senses of Cinema* Nov-Dec 2003, Issue No. 29 <http://www.sensesofcinema.com/contents/03/29/sopranos_televisuality.html>.

___. "Waddaya Lookin' At? Re-reading the Gangster Genre Through *The Sopranos*." *Film Quarterly* 56.2 (2003): 2-13.

Nozick, Robert. *Anarchy, State, and Utopia*. New York: Basic Books, 1977.

Orban, Clara. "Stereotyping in *The Sopranos*." *VIA: Voices in Italian Americana* 12.1 (2001): 35-56.

Paglia, Camille. "The Energy Mess and Fascist Fays." *Salon* 23 May 2001. http://www.salon.com/people/col/pagl/2001/05/23/oil/index2.html.

___. "Feinstein for President, Buchanan for Emperor." http://www.salon.com/people/col/pagl/1999/10/27/paglia1027/index.html.

Paoli, Letizia. *Mafia Brotherhoods: Organized Crime, Italian Style*. Oxford: Oxford UP, 2003.

Papke, David Ray. "Myth and Meaning: Francis Ford Coppola and Popular Response to the Godfather Trilogy." *Legal Reelism: Movies as Legal Texts*. Ed. John Denver. Urbana and Chicago: U of Illinois P, 1996. 2-22.

Parini, Jay. "The Cultural Work of *The Sopranos*." Barreca 75-88.

Pattie, David. "Mobbed Up: *The Sopranos* and the Modern Gangster Film." Lavery 135-45.

Pestana, Carla Gardina, "Catholicism, Identity, and Ethics in *The Sopranos*." 129-48.

"Peter Bogdanovich Interviews David Chase." *The Sopranos: The Complete First Season*. DVD. NY: HBO-Time-Warner Prod., 2000.

Pinar, William F. "The Queer Character of Lynching." Lecture transcript. *Interdisciplinary Nineteenth Century Studies Conference*. Louisiana State University, April 23, 2005.

Plummer, David. *One of the Boys: Masculinity, Homophobia, and Modern Manhood*. New York: Haworth, 1999.

Poniewozik, James. "Back in business: next month *The Sopranos* gives some bada-bing to a too-safe fall TV season. We've got a sneak peak." *Time* 2 Sept 2002: 48-51, 53.

Quinn, Roseanne Giannini. "Mothers, molls, and misogynists: resisting Italian American womanhood in *The Sopranos*." *Journal of American Culture* 27.2 (2004): 166-75.

Radway, Janice. *Reading the Romance: Women, Patriarchy and Popular Literature*. London: Verso, 1987.

Remnick, David. "Is This the End of Rico? With *The Sopranos* the Mob Genre is on the Brink." *New Yorker* 2 April 2001: 38-44.

Reynolds, Mike. " HBO Gets In the Game: Network Puts Top Properties Onto Toy Store Shelves." *Multichannel News* 20 Sept. 2004, marketing/advertising: 50.

Rice, Lynette. "Sexual Healing; For HBO, the Future is Now. So Guess Who It Hopes Has Some New Ideas?" *Entertainment Weekly* 25 Mar. 2005: 9.

Rogers, Mark C., Michael M. Epstein, and Jimmie R. Reeves. "*The Sopranos* as HBO Brand Equity: The Art of Commerce in the Age of Digital Reproduction." Lavery, *This Thing* 42-57.

Ross, Marlon B. "Race, Rape, Castration: Feminist Theories of Sexual Violence and Masculine Strategies of Black Protest." *Masculinity Studies and Feminist Theory: New Directions*. Ed. Judith Kegan Gardiner. New York: Columbia UP, 2002. 305-43.

Rotundo, E. Anthony. "Wonderbread and Stugots: Italian American Manhood and *The Sopranos*." Barreca 47-74.

Rowe, Kathleen. *The Unruly Woman: Gender and the Genres of Laughter*. Austin: U of Texas P, 1995.

Rozdeba, Suzanne. "*The Sopranos'* Joe Gannascoli Loves Playing A Gay Mobster." *Star*, May 24, 2004.

Rucker, Allen. *The Sopranos: A Family History*. New York: New American Library, 2004.

___. *The Sopranos Family Cookbook, as Compiled by Artie Bucco*. New York: Warner, 2002.

Ruth, David E. *Inventing the Public Enemy: The Gangster in American Culture, 1918-1934*. Chicago and London: U of Chicago P, 1996.

Santo, Avi. "'Fat fuck! Why don't you take a look in the mirror?': Weight, Body Image, and Masculinity in *The Sopranos*." Lavery, *This Thing* 72-94.

Schechner, Richard. *Performance Theory*. Revised ed. London and New York: Routledge Classics, 2003.

Scheie, Timothy. "'Questionable Terms': Shylock, Céline's *L'Eglise*, and the Performative." *Text and Performance Quarterly* 17 (1997): 153-69.

Schneider, Anthony. *Tony Soprano on Management: Leadership Lessons Inspired by America's Favorite Mobster*. New York: Berkeley Publishing, 2004.

Seay, Chris. *The Gospel According to Tony Soprano*. New York: Jeremy P. Tarcher, 2002.

Sepinwall, Alan. "Chase continues to follow his inner-mobster" (interview with David Chase). *The Star Ledger* 2 March 2004.

Seshadri-Crooks, Kalpana. *Desiring Whiteness: A Lacanian Analysis of Race*. London and New York: Routledge, 2000.

Shadoian, Jack. *Dreams and Dead Ends: The American Gangster Film*. 2nd ed. Oxford: Oxford UP, 2003.

Short, Martin. "All in the Family." *Crime Inc: The Real Story of the Mafia*. Episode 1, Disc 1, United Kingdom, Thames Television Ltd., 1984.

Siegel, Deborah. "Reading Between the Waves: Feminist Historiography in a 'Postfeminist' Moment." Heywood and Drake, *Third Wave Agenda* 55-82.

Siegel, Lee. "The Attraction of Repulsion." *The New Republic* (December 13, 2004): 40-47.

Simon, David. *Tony Soprano's America: The Criminal Side of the American Dream.* Boulder, CO: Westview, 2004.

Smith, Alane Salierno. "Respect." *Beyond the Godfather: Italian American Writers on the Real Italian American Experience.* NY: UP of New England, 1998. 62-73.

Sopranoland.com. 16 June 2005. Sopranoland. July 2005 <http://www.sopranoland.com/>.

Staples, Robert. "Stereotypes of Black Male Sexuality: The Facts Behind the Myths." *Men's Lives.* Eds. Michael S. Kimmel and Michael A. Messner. 3rd ed. Needham Heights, MA: Allyn & Bacon, 1995. 375-80.

Steeves, H. Peter. "Dying in Our Own Arms: Liberalism, Communitarianism, and the Construction of Identity on *The Sopranos.*" Greene and Vernezze 108-18.

Steinberg, Jacques. "A&E Buys Rights To Rerun 'Sopranos'." *The New York Times* 1 Feb. 2005, final late ed.: E1.

Stoehr, Kevin L. "'It's All a Big Nothing': The Nihilistic Vision of *The Sopranos.*" Greene and Vernezze 37-47.

Strate, Lance. "No(rth Jersey) Sense of Place: The Cultural Geography (and Media Ecology) of *The Sopranos.*" Lavery, *This Thing* 178-94.

The Sopranos: Selected Scripts from Three Seasons. New York: Warner Books, 2002.

Tillich, Paul. *The Courage to Be.* New Haven: Yale UP, 1959.

Vernezze, Peter. "Tony Soprano in Hell: Chase's Mob in Dante's Inferno." Greene and Vernezze 185-94.

Waggoner, Catherine and D. Lynn O'Brien Hallstein. "Feminist Ideologies Meet Fashionable Bodies: Managing the Agency/Constraint Conundrum." *Text and Performance Quarterly* 21 (2001): 26-46.

Walker, Joseph S. "'Cunnilingus and Psychiatry Have Brought Us To This': Livia and the Logic of False Hoods in the First Season of *The Sopranos.*" Lavery, *This Thing* 109-23.

Walker, Rebecca, ed. (1995), *To Be Real: Telling the Truth and Changing the Face of Feminism.* New York: Doubleday, 1995.

Walter, Natasha. *The New Feminism.* London: Little, Brown and Company, 1998.

Warshow, Robert. "The Gangster as Tragic Hero." *The Immediate Experience. Movies, Comics, Theatre and other Aspects of Popular Culture.* New York: Doubleday & Co. Inc, 1962: 127-133.

Weber, Samuel. *Theatricality as Medium.* New York: Fordham UP, 2004.

White, Walter. *Rope and Faggot: A Biography of Judge Lynch.* New York: Knopf, 1929.

Whitney, Daisy. "The Scramble for Bandwidth: MSOs Create Services to Compete With Telcos, Now Must Devise Reliable Pipeline." *Television Week* 20 June 2005, TV technology: 12.

Wiegman, Robyn. *American Anatomies: Theorizing Race and Gender.* Durham, NC: Duke UP, 1995.

Williams, Joan. *Unbending Gender: Why Family and Work Conflict and What to do About it.* Oxford: Oxford UP., 2000.

Williamson, Joel. *The Crucible of Race: Black-White Relations in the American South Since Emancipation.* New York: Oxford UP, 1984.

Willis, Ellen. "Our Mobsters, Ourselves." Lavery, *This Thing* 2-9.

Wilson, Scott D. "Staying within the Family: Tony Soprano's Ethical Obligations." Greene and Vernezze 86-96.

Wise, Tim. "Tony Soprano, Christopher Columbus and the Irony of Ethnic Stereotypes." *ZNet Daily Commentaries*, Oct. 15, 2002. http://www.zmag.org/sustainers/content/2002-10/15wise.cfm.

Wolf, Naomi. *Fire With Fire: The New Female Power and How It Will Change the 21st-Century.* New York: Random House, 1993.

Wood, Amy Louise. "Lynching Photography and the 'Black Beast Rapist' in the Southern White Masculine Imagination." *Masculinity: Bodies, Movies, Culture.* Ed. Peter Lehman. New York: Routledge, 2001. 193-211.

Yacowar, Maurice. *The Sopranos on the Couch: Analyzing Television's Greatest Series.* New and expanded edition. New York: Continuum, 2003.

Young-Bruehl, Elisabeth. *The Anatomy of Prejudices.* Cambridge, MA: Harvard UP, 1996.

Zinn, Howard, *A People's History of the United States.* New York: Harper Perennial, 2003.

INDEX